C-1886   CAREER EXAMINATION SERIES

This is your
PASSBOOK for...

Traffic Engineer I

Test Preparation Study Guide
Questions & Answers

COPYRIGHT NOTICE

This book is SOLELY intended for, is sold ONLY to, and its use is RESTRICTED to individual, bona fide applicants or candidates who qualify by virtue of having seriously filed applications for appropriate license, certificate, professional and/or promotional advancement, higher school matriculation, scholarship, or other legitimate requirements of education and/or governmental authorities.

This book is NOT intended for use, class instruction, tutoring, training, duplication, copying, reprinting, excerption, or adaptation, etc., by:

1) Other publishers
2) Proprietors and/or Instructors of "Coaching" and/or Preparatory Courses
3) Personnel and/or Training Divisions of commercial, industrial, and governmental organizations
4) Schools, colleges, or universities and/or their departments and staffs, including teachers and other personnel
5) Testing Agencies or Bureaus
6) Study groups which seek by the purchase of a single volume to copy and/or duplicate and/or adapt this material for use by the group as a whole without having purchased individual volumes for each of the members of the group
7) Et al.

Such persons would be in violation of appropriate Federal and State statutes.

PROVISION OF LICENSING AGREEMENTS – Recognized educational, commercial, industrial, and governmental institutions and organizations, and others legitimately engaged in educational pursuits, including training, testing, and measurement activities, may address request for a licensing agreement to the copyright owners, who will determine whether, and under what conditions, including fees and charges, the materials in this book may be used them. In other words, a licensing facility exists for the legitimate use of the material in this book on other than an individual basis. However, it is asseverated and affirmed here that the material in this book CANNOT be used without the receipt of the express permission of such a licensing agreement from the Publishers. Inquiries re licensing should be addressed to the company, attention rights and permissions department.

All rights reserved, including the right of reproduction in whole or in part, in any form or by any means, electronic or mechanical, including photocopying, recording, or by any information storage and retrieval system, without permission in writing from the Publisher.

Copyright © 2025 by
National Learning Corporation

212 Michael Drive, Syosset, NY 11791
(516) 921-8888 • www.passbooks.com
E-mail: info@passbooks.com

PASSBOOK® SERIES

THE *PASSBOOK® SERIES* has been created to prepare applicants and candidates for the ultimate academic battlefield – the examination room.

At some time in our lives, each and every one of us may be required to take an examination – for validation, matriculation, admission, qualification, registration, certification, or licensure.

Based on the assumption that every applicant or candidate has met the basic formal educational standards, has taken the required number of courses, and read the necessary texts, the *PASSBOOK® SERIES* furnishes the one special preparation which may assure passing with confidence, instead of failing with insecurity. Examination questions – together with answers – are furnished as the basic vehicle for study so that the mysteries of the examination and its compounding difficulties may be eliminated or diminished by a sure method.

This book is meant to help you pass your examination provided that you qualify and are serious in your objective.

The entire field is reviewed through the huge store of content information which is succinctly presented through a provocative and challenging approach – the question-and-answer method.

A climate of success is established by furnishing the correct answers at the end of each test.

You soon learn to recognize types of questions, forms of questions, and patterns of questioning. You may even begin to anticipate expected outcomes.

You perceive that many questions are repeated or adapted so that you can gain acute insights, which may enable you to score many sure points.

You learn how to confront new questions, or types of questions, and to attack them confidently and work out the correct answers.

You note objectives and emphases, and recognize pitfalls and dangers, so that you may make positive educational adjustments.

Moreover, you are kept fully informed in relation to new concepts, methods, practices, and directions in the field.

You discover that you are actually taking the examination all the time: you are preparing for the examination by "taking" an examination, not by reading extraneous and/or supererogatory textbooks.

In short, this PASSBOOK®, used directedly, should be an important factor in helping you to pass your test.

TRAFFIC ENGINEER I

DUTIES:
    Directs an assigned phase of the highway planning or traffic control program. Assignments are received with general instruction, but incumbents are expected to use initiative and judgment in completing them. Supervision may be exercised over technical assistants in any phase of their assigned duties, and work is checked and reviewed frequently throughout its progress and at its conclusion by a technical supervisor. Does related work as required.

SCOPE OF THE EXAMINATION:
The written test designed to evaluate knowledge, skills and /or abilities in the following areas:
1. **Engineering plans, specifications and estimates** - These questions test for knowledge of and the ability to read and interpret construction drawings and technical specifications, and for the ability to calculate cost and quantity estimates from technical presentations and/or engineering and construction drawings. Knowledge of estimating techniques and the proper method of construction for specified projects will be required.
2. **Preparing written material** - These questions test for the ability to present information clearly and accurately, and to organize paragraphs logically and comprehensibly. For some questions, you will be given information in two or three sentences followed by four restatements of the information. You must then choose the best version. For other questions, you will be given paragraphs with their sentences out of order. You must then choose, from four suggestions, the best order for the sentences.
3. **Principles and practices of traffic and transportation engineering** - These questions test for knowledge of traffic and transportation engineering concepts and their practical applications, including materials, terminology and procedures used, computations related to the design, construction and operation of roadways and related facilities, traffic and transportation studies and data interpretation, and safety issues.
4. **Traffic control devices and regulations and collection, analysis and presentation of data** - These questions test for knowledge of the uses, placement, laws, rules and regulations related to various types of traffic safety and traffic control devices such as pavement markings, work zone markings, signs and traffic signals, and the proper procedures and terminology used to gather, evaluate, organize and utilize various types of technical data related to transportation and traffic studies.
5. **Highway planning, design, safety and laws** - These questions test for knowledge of the concepts, economics, computations and federal and state rules and regulations involved in the planning, design, construction and operation of roadway systems, including the safety of workers and the traveling public.

HOW TO TAKE A TEST

I. YOU MUST PASS AN EXAMINATION

A. WHAT EVERY CANDIDATE SHOULD KNOW

Examination applicants often ask us for help in preparing for the written test. What can I study in advance? What kinds of questions will be asked? How will the test be given? How will the papers be graded?

As an applicant for a civil service examination, you may be wondering about some of these things. Our purpose here is to suggest effective methods of advance study and to describe civil service examinations.

Your chances for success on this examination can be increased if you know how to prepare. Those "pre-examination jitters" can be reduced if you know what to expect. You can even experience an adventure in good citizenship if you know why civil service exams are given.

B. WHY ARE CIVIL SERVICE EXAMINATIONS GIVEN?

Civil service examinations are important to you in two ways. As a citizen, you want public jobs filled by employees who know how to do their work. As a job seeker, you want a fair chance to compete for that job on an equal footing with other candidates. The best-known means of accomplishing this two-fold goal is the competitive examination.

Exams are widely publicized throughout the nation. They may be administered for jobs in federal, state, city, municipal, town or village governments or agencies.

Any citizen may apply, with some limitations, such as the age or residence of applicants. Your experience and education may be reviewed to see whether you meet the requirements for the particular examination. When these requirements exist, they are reasonable and applied consistently to all applicants. Thus, a competitive examination may cause you some uneasiness now, but it is your privilege and safeguard.

C. HOW ARE CIVIL SERVICE EXAMS DEVELOPED?

Examinations are carefully written by trained technicians who are specialists in the field known as "psychological measurement," in consultation with recognized authorities in the field of work that the test will cover. These experts recommend the subject matter areas or skills to be tested; only those knowledges or skills important to your success on the job are included. The most reliable books and source materials available are used as references. Together, the experts and technicians judge the difficulty level of the questions.

Test technicians know how to phrase questions so that the problem is clearly stated. Their ethics do not permit "trick" or "catch" questions. Questions may have been tried out on sample groups, or subjected to statistical analysis, to determine their usefulness.

Written tests are often used in combination with performance tests, ratings of training and experience, and oral interviews. All of these measures combine to form the best-known means of finding the right person for the right job.

II. HOW TO PASS THE WRITTEN TEST

A. NATURE OF THE EXAMINATION

To prepare intelligently for civil service examinations, you should know how they differ from school examinations you have taken. In school you were assigned certain definite pages to read or subjects to cover. The examination questions were quite detailed and usually emphasized memory. Civil service exams, on the other hand, try to discover your present ability to perform the duties of a position, plus your potentiality to learn these duties. In other words, a civil service exam attempts to predict how successful you will be. Questions cover such a broad area that they cannot be as minute and detailed as school exam questions.

In the public service similar kinds of work, or positions, are grouped together in one "class." This process is known as *position-classification*. All the positions in a class are paid according to the salary range for that class. One class title covers all of these positions, and they are all tested by the same examination.

B. FOUR BASIC STEPS

1) Study the announcement

How, then, can you know what subjects to study? Our best answer is: "Learn as much as possible about the class of positions for which you've applied." The exam will test the knowledge, skills and abilities needed to do the work.

Your most valuable source of information about the position you want is the official exam announcement. This announcement lists the training and experience qualifications. Check these standards and apply only if you come reasonably close to meeting them.

The brief description of the position in the examination announcement offers some clues to the subjects which will be tested. Think about the job itself. Review the duties in your mind. Can you perform them, or are there some in which you are rusty? Fill in the blank spots in your preparation.

Many jurisdictions preview the written test in the exam announcement by including a section called "Knowledge and Abilities Required," "Scope of the Examination," or some similar heading. Here you will find out specifically what fields will be tested.

2) Review your own background

Once you learn in general what the position is all about, and what you need to know to do the work, ask yourself which subjects you already know fairly well and which need improvement. You may wonder whether to concentrate on improving your strong areas or on building some background in your fields of weakness. When the announcement has specified "some knowledge" or "considerable knowledge," or has used adjectives like "beginning principles of…" or "advanced … methods," you can get a clue as to the number and difficulty of questions to be asked in any given field. More questions, and hence broader coverage, would be included for those subjects which are more important in the work. Now weigh your strengths and weaknesses against the job requirements and prepare accordingly.

3) Determine the level of the position

Another way to tell how intensively you should prepare is to understand the level of the job for which you are applying. Is it the entering level? In other words, is this the position in which beginners in a field of work are hired? Or is it an intermediate or advanced level? Sometimes this is indicated by such words as "Junior" or "Senior" in the class title. Other jurisdictions use Roman numerals to designate the level – Clerk I, Clerk II, for example. The word "Supervisor" sometimes appears in the title. If the level is not indicated by the title, check the description of duties. Will you be working under very close supervision, or will you have responsibility for independent decisions in this work?

4) Choose appropriate study materials

Now that you know the subjects to be examined and the relative amount of each subject to be covered, you can choose suitable study materials. For beginning level jobs, or even advanced ones, if you have a pronounced weakness in some aspect of your training, read a modern, standard textbook in that field. Be sure it is up to date and has general coverage. Such books are normally available at your library, and the librarian will be glad to help you locate one. For entry-level positions, questions of appropriate difficulty are chosen – neither highly advanced questions, nor those too simple. Such questions require careful thought but not advanced training.

If the position for which you are applying is technical or advanced, you will read more advanced, specialized material. If you are already familiar with the basic principles of your field, elementary textbooks would waste your time. Concentrate on advanced textbooks and technical periodicals. Think through the concepts and review difficult problems in your field.

These are all general sources. You can get more ideas on your own initiative, following these leads. For example, training manuals and publications of the government agency which employs workers in your field can be useful, particularly for technical and professional positions. A letter or visit to the government department involved may result in more specific study suggestions, and certainly will provide you with a more definite idea of the exact nature of the position you are seeking.

III. KINDS OF TESTS

Tests are used for purposes other than measuring knowledge and ability to perform specified duties. For some positions, it is equally important to test ability to make adjustments to new situations or to profit from training. In others, basic mental abilities not dependent on information are essential. Questions which test these things may not appear as pertinent to the duties of the position as those which test for knowledge and information. Yet they are often highly important parts of a fair examination. For very general questions, it is almost impossible to help you direct your study efforts. What we can do is to point out some of the more common of these general abilities needed in public service positions and describe some typical questions.

1) General information

Broad, general information has been found useful for predicting job success in some kinds of work. This is tested in a variety of ways, from vocabulary lists to questions about current events. Basic background in some field of work, such as sociology or economics, may be sampled in a group of questions. Often these are principles which have become familiar to most persons through exposure rather than through formal training. It is difficult to advise you how to study for these questions; being alert to the world around you is our best suggestion.

2) Verbal ability

An example of an ability needed in many positions is verbal or language ability. Verbal ability is, in brief, the ability to use and understand words. Vocabulary and grammar tests are typical measures of this ability. Reading comprehension or paragraph interpretation questions are common in many kinds of civil service tests. You are given a paragraph of written material and asked to find its central meaning.

3) Numerical ability

Number skills can be tested by the familiar arithmetic problem, by checking paired lists of numbers to see which are alike and which are different, or by interpreting charts and graphs. In the latter test, a graph may be printed in the test booklet which you are asked to use as the basis for answering questions.

4) Observation

A popular test for law-enforcement positions is the observation test. A picture is shown to you for several minutes, then taken away. Questions about the picture test your ability to observe both details and larger elements.

5) Following directions

In many positions in the public service, the employee must be able to carry out written instructions dependably and accurately. You may be given a chart with several columns, each column listing a variety of information. The questions require you to carry out directions involving the information given in the chart.

6) Skills and aptitudes

Performance tests effectively measure some manual skills and aptitudes. When the skill is one in which you are trained, such as typing or shorthand, you can practice. These tests are often very much like those given in business school or high school courses. For many of the other skills and aptitudes, however, no short-time preparation can be made. Skills and abilities natural to you or that you have developed throughout your lifetime are being tested.

Many of the general questions just described provide all the data needed to answer the questions and ask you to use your reasoning ability to find the answers. Your best preparation for these tests, as well as for tests of facts and ideas, is to be at your physical and mental best. You, no doubt, have your own methods of getting into an exam-taking mood and keeping "in shape." The next section lists some ideas on this subject.

IV. KINDS OF QUESTIONS

Only rarely is the "essay" question, which you answer in narrative form, used in civil service tests. Civil service tests are usually of the short-answer type. Full instructions for answering these questions will be given to you at the examination. But in case this is your first experience with short-answer questions and separate answer sheets, here is what you need to know:

1) Multiple-choice Questions

Most popular of the short-answer questions is the "multiple choice" or "best answer" question. It can be used, for example, to test for factual knowledge, ability to solve problems or judgment in meeting situations found at work.

A multiple-choice question is normally one of three types—
- It can begin with an incomplete statement followed by several possible endings. You are to find the one ending which *best* completes the statement, although some of the others may not be entirely wrong.
- It can also be a complete statement in the form of a question which is answered by choosing one of the statements listed.

- It can be in the form of a problem – again you select the best answer.

Here is an example of a multiple-choice question with a discussion which should give you some clues as to the method for choosing the right answer:

When an employee has a complaint about his assignment, the action which will *best* help him overcome his difficulty is to
  A. discuss his difficulty with his coworkers
  B. take the problem to the head of the organization
  C. take the problem to the person who gave him the assignment
  D. say nothing to anyone about his complaint

In answering this question, you should study each of the choices to find which is best. Consider choice "A" – Certainly an employee may discuss his complaint with fellow employees, but no change or improvement can result, and the complaint remains unresolved. Choice "B" is a poor choice since the head of the organization probably does not know what assignment you have been given, and taking your problem to him is known as "going over the head" of the supervisor. The supervisor, or person who made the assignment, is the person who can clarify it or correct any injustice. Choice "C" is, therefore, correct. To say nothing, as in choice "D," is unwise. Supervisors have and interest in knowing the problems employees are facing, and the employee is seeking a solution to his problem.

2) True/False Questions

The "true/false" or "right/wrong" form of question is sometimes used. Here a complete statement is given. Your job is to decide whether the statement is right or wrong.

SAMPLE: A roaming cell-phone call to a nearby city costs less than a non-roaming call to a distant city.

This statement is wrong, or false, since roaming calls are more expensive.

This is not a complete list of all possible question forms, although most of the others are variations of these common types. You will always get complete directions for answering questions. Be sure you understand *how* to mark your answers – ask questions until you do.

V. RECORDING YOUR ANSWERS

Computer terminals are used more and more today for many different kinds of exams.
For an examination with very few applicants, you may be told to record your answers in the test booklet itself. Separate answer sheets are much more common. If this separate answer sheet is to be scored by machine – and this is often the case – it is highly important that you mark your answers correctly in order to get credit.
An electronic scoring machine is often used in civil service offices because of the speed with which papers can be scored. Machine-scored answer sheets must be marked with a pencil, which will be given to you. This pencil has a high graphite content which responds to the electronic scoring machine. As a matter of fact, stray dots may register as answers, so do not let your pencil rest on the answer sheet while you are pondering the correct answer. Also, if your pencil lead breaks or is otherwise defective, ask for another.

Since the answer sheet will be dropped in a slot in the scoring machine, be careful not to bend the corners or get the paper crumpled.

The answer sheet normally has five vertical columns of numbers, with 30 numbers to a column. These numbers correspond to the question numbers in your test booklet. After each number, going across the page are four or five pairs of dotted lines. These short dotted lines have small letters or numbers above them. The first two pairs may also have a "T" or "F" above the letters. This indicates that the first two pairs only are to be used if the questions are of the true-false type. If the questions are multiple choice, disregard the "T" and "F" and pay attention only to the small letters or numbers.

Answer your questions in the manner of the sample that follows:

32. The largest city in the United States is
    A. Washington, D.C.
    B. New York City
    C. Chicago
    D. Detroit
    E. San Francisco

1) Choose the answer you think is best. (New York City is the largest, so "B" is correct.)
2) Find the row of dotted lines numbered the same as the question you are answering. (Find row number 32)
3) Find the pair of dotted lines corresponding to the answer. (Find the pair of lines under the mark "B.")
4) Make a solid black mark between the dotted lines.

VI. BEFORE THE TEST

Common sense will help you find procedures to follow to get ready for an examination. Too many of us, however, overlook these sensible measures. Indeed, nervousness and fatigue have been found to be the most serious reasons why applicants fail to do their best on civil service tests. Here is a list of reminders:

- Begin your preparation early – Don't wait until the last minute to go scurrying around for books and materials or to find out what the position is all about.
- Prepare continuously – An hour a night for a week is better than an all-night cram session. This has been definitely established. What is more, a night a week for a month will return better dividends than crowding your study into a shorter period of time.
- Locate the place of the exam – You have been sent a notice telling you when and where to report for the examination. If the location is in a different town or otherwise unfamiliar to you, it would be well to inquire the best route and learn something about the building.
- Relax the night before the test – Allow your mind to rest. Do not study at all that night. Plan some mild recreation or diversion; then go to bed early and get a good night's sleep.
- Get up early enough to make a leisurely trip to the place for the test – This way unforeseen events, traffic snarls, unfamiliar buildings, etc. will not upset you.
- Dress comfortably – A written test is not a fashion show. You will be known by number and not by name, so wear something comfortable.

- Leave excess paraphernalia at home – Shopping bags and odd bundles will get in your way. You need bring only the items mentioned in the official notice you received; usually everything you need is provided. Do not bring reference books to the exam. They will only confuse those last minutes and be taken away from you when in the test room.
- Arrive somewhat ahead of time – If because of transportation schedules you must get there very early, bring a newspaper or magazine to take your mind off yourself while waiting.
- Locate the examination room – When you have found the proper room, you will be directed to the seat or part of the room where you will sit. Sometimes you are given a sheet of instructions to read while you are waiting. Do not fill out any forms until you are told to do so; just read them and be prepared.
- Relax and prepare to listen to the instructions
- If you have any physical problem that may keep you from doing your best, be sure to tell the test administrator. If you are sick or in poor health, you really cannot do your best on the exam. You can come back and take the test some other time.

VII. AT THE TEST

The day of the test is here and you have the test booklet in your hand. The temptation to get going is very strong. Caution! There is more to success than knowing the right answers. You must know how to identify your papers and understand variations in the type of short-answer question used in this particular examination. Follow these suggestions for maximum results from your efforts:

1) Cooperate with the monitor

The test administrator has a duty to create a situation in which you can be as much at ease as possible. He will give instructions, tell you when to begin, check to see that you are marking your answer sheet correctly, and so on. He is not there to guard you, although he will see that your competitors do not take unfair advantage. He wants to help you do your best.

2) Listen to all instructions

Don't jump the gun! Wait until you understand all directions. In most civil service tests you get more time than you need to answer the questions. So don't be in a hurry. Read each word of instructions until you clearly understand the meaning. Study the examples, listen to all announcements and follow directions. Ask questions if you do not understand what to do.

3) Identify your papers

Civil service exams are usually identified by number only. You will be assigned a number; you must not put your name on your test papers. Be sure to copy your number correctly. Since more than one exam may be given, copy your exact examination title.

4) Plan your time

Unless you are told that a test is a "speed" or "rate of work" test, speed itself is usually not important. Time enough to answer all the questions will be provided, but this does not mean that you have all day. An overall time limit has been set. Divide the total time (in minutes) by the number of questions to determine the approximate time you have for each question.

5) Do not linger over difficult questions

If you come across a difficult question, mark it with a paper clip (useful to have along) and come back to it when you have been through the booklet. One caution if you do this – be sure to skip a number on your answer sheet as well. Check often to be sure that you have not lost your place and that you are marking in the row numbered the same as the question you are answering.

6) Read the questions

Be sure you know what the question asks! Many capable people are unsuccessful because they failed to *read* the questions correctly.

7) Answer all questions

Unless you have been instructed that a penalty will be deducted for incorrect answers, it is better to guess than to omit a question.

8) Speed tests

It is often better NOT to guess on speed tests. It has been found that on timed tests people are tempted to spend the last few seconds before time is called in marking answers at random – without even reading them – in the hope of picking up a few extra points. To discourage this practice, the instructions may warn you that your score will be "corrected" for guessing. That is, a penalty will be applied. The incorrect answers will be deducted from the correct ones, or some other penalty formula will be used.

9) Review your answers

If you finish before time is called, go back to the questions you guessed or omitted to give them further thought. Review other answers if you have time.

10) Return your test materials

If you are ready to leave before others have finished or time is called, take ALL your materials to the monitor and leave quietly. Never take any test material with you. The monitor can discover whose papers are not complete, and taking a test booklet may be grounds for disqualification.

VIII. EXAMINATION TECHNIQUES

1) Read the general instructions carefully. These are usually printed on the first page of the exam booklet. As a rule, these instructions refer to the timing of the examination; the fact that you should not start work until the signal and must stop work at a signal, etc. If there are any *special* instructions, such as a choice of questions to be answered, make sure that you note this instruction carefully.

2) When you are ready to start work on the examination, that is as soon as the signal has been given, read the instructions to each question booklet, underline any key words or phrases, such as *least, best, outline, describe* and the like. In this way you will tend to answer as requested rather than discover on reviewing your paper that you *listed without describing*, that you selected the *worst* choice rather than the *best* choice, etc.

3) If the examination is of the objective or multiple-choice type – that is, each question will also give a series of possible answers: A, B, C or D, and you are called upon to select the best answer and write the letter next to that answer on your answer paper – it is advisable to start answering each question in turn. There may be anywhere from 50 to 100 such questions in the three or four hours allotted and you can see how much time would be taken if you read through all the questions before beginning to answer any. Furthermore, if you come across a question or group of questions which you know would be difficult to answer, it would undoubtedly affect your handling of all the other questions.

4) If the examination is of the essay type and contains but a few questions, it is a moot point as to whether you should read all the questions before starting to answer any one. Of course, if you are given a choice – say five out of seven and the like – then it is essential to read all the questions so you can eliminate the two that are most difficult. If, however, you are asked to answer all the questions, there may be danger in trying to answer the easiest one first because you may find that you will spend too much time on it. The best technique is to answer the first question, then proceed to the second, etc.

5) Time your answers. Before the exam begins, write down the time it started, then add the time allowed for the examination and write down the time it must be completed, then divide the time available somewhat as follows:
    - If 3-1/2 hours are allowed, that would be 210 minutes. If you have 80 objective-type questions, that would be an average of 2-1/2 minutes per question. Allow yourself no more than 2 minutes per question, or a total of 160 minutes, which will permit about 50 minutes to review.
    - If for the time allotment of 210 minutes there are 7 essay questions to answer, that would average about 30 minutes a question. Give yourself only 25 minutes per question so that you have about 35 minutes to review.

6) The most important instruction is to *read each question* and make sure you know what is wanted. The second most important instruction is to *time yourself properly* so that you answer every question. The third most important instruction is to *answer every question*. Guess if you have to but include something for each question. Remember that you will receive no credit for a blank and will probably receive some credit if you write something in answer to an essay question. If you guess a letter – say "B" for a multiple-choice question – you may have guessed right. If you leave a blank as an answer to a multiple-choice question, the examiners may respect your feelings but it will not add a point to your score. Some exams may penalize you for wrong answers, so in such cases *only*, you may not want to guess unless you have some basis for your answer.

7) Suggestions
    a. Objective-type questions
        1. Examine the question booklet for proper sequence of pages and questions
        2. Read all instructions carefully
        3. Skip any question which seems too difficult; return to it after all other questions have been answered
        4. Apportion your time properly; do not spend too much time on any single question or group of questions

5. Note and underline key words – *all, most, fewest, least, best, worst, same, opposite,* etc.
6. Pay particular attention to negatives
7. Note unusual option, e.g., unduly long, short, complex, different or similar in content to the body of the question
8. Observe the use of "hedging" words – *probably, may, most likely,* etc.
9. Make sure that your answer is put next to the same number as the question
10. Do not second-guess unless you have good reason to believe the second answer is definitely more correct
11. Cross out original answer if you decide another answer is more accurate; do not erase until you are ready to hand your paper in
12. Answer all questions; guess unless instructed otherwise
13. Leave time for review

  b. Essay questions
1. Read each question carefully
2. Determine exactly what is wanted. Underline key words or phrases.
3. Decide on outline or paragraph answer
4. Include many different points and elements unless asked to develop any one or two points or elements
5. Show impartiality by giving pros and cons unless directed to select one side only
6. Make and write down any assumptions you find necessary to answer the questions
7. Watch your English, grammar, punctuation and choice of words
8. Time your answers; don't crowd material

8) Answering the essay question

Most essay questions can be answered by framing the specific response around several key words or ideas. Here are a few such key words or ideas:

M's: manpower, materials, methods, money, management
P's: purpose, program, policy, plan, procedure, practice, problems, pitfalls, personnel, public relations

  a. Six basic steps in handling problems:
1. Preliminary plan and background development
2. Collect information, data and facts
3. Analyze and interpret information, data and facts
4. Analyze and develop solutions as well as make recommendations
5. Prepare report and sell recommendations
6. Install recommendations and follow up effectiveness

  b. Pitfalls to avoid
1. *Taking things for granted* – A statement of the situation does not necessarily imply that each of the elements is necessarily true; for example, a complaint may be invalid and biased so that all that can be taken for granted is that a complaint has been registered

2. *Considering only one side of a situation* – Wherever possible, indicate several alternatives and then point out the reasons you selected the best one
3. *Failing to indicate follow up* – Whenever your answer indicates action on your part, make certain that you will take proper follow-up action to see how successful your recommendations, procedures or actions turn out to be
4. *Taking too long in answering any single question* – Remember to time your answers properly

IX. AFTER THE TEST

Scoring procedures differ in detail among civil service jurisdictions although the general principles are the same. Whether the papers are hand-scored or graded by machine we have described, they are nearly always graded by number. That is, the person who marks the paper knows only the number – never the name – of the applicant. Not until all the papers have been graded will they be matched with names. If other tests, such as training and experience or oral interview ratings have been given, scores will be combined. Different parts of the examination usually have different weights. For example, the written test might count 60 percent of the final grade, and a rating of training and experience 40 percent. In many jurisdictions, veterans will have a certain number of points added to their grades.

After the final grade has been determined, the names are placed in grade order and an eligible list is established. There are various methods for resolving ties between those who get the same final grade – probably the most common is to place first the name of the person whose application was received first. Job offers are made from the eligible list in the order the names appear on it. You will be notified of your grade and your rank as soon as all these computations have been made. This will be done as rapidly as possible.

People who are found to meet the requirements in the announcement are called "eligibles." Their names are put on a list of eligible candidates. An eligible's chances of getting a job depend on how high he stands on this list and how fast agencies are filling jobs from the list.

When a job is to be filled from a list of eligibles, the agency asks for the names of people on the list of eligibles for that job. When the civil service commission receives this request, it sends to the agency the names of the three people highest on this list. Or, if the job to be filled has specialized requirements, the office sends the agency the names of the top three persons who meet these requirements from the general list.

The appointing officer makes a choice from among the three people whose names were sent to him. If the selected person accepts the appointment, the names of the others are put back on the list to be considered for future openings.

That is the rule in hiring from all kinds of eligible lists, whether they are for typist, carpenter, chemist, or something else. For every vacancy, the appointing officer has his choice of any one of the top three eligibles on the list. This explains why the person whose name is on top of the list sometimes does not get an appointment when some of the persons lower on the list do. If the appointing officer chooses the second or third eligible, the No. 1 eligible does not get a job at once, but stays on the list until he is appointed or the list is terminated.

X. HOW TO PASS THE INTERVIEW TEST

The examination for which you applied requires an oral interview test. You have already taken the written test and you are now being called for the interview test – the final part of the formal examination.

You may think that it is not possible to prepare for an interview test and that there are no procedures to follow during an interview. Our purpose is to point out some things you can do in advance that will help you and some good rules to follow and pitfalls to avoid while you are being interviewed.

What is an interview supposed to test?

The written examination is designed to test the technical knowledge and competence of the candidate; the oral is designed to evaluate intangible qualities, not readily measured otherwise, and to establish a list showing the relative fitness of each candidate – as measured against his competitors – for the position sought. Scoring is not on the basis of "right" and "wrong," but on a sliding scale of values ranging from "not passable" to "outstanding." As a matter of fact, it is possible to achieve a relatively low score without a single "incorrect" answer because of evident weakness in the qualities being measured.

Occasionally, an examination may consist entirely of an oral test – either an individual or a group oral. In such cases, information is sought concerning the technical knowledges and abilities of the candidate, since there has been no written examination for this purpose. More commonly, however, an oral test is used to supplement a written examination.

Who conducts interviews?

The composition of oral boards varies among different jurisdictions. In nearly all, a representative of the personnel department serves as chairman. One of the members of the board may be a representative of the department in which the candidate would work. In some cases, "outside experts" are used, and, frequently, a businessman or some other representative of the general public is asked to serve. Labor and management or other special groups may be represented. The aim is to secure the services of experts in the appropriate field.

However the board is composed, it is a good idea (and not at all improper or unethical) to ascertain in advance of the interview who the members are and what groups they represent. When you are introduced to them, you will have some idea of their backgrounds and interests, and at least you will not stutter and stammer over their names.

What should be done before the interview?

While knowledge about the board members is useful and takes some of the surprise element out of the interview, there is other preparation which is more substantive. It *is* possible to prepare for an oral interview – in several ways:

1) Keep a copy of your application and review it carefully before the interview

This may be the only document before the oral board, and the starting point of the interview. Know what education and experience you have listed there, and the sequence and dates of all of it. Sometimes the board will ask you to review the highlights of your experience for them; you should not have to hem and haw doing it.

2) Study the class specification and the examination announcement

Usually, the oral board has one or both of these to guide them. The qualities, characteristics or knowledges required by the position sought are stated in these documents. They offer valuable clues as to the nature of the oral interview. For example, if the job involves supervisory responsibilities, the announcement will usually indicate that knowledge of modern supervisory methods and the qualifications of the candidate as a supervisor will be tested. If so, you can expect such questions, frequently in the form of a hypothetical situation which you are expected to solve. NEVER go into an oral without knowledge of the duties and responsibilities of the job you seek.

3) Think through each qualification required

Try to visualize the kind of questions you would ask if you were a board member. How well could you answer them? Try especially to appraise your own knowledge and background in each area, *measured against the job sought*, and identify any areas in which you are weak. Be critical and realistic – do not flatter yourself.

4) Do some general reading in areas in which you feel you may be weak

For example, if the job involves supervision and your past experience has NOT, some general reading in supervisory methods and practices, particularly in the field of human relations, might be useful. Do NOT study agency procedures or detailed manuals. The oral board will be testing your understanding and capacity, not your memory.

5) Get a good night's sleep and watch your general health and mental attitude

You will want a clear head at the interview. Take care of a cold or any other minor ailment, and of course, no hangovers.

What should be done on the day of the interview?

Now comes the day of the interview itself. Give yourself plenty of time to get there. Plan to arrive somewhat ahead of the scheduled time, particularly if your appointment is in the fore part of the day. If a previous candidate fails to appear, the board might be ready for you a bit early. By early afternoon an oral board is almost invariably behind schedule if there are many candidates, and you may have to wait. Take along a book or magazine to read, or your application to review, but leave any extraneous material in the waiting room when you go in for your interview. In any event, relax and compose yourself.

The matter of dress is important. The board is forming impressions about you – from your experience, your manners, your attitude, and your appearance. Give your personal appearance careful attention. Dress your best, but not your flashiest. Choose conservative, appropriate clothing, and be sure it is immaculate. This is a business interview, and your appearance should indicate that you regard it as such. Besides, being well groomed and properly dressed will help boost your confidence.

Sooner or later, someone will call your name and escort you into the interview room. *This is it.* From here on you are on your own. It is too late for any more preparation. But remember, you asked for this opportunity to prove your fitness, and you are here because your request was granted.

What happens when you go in?

The usual sequence of events will be as follows: The clerk (who is often the board stenographer) will introduce you to the chairman of the oral board, who will introduce you to the other members of the board. Acknowledge the introductions before you sit down. Do not be surprised if you find a microphone facing you or a stenotypist sitting by. Oral interviews are usually recorded in the event of an appeal or other review.

Usually the chairman of the board will open the interview by reviewing the highlights of your education and work experience from your application – primarily for the benefit of the other members of the board, as well as to get the material into the record. Do not interrupt or comment unless there is an error or significant misinterpretation; if that is the case, do not hesitate. But do not quibble about insignificant matters. Also, he will usually ask you some question about your education, experience or your present job – partly to get you to start talking and to establish the interviewing "rapport." He may start the actual questioning, or turn it over to one of the other members. Frequently, each member undertakes the questioning on a particular area, one in which he is perhaps most competent, so you can expect each member to participate in the examination. Because time is limited, you may also expect some rather abrupt switches in the direction the questioning takes, so do not be upset by it. Normally, a board member will not pursue a single line of questioning unless he discovers a particular strength or weakness.

After each member has participated, the chairman will usually ask whether any member has any further questions, then will ask you if you have anything you wish to add. Unless you are expecting this question, it may floor you. Worse, it may start you off on an extended, extemporaneous speech. The board is not usually seeking more information. The question is principally to offer you a last opportunity to present further qualifications or to indicate that you have nothing to add. So, if you feel that a significant qualification or characteristic has been overlooked, it is proper to point it out in a sentence or so. Do not compliment the board on the thoroughness of their examination – they have been sketchy, and you know it. If you wish, merely say, "No thank you, I have nothing further to add." This is a point where you can "talk yourself out" of a good impression or fail to present an important bit of information. Remember, *you close the interview yourself*.

The chairman will then say, "That is all, Mr. _____, thank you." Do not be startled; the interview is over, and quicker than you think. Thank him, gather your belongings and take your leave. Save your sigh of relief for the other side of the door.

How to put your best foot forward

Throughout this entire process, you may feel that the board individually and collectively is trying to pierce your defenses, seek out your hidden weaknesses and embarrass and confuse you. Actually, this is not true. They are obliged to make an appraisal of your qualifications for the job you are seeking, and they want to see you in your best light. Remember, they must interview all candidates and a non-cooperative candidate may become a failure in spite of their best efforts to bring out his qualifications. Here are 15 suggestions that will help you:

1) Be natural – Keep your attitude confident, not cocky

If you are not confident that you can do the job, do not expect the board to be. Do not apologize for your weaknesses, try to bring out your strong points. The board is interested in a positive, not negative, presentation. Cockiness will antagonize any board member and make him wonder if you are covering up a weakness by a false show of strength.

2) Get comfortable, but don't lounge or sprawl

Sit erectly but not stiffly. A careless posture may lead the board to conclude that you are careless in other things, or at least that you are not impressed by the importance of the occasion. Either conclusion is natural, even if incorrect. Do not fuss with your clothing, a pencil or an ashtray. Your hands may occasionally be useful to emphasize a point; do not let them become a point of distraction.

3) Do not wisecrack or make small talk

This is a serious situation, and your attitude should show that you consider it as such. Further, the time of the board is limited – they do not want to waste it, and neither should you.

4) Do not exaggerate your experience or abilities

In the first place, from information in the application or other interviews and sources, the board may know more about you than you think. Secondly, you probably will not get away with it. An experienced board is rather adept at spotting such a situation, so do not take the chance.

5) If you know a board member, do not make a point of it, yet do not hide it

Certainly you are not fooling him, and probably not the other members of the board. Do not try to take advantage of your acquaintanceship – it will probably do you little good.

6) Do not dominate the interview

Let the board do that. They will give you the clues – do not assume that you have to do all the talking. Realize that the board has a number of questions to ask you, and do not try to take up all the interview time by showing off your extensive knowledge of the answer to the first one.

7) Be attentive

You only have 20 minutes or so, and you should keep your attention at its sharpest throughout. When a member is addressing a problem or question to you, give him your undivided attention. Address your reply principally to him, but do not exclude the other board members.

8) Do not interrupt

A board member may be stating a problem for you to analyze. He will ask you a question when the time comes. Let him state the problem, and wait for the question.

9) Make sure you understand the question

Do not try to answer until you are sure what the question is. If it is not clear, restate it in your own words or ask the board member to clarify it for you. However, do not haggle about minor elements.

10) Reply promptly but not hastily

A common entry on oral board rating sheets is "candidate responded readily," or "candidate hesitated in replies." Respond as promptly and quickly as you can, but do not jump to a hasty, ill-considered answer.

11) Do not be peremptory in your answers

A brief answer is proper – but do not fire your answer back. That is a losing game from your point of view. The board member can probably ask questions much faster than you can answer them.

12) Do not try to create the answer you think the board member wants

He is interested in what kind of mind you have and how it works – not in playing games. Furthermore, he can usually spot this practice and will actually grade you down on it.

13) Do not switch sides in your reply merely to agree with a board member

Frequently, a member will take a contrary position merely to draw you out and to see if you are willing and able to defend your point of view. Do not start a debate, yet do not surrender a good position. If a position is worth taking, it is worth defending.

14) Do not be afraid to admit an error in judgment if you are shown to be wrong

The board knows that you are forced to reply without any opportunity for careful consideration. Your answer may be demonstrably wrong. If so, admit it and get on with the interview.

15) Do not dwell at length on your present job

The opening question may relate to your present assignment. Answer the question but do not go into an extended discussion. You are being examined for a *new* job, not your present one. As a matter of fact, try to phrase ALL your answers in terms of the job for which you are being examined.

Basis of Rating

Probably you will forget most of these "do's" and "don'ts" when you walk into the oral interview room. Even remembering them all will not ensure you a passing grade. Perhaps you did not have the qualifications in the first place. But remembering them will help you to put your best foot forward, without treading on the toes of the board members.

Rumor and popular opinion to the contrary notwithstanding, an oral board wants you to make the best appearance possible. They know you are under pressure – but they also want to see how you respond to it as a guide to what your reaction would be under the pressures of the job you seek. They will be influenced by the degree of poise you display, the personal traits you show and the manner in which you respond.

ABOUT THIS BOOK

This book contains tests divided into Examination Sections. Go through each test, answering every question in the margin. We have also attached a sample answer sheet at the back of the book that can be removed and used. At the end of each test look at the answer key and check your answers. On the ones you got wrong, look at the right answer choice and learn. Do not fill in the answers first. Do not memorize the questions and answers, but understand the answer and principles involved. On your test, the questions will likely be different from the samples. Questions are changed and new ones added. If you understand these past questions you should have success with any changes that arise. Tests may consist of several types of questions. We have additional books on each subject should more study be advisable or necessary for you. Finally, the more you study, the better prepared you will be. This book is intended to be the last thing you study before you walk into the examination room. Prior study of relevant texts is also recommended. NLC publishes some of these in our Fundamental Series. Knowledge and good sense are important factors in passing your exam. Good luck also helps. So now study this Passbook, absorb the material contained within and take that knowledge into the examination. Then do your best to pass that exam.

EXAMINATION SECTION

EXAMINATION SECTION
TEST 1

DIRECTIONS: Each question or incomplete statement is followed by several suggested answers or completions. Select the one that BEST answers the question or completes the statement. *PRINT THE LETTER OF THE CORRECT ANSWER IN THE SPACE AT THE RIGHT.*

Questions 1-2.

DIRECTIONS: Questions 1 and 2 refer to the formula below.

The formula for stopping sight distance SSD13

$$SSD = 1.47tV + \frac{V^2}{30(f+G)}$$

1. The number 1.47 is a(n)

   A. empirically derived constant
   B. conversion factor
   C. factor based on perception reaction time
   D. factor of safety

   1.____

2. The term t is usually assumed to be _____ seconds.

   A. 1.5   B. 2.0   C. 2.5   D. 3.0

   2.____

3. An automobile weighing W is rounding a curve of radius R with a velocity V. Neglecting the friction between the tires and the roadway, if the forces acting on the car are in equilibrium, then

   3.____

   A. $\sin\theta = \dfrac{V^2}{gR}$

   B. $\cos\theta = \dfrac{V^2}{gR}$

   C. $\tan\theta = \dfrac{V^2}{gR}$

   D. $\cot\theta = \dfrac{V^2}{gR}$

Questions 4-5.

DIRECTIONS: Questions 4 and 5 refer to the horizontal curve below.

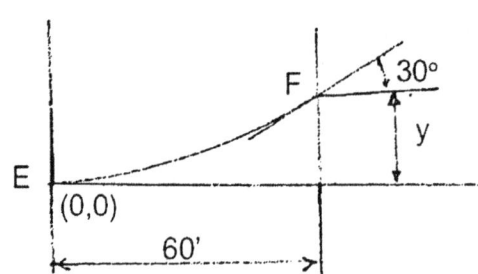

The equation of the curve is $y = kx^3$. The slope of the curve at F is 30°.

4. The value of k is

   A. .000023   B. .000033   C. .000043   D. .000053

5. The value of y is

   A. 5.0   B. 7.1   C. 9.3   D. 11.5

6. A 4° horizontal curve has a radius of _____ feet.

   A. 1232.4   B. 1332.4   C. 1432.4   D. 1532.4

Questions 7-10.

DIRECTIONS: Questions 7 through 10, inclusive, refer to the diagram of a horizontal circular highway curve.

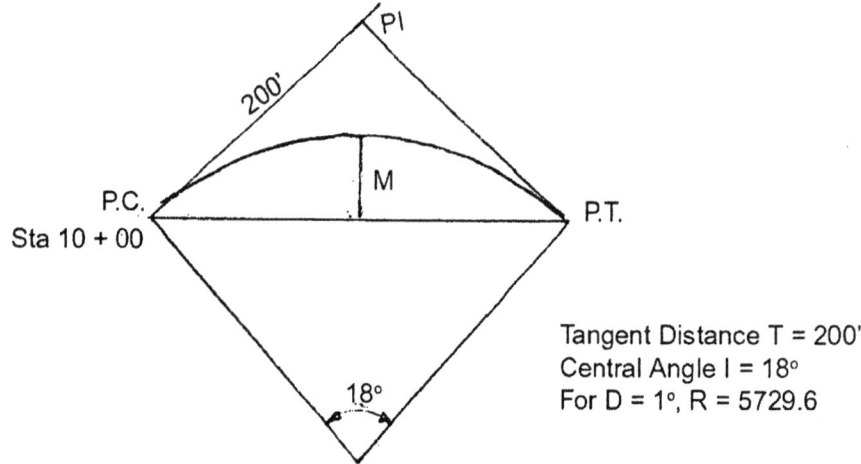

Tangent Distance T = 200'
Central Angle I = 18°
For D = 1°, R = 5729.6

7. The radius of the curve is _____ feet.

   A. 1212.7   B. 1232.7   C. 1262.7   D. 1292.7

8. The length of the arc of the circular curve is MOST NEARLY _____ feet.

   A. 396.7   B. 397.0   C. 397.7   D. 398.0

9. The long chord P.C. to P.T. is MOST NEARLY _____ feet.

   A. 392.06   B. 393.06   C. 394.06   D. 395.06

10. The middle ordinate M is most nearly _____ feet.

    A. 14.95   B. 15.15   C. 15.35   D. 15.55

11.

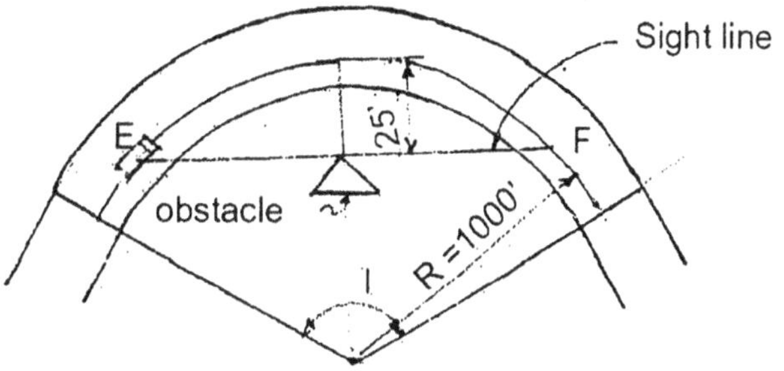

    The sight distance EF is MOST NEARLY _____ feet.

    A. 324   B. 364   C. 404   D. 444

12. For crest vertical curves, the length of the curve depends on the change in grade and H_e and H_o where He is the driver's eye height and H_o is the object height. Their relation is usually

    A. $H_e < H_o$
    B. $H_e = H_o$
    C. $H_e > H_o$
    D. H_e is either greater, equal or less than H_o, depending on the judgment of chief of design

13. The length of a transition curve which connects a tangent to a circular curve should be sufficient to

    A. keep the rate of change of direction small
    B. achieve the superelevation of the road section
    C. prevent disruption of the drainage system
    D. prevent an abrupt change of direction when the circular curve is reached

14. It is desirable to have a minimum road grade of at least 0.3% in order to

    A. follow the land contours
    B. facilitate keeping the shoulders clear of debris
    C. secure adequate drainage for the roadway
    D. prevent drivers becoming drowsy on long stretches of level roadway

Questions 15-16.

DIRECTIONS: Questions 15 and 16 refer to the horizontal highway curve below.

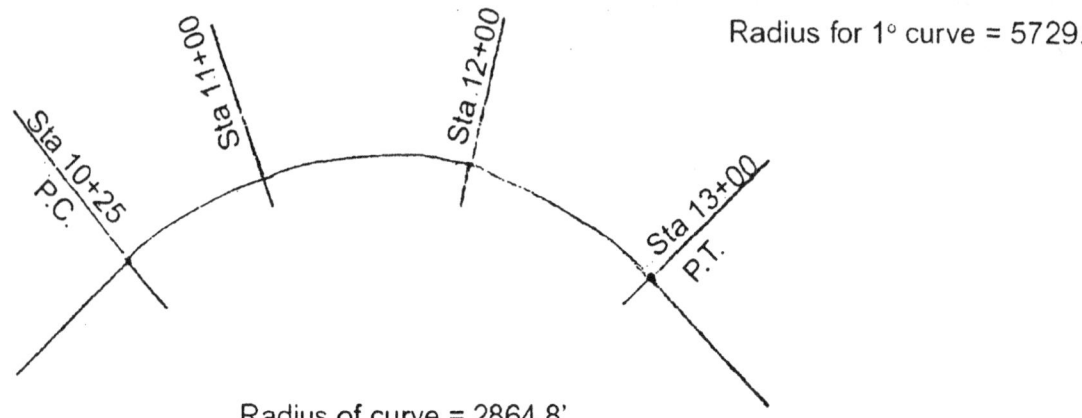

Radius for 1° curve = 5729.6'

Radius of curve = 2864.8'

15. The deflection angle from the P.C. to Sta 11+00 is 15.___

    A. 0°45'   B. 1°00'   C. 1°15'   D. 1°30'

16. The deflection angle to Sta 13+00 is 16.___

    A. 2°00'   B. 2°45'   C. 3°45'   D. 5°30'

17. Air entrained cement is used in air entrained concrete. The acceptable amount of air is generally between _____ percent of the total volume. 17.___

    A. 1 and 5   B. 2 and 6   C. 3 and 7   D. 4 and 8

18. Pumping of joints in a concrete roadway slab will occur during frequent occurrence of heavy wheel loads, the presence in the subgrade soil that is susceptible to pumping and 18.___

    A. inadequate thickness of the concrete slab
    B. air entrained cement is used in the roadway
    C. surplus water in the subgrade
    D. coarse and fine sand subgrades

19. Distributed steel reinforcing is primarily used to control cracking of a concrete roadway pavement and to maintain the integrity of the slab between transverse joints. Wire fabric or bar mats are used.
    In a concrete roadway section, the steel is usually placed at _____ of the slab. 19.___

    A. or near the center
    B. the bottom
    C. the top
    D. the bottom and at the top

20. In slipform paving for a concrete roadway, the slump in the concrete being poured should be _____ inch(es). 20.___

    A. 1/2 to 1   B. 1 to 1 1/2   C. 1 1/2 to 2   D. 2 to 2 1/2

21. The collapse of a section of the New England Thruway at Mianus was due primarily to faulty   21._____

    A. steel
    B. design
    C. construction
    D. periodic inspections

22. The coefficient of expansion of concrete due to temperature change is considered   22._____

    A. the same as that for steel
    B. less than that for steel
    C. more than that for steel
    D. more or less than that for steel, depending on the type of steel being used

23. Design hourly volume is a future hourly volume used for design. It is usually taken as the _____ hourly volume of the year.   23._____

    A. 10th   B. 15th   C. 20th   D. 30th

24. Let E be an experiment and S a sample space associated with the experiment. A function X assigned to every element SES a real number X(S) is called a   24._____

    A. relative frequency
    B. likely outcome
    C. random variable
    D. conditional probability

25. The color code brown on a traffic device denotes   25._____

    A. public recreation and scenic guidance
    B. construction and maintenance warning
    C. general warning
    D. motorist service guidance

KEY (CORRECT ANSWERS)

1.	B	11.	D
2.	C	12.	C
3.	C	13.	B
4.	D	14.	C
5.	D	15.	A
6.	C	16.	B
7.	C	17.	D
8.	A	18.	C
9.	D	19.	A
10.	D	20.	B

21. D
22. A
23. D
24. C
25. A

TEST 2

DIRECTIONS: Each question or incomplete statement is followed by several suggested answers or completions. Select the one that BEST answers the question or completes the statement. *PRINT THE LETTER OF THE CORRECT ANSWER IN THE SPACE AT THE RIGHT.*

1. The minimum headroom clearance for a sign over a roadway, according to the Federal Highway Administration, should be _____ feet.   1.____

   A. 15   B. 16   C. 17   D. 18

2. In traffic flow, time mean speed _____ space mean speed.   2.____

   A. equals
   B. is less than
   C. is greater than
   D. may be greater or less than

3. Overall speed and running speed are speeds over a relatively long section of street or highway between an origin and a destination. Test vehicles are driven over the test section of the roadway. The driver attempts to float in the traffic stream.
   This means   3.____

   A. driving as fast as he can under the speed limit
   B. driving in the middle lane of a three lane road
   C. passing as many vehicles as pass the test vehicle
   D. trying to keep his speed the same as the average speed of the vehicles on the road

4. The difference between overall speed and running speed on a test run between origin and destination is overall speed is the   4.____

   A. average of the maximum and minimum speed while running speed is the distance covered divided by the time elapsed
   B. distance traveled divided by the time required while running speed is the distance traveled divided by the time required reduced by time for stop delays
   C. distance traveled divided by the total time required while running speed is the minimum time needed to cover the distance
   D. distance traveled divided by the total time required while running speed is the effort by the driver to stay in the flow of traffic

5. The ductility test on asphalt is considered a measure of the _____ of the asphalt.   5.____

   A. impact resistance   B. elasticity
   C. durability   D. cementing power

6. In asphalt paving work, there are three different types of specific gravity: bulk, apparent, and effective. Of the following statements relating to specific gravity, the one that is CORRECT is: 6.____

   A. Water absorption is normally not used in determining the quantity of permeable voids in the volume of aggregates
   B. The apparent specific gravity is less than the bulk specific gravity

C. The effective specific gravity is less than the bulk specific gravity
D. The effective specific gravity falls between the bulk specific gravity and the apparent specific gravity

7. The temperature range of asphalt prior to entering the mixer in a batch or continuous plant is usually

   A. 150 to 250° F
   B. 175 to 275° F
   C. 200 to 300° F
   D. 225 to 325° F

8. The most likely cause of the various distress types in asphalt concrete pavements is

   A. structural failure
   B. temperature changes
   C. moisture changes
   D. faulty construction

9. Bleeding in asphalt concrete pavements is MOST likely caused by

   A. faulty mix composition
   B. structural failure
   C. temperature changes
   D. moisture changes

10. Depressions in asphalt concrete pavements is MOST likely caused by

    A. faulty construction
    B. faulty mix composition
    C. temperature changes
    D. moisture changes

11. The gradation curve of particle sizes is represented graphically with the ordinate defining the percent by weight passing a given size and the abscissa representing the particle size.
    The ordinate is plotted on a(n) _____ scale and the abscissa is plotted on a(n) _____ scale.

    A. arithmetic; arithmetic
    B. logarithmic; arithmetic
    C. arithmetic; logarithmic
    D. logarithmic; logarithmic

12. The viscosity of a liquid is a measure of its

    A. resistance to flow
    B. volatility
    C. solubility in carbon tetrachloride
    D. elasticity

13. Failures that occur in soil masses as a result of the action of highway loads are primarily _____ failures.

    A. tensile   B. torsion   C. shear   D. buckling

14. Bitumens composed primarily of high molecular weight hydrocarbons are soluble in

    A. toluene
    B. carbon sulfate
    C. carbon disulfide
    D. ammonium chloride

15. One pascal-second equals _____ poise(s).

    A. 1   B. 5   C. 10   D. 20

16. RS emulsions are best used

    A. where deep penetration is desired
    B. with coarse aggregates
    C. in warm weather
    D. in spraying applications

17. The specific gravity of bituminous material is generally determined

    A. with a pyenometer
    B. with a hygrometer
    C. by displacement
    D. with a hydrometer

18. The principal reason for determining the specific gravity of a bituminous material is

    A. converting from volume to weight measurements and vice versa
    B. identifying the type of bituminous material used in a mix
    C. for checking the uniformity of a mix where large quantities are involved
    D. insure that the properties of the mix continue to meet specifications

19. The specific gravity of asphaltic products derived from petroleum vary from

    A. .80 to .84
    B. .92 to 1.06
    C. 1.04 to 1.18
    D. 1.16 to 1.30

20. The flash point is an indirect measurement of the quality and kind of volatiles present in the asphalt being tested.
    Rapid cure cutback asphalts have a flashpoint of _____ or less.

    A. 100° F   B. 130° F   C. 150° F   D. 180° F

21. Traffic density is defined as the

    A. number of vehicles passing a given point in a given period of time
    B. average number of vehicles occupying a given length of roadway at a given instant
    C. average center to center distance of vehicles on a given stretch of roadway at a given instant
    D. minimum distance center to center of vehicles on a given stretch of roadway at a given instant

22. Of the following, the best distribution that describes the vehicle distribution on a given stretch of highway at a given instant is the _____ distribution.

    A. Poisson
    B. Pascal
    C. normal
    D. hypergeometric

23. In slipform paving for a concrete roadway, the slump in the concrete being poured should be _____ inch(es).

    A. 1/2 to 1   B. 1 to 1 1/2   C. 1 1/2 to 2   D. 2 to 2 1/2

24. A water-cement ratio of 6 gallons per sack of cement is equal to a water-cement ratio of _____ by weight.

    A. .50   B. .53   C. .56   D. .59

25. One micron is equal to _____ centimeters.   25.____

    A. 10^{-2} B. 10^{-3} C. 10^{-4} D. 10^{-5}

KEY (CORRECT ANSWERS)

1. C
2. C
3. C
4. B
5. D
6. D
7. D
8. D
9. A
10. A

11. C
12. A
13. C
14. C
15. C
16. D
17. A
18. A
19. B
20. A

21. B
22. A
23. B
24. B
25. C

EXAMINATION SECTION
TEST 1

DIRECTIONS: Each question or incomplete statement is followed by several suggested answers or completions. Select the one that BEST answers the question or completes the statement. *PRINT THE LETTER OF THE CORRECT ANSWER IN THE SPACE AT THE RIGHT.*

1. Reflective cracks in asphalt overlays   1.____

    A. are cracks in asphalt overlays that show the crack pattern of the pavement underneath
    B. are cracks that reflect caused by weakness in the base soil
    C. are the result of change in weights and frequency of truck travel in that they are greater than the loads the pavement was designed for
    D. reflect the type of cracks that normally could be expected for this type of pavement

2. In a guide for the estimation of Pavement Condition Rating for asphalt concrete pavement on a highway is the following classification: *Pavement is in fairly good condition with frequent slight cracking or very slight channeling and a few areas with slight alligatoring. Rideability is fairly good with intermittent rough and uneven sections.*   2.____
The maintenance recommendation for this class of pavement condition is

    A. no maintenance required
    B. normal maintenance only
    C. resurface in 3 to 5 years
    D. resurface within 3 years

3. A major problem in bituminous asphalt plants is   3.____

    A. varying water content in the bituminous aggregate
    B. accuracy in the weighing equipment
    C. air pollution caused by plant exhausts
    D. producing a uniform mixture

4. The primary difference between asphalt concrete and sheet asphalt is asphalt concrete   4.____

    A. uses a finer sand than sheet asphalt
    B. uses a lower viscosity asphalt than sheet asphalt
    C. generally has a thinner layer than sheet asphalt
    D. contains coarse aggregate whereas sheet asphalt does not have coarse aggregate

5. It is common practice to apply a prime coat over untreated and some treated bases before asphalt concrete is placed. Of the following, the reasons for applying a prime coat are to   5.____

    A. bind loose particles of the base and minimize heat loss in the applied asphalt concrete
    B. act as a bond between base and pavement and prevent loss of asphalt in the asphalt concrete due to seepage
    C. deter rising moisture from penetrating the pavement and minimize heat loss in the applied asphalt concrete
    D. bind loose particles in the base and deter rising moisture from penetrating the asphalt pavement

6. The asphalt content of open graded mixes is generally at

   A. the same level as dense graded asphalt
   B. a higher level than dense graded asphalt
   C. a lower level than dense graded asphalt
   D. at a higher or lower level than dense graded asphalt depending on the percent of fine aggregate in the open graded asphalt mix

7. Sheet asphalt was extensively used in the past with a thickness of _____ inch(es).

   A. 1/2　　　B. 3/4　　　C. 1　　　D. 1 1/2

8. The progressive separation of aggregate particles in a pavement from the surface downward or from the edges inward in an asphalt concrete pavement is known as

   A. raveling
   B. spalling
   C. scaling
   D. reflective cracks

9. A profilometer used on an asphalt concrete road measures the _____ the road.

   A. grade of
   B. roughness of
   C. impact resistance of
   D. channels in

10. Reinforcing steel is used in a footing. The minimum distance the bottom of the steel is above the subgrade should be _____ inch(es).

    A. 1　　　B. 2　　　C. 3　　　D. 4

11. Loose sand weighs 120 pounds per cubic foot and the specific gravity of sand is 2.65. The absolute volume of a cubic foot of loose sand is, in cubic feet, most nearly

    A. .73　　　B. .75　　　C. .77　　　D. .79

12. The maximum size of coarse aggregate in a concrete mix for a reinforced concrete structure is determined by the size of the concrete section and the

    A. type of cement used
    B. proportion of fine aggregate
    C. minimum distance between reinforcing bars
    D. yield point of the reinforcing steel

13. Cement (High Early Strength) is Type _____ cement.

    A. I　　　B. II　　　C. III　　　D. IV

14. Slunp in concrete is a measure of

    A. strength
    B. porosity
    C. permeability
    D. workability

15. The cross section area of a #8 bar is _____ square inches.

    A. .60　　　B. .79　　　C. 1.00　　　D. 1.25

16. Construction joints for slabs in a building shall be made 16.____
    A. at the supports
    B. within 1/8 of the span of the slab from the supports
    C. from 1/8 to 3/8 of the span of the slab from the supports
    D. near the center of the span

17. Chutes for depositing concrete shall have a slope no greater than 17.____

    A. (triangle 1:1)   B. (triangle 1:1½)   C. (triangle 1:2)   D. (triangle 1:2½)

18. Air entrained cement is used in a concrete mix on highways primarily to 18.____
    A. make the concrete stronger after 28 days
    B. have a higher early strength
    C. make the surface more resistant to freezing and thawing
    D. make the surface less porous to better resist the impact of trucks

19. Beach sand is unsuitable as a fine aggregate in concrete because it has salt contamination and the sand particles are 19.____
    A. smooth   B. rough
    C. uniform in size   D. too fine

20. The fineness modulus of sand for concrete is taken on the job to insure 20.____
    A. the quality of the sand
    B. that the gradation of the sand does not change
    C. that there is not an excess of fines in the sand
    D. that there is not an excess of oversized particles in the sand

21. The coarse and fine aggregate for concrete are usually tested 21.____
    A. at the quarry site
    B. at the job site
    C. by sampling a loaded truck
    D. in the design engineering office

22. The slump in concrete for highway mixtures range from _____ inches. 22.____
    A. 1 to 3   B. 2 to 5   C. 3 to 6   D. 4 to 7

23. A bag of cement weighs _____ pounds. 23.____
    A. 90   B. 94   C. 97   D. 100

24. The design strength of concrete is to be reached at the end of _____ days. 24.____
    A. 7   B. 14   C. 21   D. 28

25. Of the following, water-cement ratio may be defined as _____ of water per _____ of cement. 25.____
    A. gallons; bag   B. gallons; 100 pounds
    C. quarts; bag   D. quarts; 100 pounds

KEY (CORRECT ANSWERS)

1. A
2. C
3. C
4. D
5. D

6. B
7. D
8. A
9. B
10. C

11. A
12. C
13. C
14. D
15. B

16. D
17. C
18. C
19. C
20. B

21. A
22. A
23. B
24. D
25. A

TEST 2

DIRECTIONS: Each question or incomplete statement is followed by several suggested answers or completions. Select the one that BEST answers the question or completes the statement. *PRINT THE LETTER OF THE CORRECT ANSWER IN THE SPACE AT THE RIGHT.*

1. The maximum size of coarse aggregate in a concrete mix for a reinforced concrete structure is determined by the size of the section and the

    A. type of cement used
    B. proportion of fine aggregate
    C. minimum distance between reinforcing bars
    D. the yield point of the reinforcing steel

1.____

Questions 2-3.

DIRECTIONS: Questions 2 and 3 refer to concrete mix design.

2. The present and most popular method of rational mixture design is sponsored by ACI committee 211, 1994. In this method, the design using ordinary cement is based on

    A. slump and water-cement ratio
    B. aggregate size and water-cement ratio
    C. slump, aggregate size, and water-cement ratio
    D. slump and water content

2.____

3. In the method of mix design of ACI committee 211, 1994, water content is expressed in

    A. pounds of water per bag of cement
    B. pounds of water per cubic foot of concrete
    C. gallons of water per cubic yard of concrete
    D. pounds of water per cubic yard of concrete

3.____

4. The right to use or control the property of another for designated purposes is the definition of

    A. property acquisition   B. right-of-way
    C. an air right   D. an easement

4.____

5. A 24 inch circular drainage pipe is shown on a profile drawing of a highway as an ellipse with the major axis vertical. The reason for this is

    A. the horizontal and vertical scales of the profile drawing are different
    B. the pipe is not perpendicular to the center line of the roadway
    C. to emphasize the height of the pipe
    D. the slope of the pipe is taken into account

5.____

6. On a highway plan is a note for #4 wire game fence reading Lt Sta 2970 + 00 to 2979 + 85, Rt Sta 2970 + 00 to 2980 + 70. The total number of linear feet of new #4 wire game fence is, in feet, most nearly

    A. 1955   B. 2005   C. 2055   D. 2105

6.____

7. The superelevation of a curve is .075 feet. The superelevation, in inches, is most nearly

   A. 9   B. 5/8   C. 3/4   D. 7/8

8. On a plan for a highway is a note $\dfrac{\text{S.C.}}{\text{Sta } 2968+56.50}$ The S.C. is an abbreviation for

   A. slope at curve
   B. spiral to circular curve
   C. superelevated curve
   D. separation at center

9. Of the following methods of soil stabilization for the base of a highway pavement, the one that is most effective is

   A. a cement admixture
   B. a lime admixture
   C. an emulsified asphalt treated soil
   D. mechanical soil stabilization

10. An asphalt pavement mixture having a brownish dull appearance and lacking a shiny black luster

    A. is normal for an asphalt mixture
    B. contains too little aggregate
    C. is too cold
    D. contains too little asphalt

11. Steam rising from an asphalt mix when it is dumped into a hopper indicates

    A. there is excessive moisture in the aggregate
    B. the mix is overheated
    C. emulsification is taking place
    D. the mixture has not been adequately mixed

12. The disadvantage of excessive fine aggregate in an asphalt mix is

    A. it is difficult to get a uniform mix
    B. it will require an excessive amount of asphalt
    C. it is difficult to apply because of the grittiness of the mix
    D. the final surface will tend to be rough

13. On highways where heavy trucks are permitted, the percent of total traffic that are heavy trucks is, in percent, MOST NEARLY

    A. 4   B. 11   C. 18   D. 25

14. A single axle 80 kN load is equal to _____ pounds per axle.

    A. 12,000   B. 14,000   C. 16,000   D. 18,000

15. Normal traffic growth in the United States is _____ percent per year.

    A. 1-2   B. 3-5   C. 5-7   D. 7-9

16. EAL is an abbreviation for _____ axle load

    A. equal
    B. equivalent
    C. effective
    D. estimated

17. A roughometer is a single-wheeled trailer instrumented to measure the roughness of a pavement surface. The measure is in inches per

    A. foot　　　　B. yard　　　　C. hundred yards　　D. mile

18. The Atterberg Limit is a test on

    A. coarse aggregate　　　　B. asphalt
    C. soil　　　　　　　　　　D. Portland cement

19. Of the following, the one that is a high strength bolt is designated

    A. A7　　　　B. A36　　　　C. A180　　　　D. A325

20. Construction contracts in a broad sense fall into two categories - fixed price and

    A. cost-plus　　　　　　　　B. fixed price plus overhead and profit
    C. negotiated price　　　　　D. arbitrated price

21. A punch list on a construction job is usually made by the inspector

    A. weekly
    B. monthly
    C. continuously during the last half of the job
    D. near the end of the job

22. When an accident occurs on a construction job in which someone is injured, an accident report is usually made out by the

    A. insurance carrier　　　　B. contractor
    C. inspector　　　　　　　　D. inspector's superior

23. The inspector and the contractor share common goals. The one of the goals listed below that is NOT shared by the contractor and the inspector is

    A. get a good job done
    B. see that the contractor makes a reasonable profit
    C. get the job done as speedily as possible
    D. have the job done at as low a cost as possible

24. A crack relief layer is placed over an existing Portland cement concrete pavement followed by a well-graded intermediate course, then a dense graded surface course. The crack relief layer consists of an open graded

    A. mix of 100% crushed material with 25-35% interconnected voids
    B. crushed material heavily compacted with no binder
    C. hot mix made up of 80% crushed material with 20% shredded rubber
    D. dense crushed material with voids filled by asphalt

25. Most of the major work performed on the nation's bridges involves

    A. painting the bridges
    B. upgrading the bridges to carry heavier loads
    C. replacing the concrete decks
    D. replacing the suspenders on cable supported bridges

KEY (CORRECT ANSWERS)

1. C
2. C
3. D
4. D
5. A

6. C
7. D
8. B
9. A
10. D

11. A
12. B
13. B
14. D
15. B

16. B
17. D
18. C
19. D
20. A

21. D
22. B
23. B
24. A
25. C

———

EXAMINATION SECTION
TEST 1

DIRECTIONS: Each question or incomplete statement is followed by several suggested answers or completions. Select the one that BEST answers the question or completes the statement. *PRINT THE LETTER OF THE CORRECT ANSWER IN THE SPACE AT THE RIGHT.*

1. 0.8021 feet is, in inches, MOST NEARLY

   A. 9 1/4   B. 9 3/8   C. 9 1/2   D. 9 5/8

2. The structural steel shape MOST often used as a stair stringer is a

   A. channel   B. angle   C. tee   D. zee

3. The abbreviation M.S.L. appearing on a topographic map means

   A. measure straight lengths
   B. make side longer
   C. mean sea level
   D. most safe lintel

4. A specification for sand to be used in concrete requires that sand be well graded. *Well graded* means that the particles be

   A. minute   B. coarse
   C. of variable sizes   D. of one size

5. A vertical transverse profile in a street showing the underground utilities is called a(n) ____-section.

   A. cross   B. contour   C. invert   D. front

6. The seepage of ground water into a sewer line is known as

   A. ingestion   B. infiltration
   C. attrition   D. dilution

7. The number of board feet in 15 pieces of 2' x 6" x 12' feet of lumber is

   A. 180   B. 360   C. 1080   D. 2160

8. The diameter of pipe, in inches, required to carry a flow of 1200 G.P.M. at a velocity of 4.91 f.p.s. is MOST NEARLY (7.48 gal. =1 cu.ft.)

   A. 8   B. 10   C. 12   D. 14

9. If the thickness of the steel wall of a 24 inch diameter water main is 1/2 inch and the water pressure in the water main is 125 p.s.i., then the unit stress in the steel, in p.s.i., is MOST NEARLY

   A. 1500   B. 2000   C. 2500   D. 3000

10. An interior angle of a five-sided traverse is measured six times and recorded as 250°55'30".
    The angle is MOST NEARLY

    A. 40°12'30"   B. 40°18'5"   C. 41°19'15"   D. 41°49'15"

11. The total number of square feet of floor area in three rooms whose measurements are 12'8" x 10'0", 10'2" x 11'8", and 12'5" x 13'8", respectively, is MOST NEARLY

   A. 410   B. 415   C. 420   D. 425

Questions 12-13.

DIRECTIONS: Questions 12 and 13 refer to the following surveying leveling notes.

STA	BS	HI	FS	ELEV
BM_1	6.23'			84.47'
TP_1	5.67'		8.29'	
TP_2	7.48'		3.41'	
BM_2			4.53'	

12. The HI of BM_1 is, in feet,

   A. 77.24   B. 79.36   C. 87.58   D. 89.70

13. The ELEV TP_2 is, in feet,

   A. 82.59   B. 83.67   C. 85.70   D. 87.18

14. A #6 bar has an area equivalent to a circle whose diameter is

   A. 1/4"   B. 1/2"   C. 3/4"   D. 1"

15.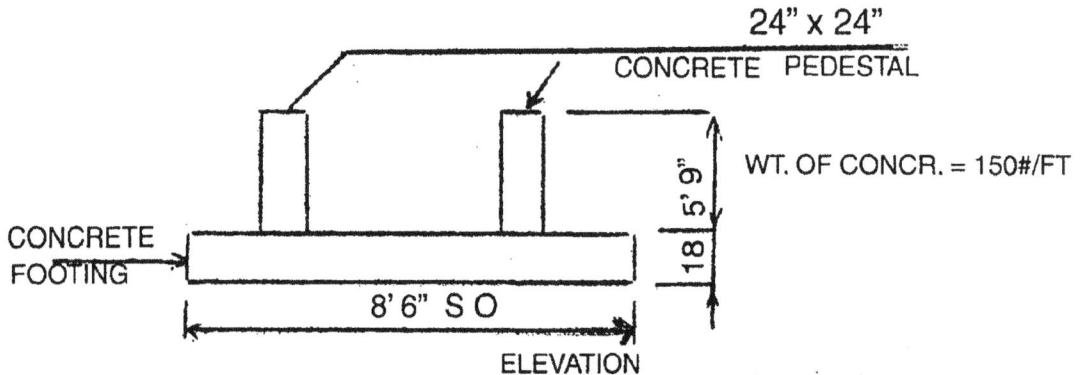

The total weight, in pounds, of the above concrete footing and pedestal is MOST NEARLY

   A. 20,200   B. 23,100   C. 32,600   D. 41,500

16. The capacity, in gallons, of a flat head steel tank 38 inches in diameter by five feet long is MOST NEARLY (7.5 gal. = 1 cu.ft.)

   A. 250   B. 275   C. 295   D. 315

17. The drafting symbol ——⊳⊲—— on a piping drawing indicates a _____ valve.

   A. globe   B. butterfly
   C. check   D. pressure relief

18. If the floor to floor height in a building is 9'6" and there are 15 equal risers, then the height of each riser is, in inches, MOST NEARLY

    A. 7.3   B. 7.4   C. 7.5   D. 7.6

19. A 2,200 feet long pipeline, 18 I.D., carries water at 5.06 feet per second. If the f is 0.02, then the total loss in head due to friction in the pipeline, in feet of water, is MOST NEARLY ($hf = flv^2/d2g$)

    A. 9.4   B. 10.5   C. 11.6   D. 12.3

20.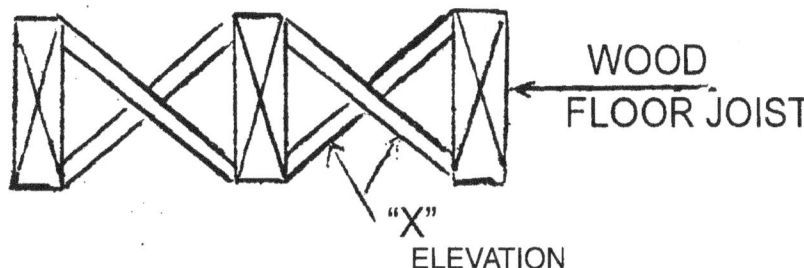

    The cross bracing labeled X on the ELEVATION shown above is called

    A. bridging   B. studding   C. shimming   D. joisting

21.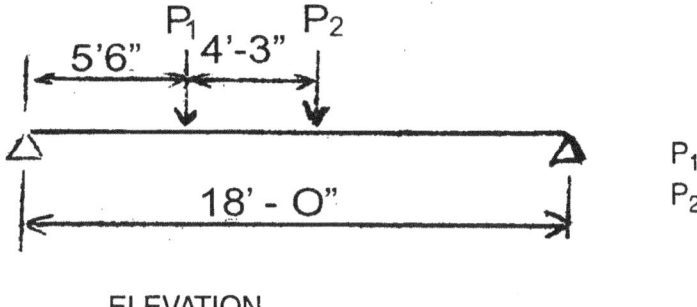

    $P_1 = 5,200$ #
    $P_2 = 4,300$ #

    ELEVATION

    The vertical shear, in pounds, one foot to the right of the concentrated load P_1, in the ELEVATION shown above, is MOST NEARLY

    A. 380   B. 520   C. 750   D. 930

22.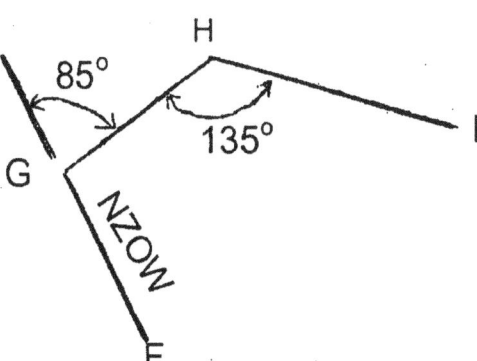

    In the layout shown on the preceding page, the bearing of line HI is

    A. N70E   B. N10W   C. S70E   D. N70W

23. A stairway with 7 treads needs _____ risers.

   A. 6   B. 7   C. 8   D. 9

24.

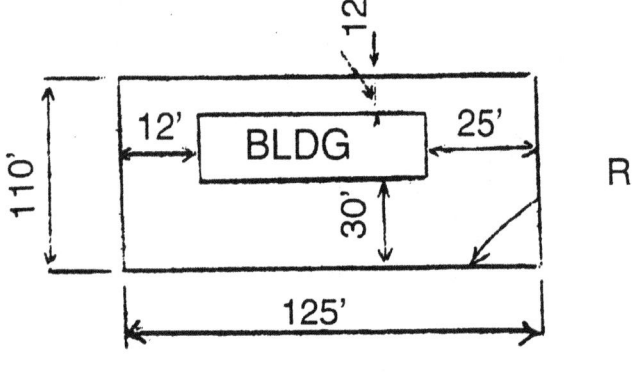

PLOT PLAN

In the above shown plot plan, the number of cubic yards of top soil, 6" deep, required to cover the tract is MOST NEARLY

   A. 115   B. 125   C. 135   D. 145

25. In structural steel work, it is usual practice NOT to paint surfaces that have been

   A. burned   B. sheared   C. milled   D. coped

KEY (CORRECT ANSWERS)

1. D   11. B
2. A   12. D
3. C   13. B
4. C   14. C
5. A   15. B

6. B   16. C
7. A   17. A
8. B   18. D
9. D   19. C
10. D   20. A

21. A
22. C
23. C
24. D
25. C

TEST 2

DIRECTIONS: Each question or incomplete statement is followed by several suggested answers or completions. Select the one that BEST answers the question or completes the statement. *PRINT THE LETTER OF THE CORRECT ANSWER IN THE SPACE AT THE RIGHT.*

Questions 1-2.

DIRECTIONS: Questions 1 and 2 refer to the following sketch.

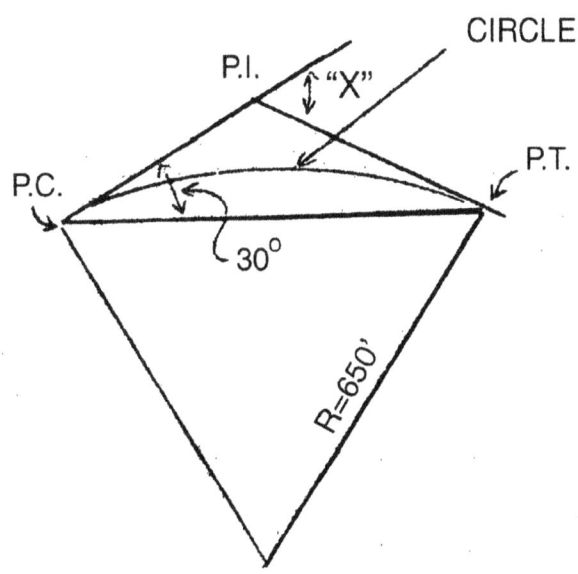

1. The angle X is

   A. 30°   B. 40°   C. 50°   D. 60°

2. The chord distance P.C. to P.T. is _____ feet.

   A. 225   B. 330   C. 650   D. 725

3. The is equal to MOST NEARLY

   A. 13.85   B. 13.90   C. 13.95   D. 14.00

4. A sounding with a lead line shows that the depth in the river is 29.8 feet. If the sounding is taken when the tide gage reads +3.4 feet above M.S.L. and the local datum is 1.9' above M.S.L., then the elevation of the bottom of the river with respect to the local datum is, in feet, MOST NEARLY

   A. -26.4   B. -28.3   C. -31.7   D. -35.1

5. The shaded area expressed algebraically is
   A. 4(X+Y/2)X
   B. $4(x^2+y^2)$
   C. (x+y)(x-y)
   D. 4(X+Y)X-2

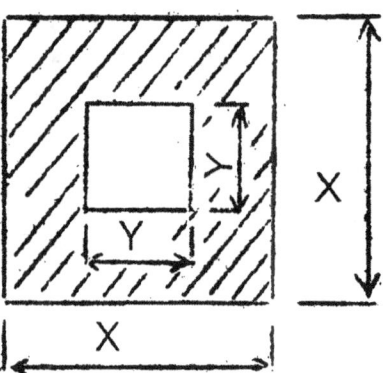

6. The valve that is placed before a fire hydrant in the city is a(n) _____ valve.
   A. angle   B. gate   C. check   D. globe

7. Of the following, the DENSEST liquid is
   A. oil   B. water   C. alcohol   D. mercury

8. The run-off, in C.F.S., from a tract 300 ft. x 830 ft., for a rainfall of 1.5 inches per hour and run-off 0.82 is MOST NEARLY (Q = C.i.A., when A is in acres. 1 acre = 43,560 sq.ft.)
   A. 4   B. 5   C. 6   D. 7

9. The resisting-moment, in foot kips, of the steel in a reinforced concrete beam whose A_s is 1.50, f_s is 24,000 p.s.i., j is 7/8, and effective depth 18 inches is MOST NEARLY ($M_s = A_s f_s j d$)
   A. 41   B. 43   C. 45   D. 47

10.

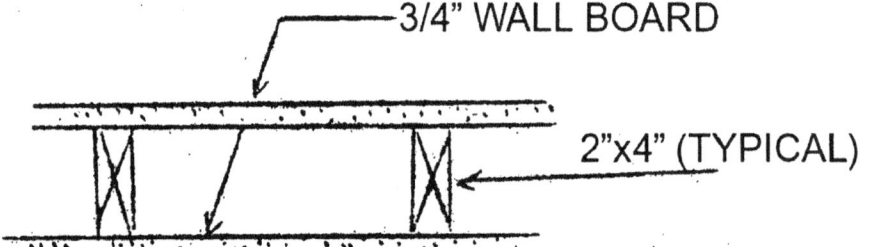

PLAN - PARTITION WALL

In the plan shown above, the 2" x 4" member is called a
   A. joist   B. stud   C. cove   D. sheath

11. In the city, reinforcing steel is bent and placed by
   A. ornamental iron workers
   B. miscellaneous iron workers
   C. carpenters
   D. metal lathers

12. The white encrustation on the face of a wall caused by the presence of salts in the mortar or bricks is called

    A. amberescence
    B. deliquescense
    C. efflorescence
    D. echinuscense

13. A dam can be built *without* diverting the river by using

    A. corewalls
    B. cofferdams
    C. channels
    D. wallpoints

14. Of the following pipe materials, the one that is MOST commonly used to convey drinking water is

    A. clay
    B. wood
    C. cast iron
    D. polyethylene plastic

15. A gooseneck is MOST often required on a(n)

    A. steam line
    B. water service line
    C. sewer house connection
    D. electric house service

16. The x——x——x——x appearing on a topographical map represents a _____ line.

    A. fence
    B. bulkhead
    C. subway
    D. water

17. In the sketch shown at the right, the horizontal molded projection at the top of the building is a
    A. camber
    B. cornice
    C. coping
    D. cant

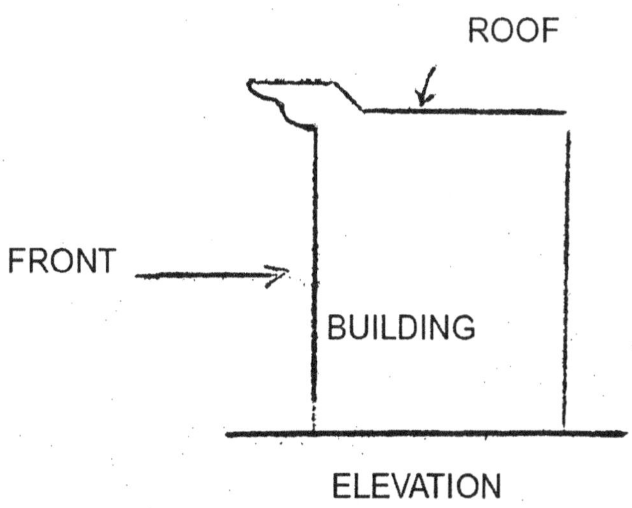

18. The moment of inertia, of the rectangle shown at the right, about the X-X axis is MOST NEARLY ($I = 1/12 bd^3$)

    A. 162 ft^3
    B. 182.3 ft^3
    C. 364.5 ft^3
    D. 729 ft^3

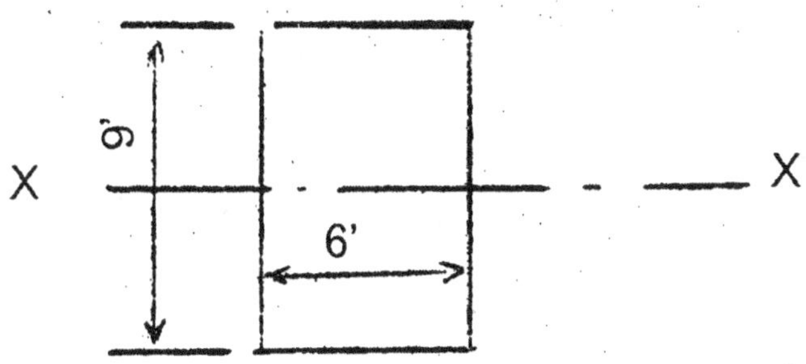

19. Galvanizing a steel surface USUALLY means coating it with

    A. cadmium
    B. zinc
    C. lead
    D. tin

20. Of the following elements, the one that is LEAST active chemically is   20.____

    A. copper   B. lead   C. zinc   D. iron

21. The hydraulic radius of a circular pipe flowing full is   21.____

    A. r/2   B. 2/r   C. r/1   D. 1/r

22. The position in which the weld shown at the right is being made is   22.____
    A. side
    B. vertical
    C. flat
    D. horizontal

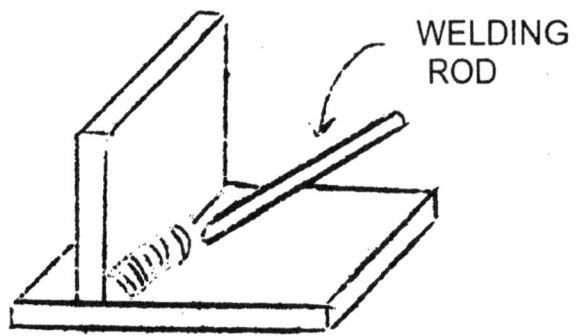

23. The figure shown at the right shows the results of a survey made with a 100.00 ft. steel tape. The tape was later standardized and found to be 99.97 feet long. The CORRECT perimeter, in feet, based on the true length of the tape is MOST NEARLY   23.____
    A. 2466.97
    B. 2467.04
    C. 2467.50
    D. 2468.57

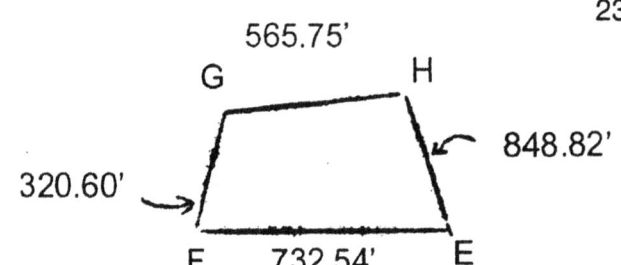

24. Of the following elements, the one that is PREDOMINANT in structural is   24.____

    A. S   B. F_e C. S_i D. M_n

25.   25.____

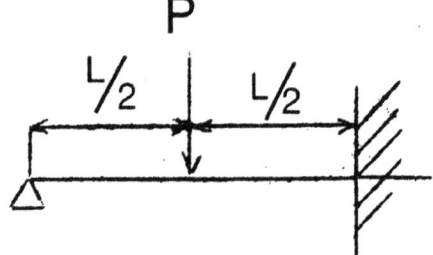

For the beam loading shown above, the shear diagram should look MOST NEARLY like

5 (#2)

A.

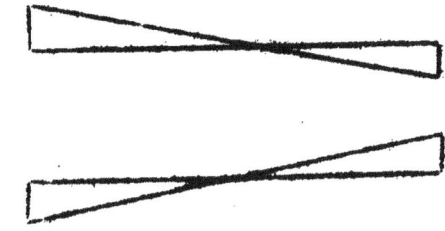

B.

C.

D.

KEY (CORRECT ANSWERS)

1. D
2. C
3. B
4. B
5. C

6. B
7. D
8. D
9. D
10. B

11. D
12. C
13. B
14. C
15. B

16. A
17. B
18. C
19. B
20. B

21. A
22. D
23. A
24. B
25. A

TEST 3

DIRECTIONS: Each question or incomplete statement is followed by several suggested answers or completions. Select the one that BEST answers the question or completes the statement. *PRINT THE LETTER OF THE CORRECT ANSWER IN THE SPACE AT THE RIGHT.*

Questions 1-2.

DIRECTIONS: Questions 1 and 2 refer to the vertical curve shown below.

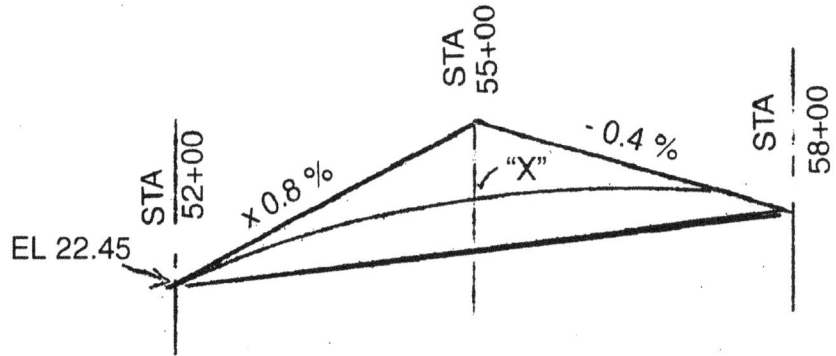

1. The algebraic difference in gradient between the two slopes is

   A. 0.6%   B. -0.8%   C. +1.0%   D. +1.2%

2. The elevation of point X on the curve is

   A. 22.80'   B. 23.25'   C. 23.55'   D. 23.95'

3. Plain concrete is USUALLY composed of

   A. cement, sand, and gravel
   B. cement and sand
   C. cement, crushed rock, and gravel
   D. gypsum and sand

4. If a 100-feet-long steel tape expands 5/64" for a temperature rise of 10°F, then the expansion of a 91-feet-long steel tape with a temperature rise of 70°F is

   A. 3/8"   B. 1/2"   C. 3/4"   D. 7/8"

5. Of the following, the one that is NOT used as a lightweight aggregate for concrete is

   A. cinders   B. traprock
   C. pumice   D. vermiculite

6. In tunnel construction, the points that mark the center line of the tunnel are USUALLY set

   A. in the roof of the tunnel
   B. on the ground four feet off the center line of the tunnel
   C. on the ground at the center line of the tunnel
   D. on the side of the tunnel at center line elevation

2 (#3)

7. The high rod reading shown at the right is
   A. 8.100
   B. 8.125
   C. 8.135
   D. 8.250

7.____

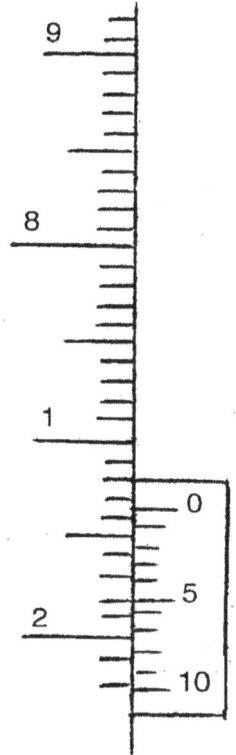

8. The value of 6!/72 is

   A. 10   B. 12   C. 14   D. 16

8.____

9. The fourth term of the binomial $(X+a)^5$ is

   A. $15a^4X^3$ B. $10a^3X^2$ C. a^5 D. $5aX^4$

9.____

10. If steel weighs 490 #/cu.ft., then the cross-sectional area, in square inches, of an 8[11.5 is MOST NEARLY

    A. 3.04   B. 3.22   C. 3.38   D. 3.45

10.____

11.

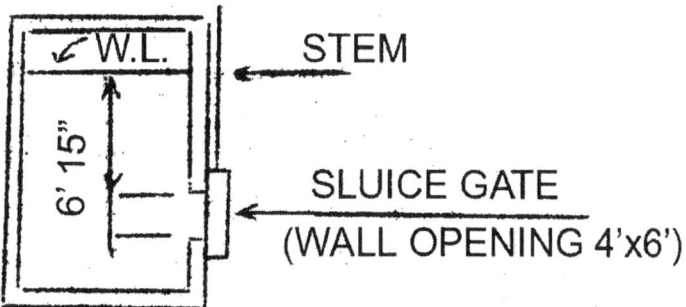

11.____

The total horizontal water pressure, in pounds, acting on the above shown sluice gate is MOST NEARLY

   A. 23,000   B. 25,000   C. 27,000   D. 29,000

12. Terrazzo would MOST likely be found on

    A. ceilings   B. floors
    C. interior walls   D. exterior walls

12.____

13. In the laying out of a building foundation, batter boards are set 13.____

    A. outside the corners of the building
    B. inside the sides of the building
    C. inside diagonally opposite corners of the building only
    D. outside one side and inside one corner of the building only

14. The value of the determinant shown at the right is 14.____

    $\begin{vmatrix} 8 & 5 \\ 2 & 1 \end{vmatrix}$

    A. 37
    B. 16
    C. 10
    D. -2

15. If the product of the slopes of two lines is -1, then the lines are 15.____

    A. 30° to each other
    B. perpendicular
    C. parallel
    D. collinear

16. Blowoffs are provided on water mains to 16.____

    A. provide access to inspect the main
    B. remove sediment in the lines
    C. prevent the buildup of excessive pressure
    D. minimize the effect of water hammer

17. A 10-foot section of a 48" round sewer settles 6 inches. 17.____
    Of the following, the MOST probable consequence of this condition is the

    A. reduction in the carrying capacity of the pipe
    B. possibility of an air lock at this point
    C. stoppage of flow due to sediment
    D. possibility of cavitation in the pipe

18. The clearance of bridges over navigable waterways is the *official* concern of the 18.____

    A. Coast and Geodetic Survey
    B. Navy Department
    C. U.S. Army
    D. Department of the Interior

19. On a highway project, a test that is USUALLY performed to determine the compaction of 19.____
    the subbase is a _____ test.

    A. density
    B. slump
    C. compression
    D. grain size

20. Of the following, the statement that is CORRECT with respect to transverse joints in 20.____
    pavements is:
    A(n)

    A. expansion joint allows for both expansion and contraction
    B. contraction joint allows for both expansion and contraction
    C. warping joint allows for both expansion and contraction
    D. warping joint allows for both contraction and warping

21. The curve that facilitates the transition from the normal crowned straight section of a roadway to the banked curved section of roadway is known as a(n)   21.____

    A. spiral easement   B. parabola
    C. simple circle   D. hyperbola

22. In trench excavation, a pair of vertical boards placed on opposite sides of a trench with two cross braces holding then is known as   22.____

    A. vertical sheeting   B. poling boards
    C. box sheeting   D. stay bracing

23. The penetration test on asphalt cement is used to determine its   23.____

    A. density   B. hardness
    C. elasticity   D. time of set

24. A concrete column with an effective cross-section 20 inches square has one percent vertical steel reinforcing with proper ties.   24.____
    Assuming fc = 500 pounds per square inch and n = 15, the capacity of the column for taking axial load, in pounds, is APPROXIMATELY (P = fc[1+(n-1)Po])

    A. 175,000   B. 200,000   C. 225,000   D. 250,000

25. Turning of metals is USUALLY performed on a   25.____

    A. radial drill press   B. lathe
    C. milling machine   D. shaper

KEY (CORRECT ANSWERS)

1. D
2. D
3. A
4. B
5. B

6. A
7. C
8. A
9. B
10. C

11. C
12. B
13. A
14. D
15. B

16. B
17. A
18. C
19. A
20. A

21. A
22. D
23. B
24. C
25. B

———

TEST 4

DIRECTIONS: Each question or incomplete statement is followed by several suggested answers or completions. Select the one that BEST answers the question or completes the statement. *PRINT THE LETTER OF THE CORRECT ANSWER IN THE SPACE AT THE RIGHT.*

1. An eighth of an inch is equal MOST NEARLY to _____ of a foot.   1._____
   A. 1/10   B. 1/100   C. 1/64   D. 1/84

2.   2._____

   In the sketch above, the type of internal stress acting on the member along line A-A due to the load P shown above is

   A. tension and compression *only*
   B. tension and shear *only*
   C. tension, compression, and shear
   D. shear *only*

3. Lime used in mortar is USUALLY   3._____
   A. hydrated lime   B. quicklime
   C. unslaked lime   D. plaster of paris

4. An air entraining compound is PRIMARILY added to concrete to   4._____
   A. make it light
   B. make it set early
   C. eliminate the need for curing
   D. make it more durable

5. The arrangement of bricks shown at the right is _____ Bond.   5._____
   A. English
   B. Flemish
   C. Common
   D. Danish

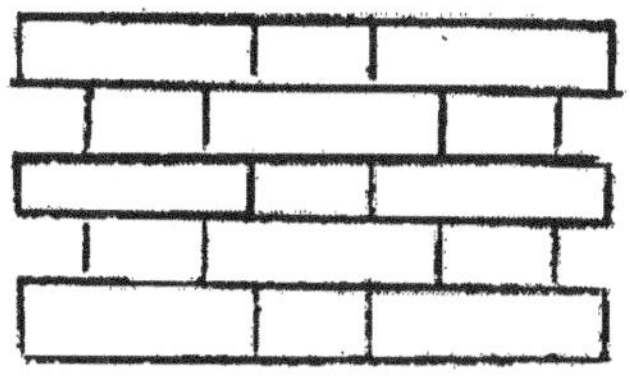

6. The coverage of a paint is 360 sq.ft./gallon.   6._____
   The number of gallons required to paint the walls of four rooris, 11'1" x 12'8" by 7'6" high, with one coat, is MOST NEARLY (do not count windows or doors)
   A. 2   B. 3   C. 4   D. 5

33

7. In the ELEVATION shown at the right, stone X is known as a
   A. reglet
   B. baffle
   C. perron
   D. coping

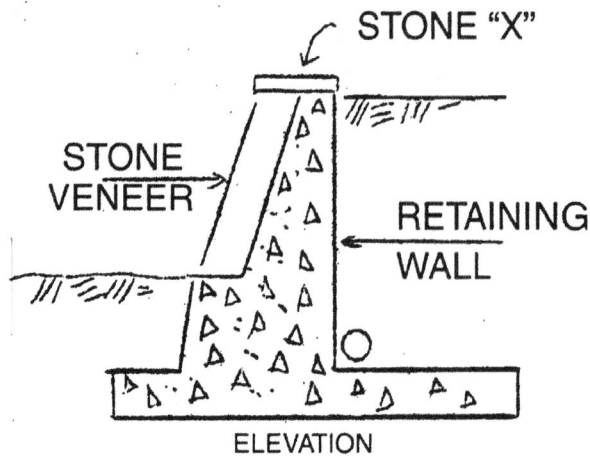

8. The material MOST commonly used as a conductor in ordinary electric wiring is
   A. brass   B. zinc   C. copper   D. aluminum

9. In trigonometry, the expression Cos X cos Y - Sin X sin Y
   A. Sin(X+Y)   B. Sin(X-Y)   C. Cos(X+Y)   D. Cos(X-Y)

10. In the window shown at the right, X is called a
    A. jamb
    B. muntin
    C. stool
    D. mullion

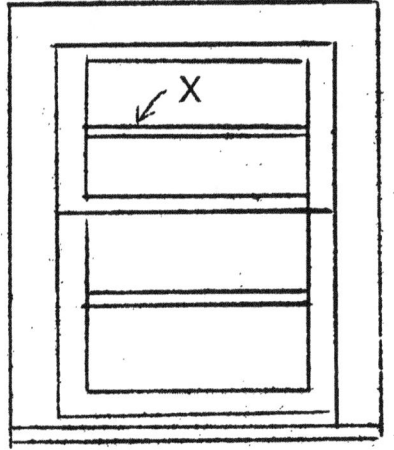

11. If the Sin X = .60, then the Cos X =
    A. .50   B. .60   C. .70   D. .80

12. The length of a meter is, in inches, MOST NEARLY
    A. 39.4   B. 38.6   C. 37.2   D. 36.9

13. To complete the square in the terms $X^2 + 10X$, we would have to add
    A. 20   B. 25   C. 30   D. 100

14. In the sketch shown at the right, the distance X - Y is MOST NEARLY
    A. 8'5"
    B. 8'8"
    C. 9'0"
    D. 9'3"

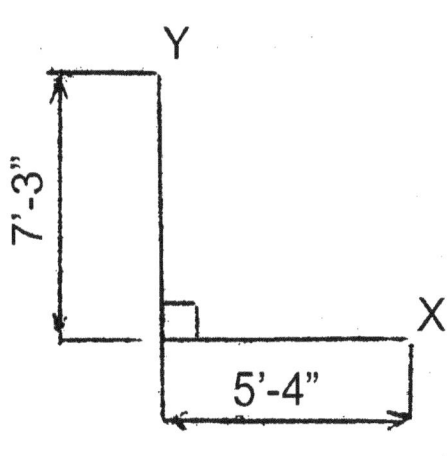

15. A rectangular footing is to have an area of 250 square feet. If the length is to be twice its width, then the width is MOST NEARLY

    A. 11.0' B. 11.2' C. 11.4' D. 11.5'

16. In the term *4000 pound concrete*, the term *4000 pound,* as applied to ordinary concrete, represents the ultimate compressive strength of the concrete at the end of _____ days.

    A. 3 B. 7 C. 14 D. 28

17.

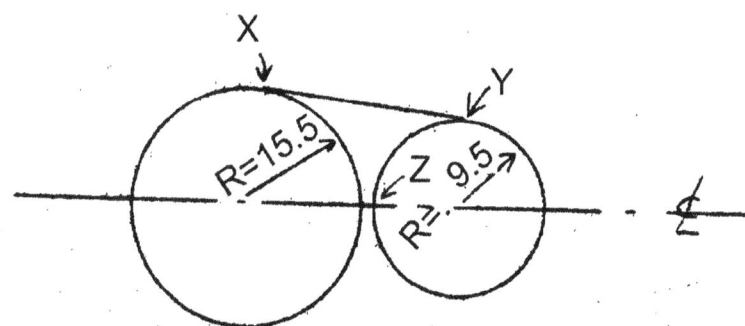

In the sketch shown above, the length of the common tangent XY to the two circles tangent at Z is

    A. 21.3 B. 22.3 C. 23.3 D. 24.3

18. $\sin(X+90)°$ is equal to

    A. Cos X B. Sin X C. - Cos X D. - Sin X

19. In a contract that includes both unit-price and lump-sum items, the one that is LEAST likely to be bid on a unit-price basis is

    A. cleaning up
    B. seeding and mulching
    C. fencing
    D. waterstops

20. The PRIMARY reason for providing sewers with manholes is to

    A. ventilate the sewage
    B. clean and inspect the sewer
    C. connect future house connections
    D. allow sewer to surcharge

21. The number of radians in the arc of a circle having a central angle of 30° is

    A. π/6 B. π/5 C. π/4 D. π/3

22. The weight of a cubic foot of cement is, in pounds, MOST NEARLY

    A. 86 B. 90 C. 94 D. 98

23. The invert elevation at a manhole of a sewer is 65.40'. If the slope of the pipe is .0063 ft./ft., then the invert elevation at a manhole 275 ft. downstream is

    A. 63.25' B. 63.67' C. 63.85' D. 63.98'

24. The cutting out of the top flange and web of a steel member so that the steel member will frame into another steel member is called

    A. coping B. crimping C. canting D. corbelling

25. The architectural symbol [∧∩∧∧] is a section representing

    A. marble
    B. glazed tile
    C. clay tile
    D. insulation

KEY (CORRECT ANSWERS)

1. B		11. D	
2. C		12. A	
3. A		13. B	
4. D		14. C	
5. B		15. B	
6. C		16. D	
7. D		17. D	
8. C		18. A	
9. C		19. A	
10. B		20. B	

21. A
22. C
23. B
24. A
25. D

EXAMINATION SECTION
TEST 1

DIRECTIONS: Each question or incomplete statement is followed by several suggested answers or completions. Select the one that BEST answers the question or completes the statement. *PRINT THE LETTER OF THE CORRECT ANSWER IN THE SPACE AT THE RIGHT.*

1. Dowels connecting adjacent roadway slabs are used primarily to 1.____

   A. transmit compressive stress to adjacent slabs
   B. reinforce against temperature stress
   C. reinforce against shrinkage stress
   D. prevent differential settlement of slabs

2. Good practice requires that the minimum overhead clearance at the crown for an underpass at the intersection of two highways be MOST NEARLY _____ feet. 2.____

   A. 10   B. 14   C. 17   D. 19

3. A simple beam on an 18'0" span carries a uniformly distributed load including its own weight of 200 pounds per foot. 3.____
   If a jack is placed under the midspan and the midpoint jacked up so it is at the same elevation as the ends, the load on the jack, in pounds, will be

   A. 960   B. 1600
   C. 1800   D. more than 1800

4. Of the following, the one which is NOT the symbol for a standard beam connection is 4.____

   A. A3   B. B3   C. H3   D. T3

5. Of the following items, the one that is NOT important in determining the minimum length of vertical curve required to connect two intersecting grades is 5.____

   A. maximum speed of vehicle
   B. grades of tangents
   C. whether intersection is at a summit or a sag
   D. crown of road

6. For an angle of intersection of 16°30', tables of the functions of a one-degree curve show the middle ordinate to be 59.30 feet. 6.____
   For the same angle of intersection, the middle ordinate for a curve whose radius is 1433 feet is MOST NEARLY

   A. 14.83   B. 24.94   C. 67.35   D. 183.72

7. The *Proctor Test* is used in testing 7.____

   A. asphalt   B. concrete   C. soils   D. mortar

8. Within the cross-section of a WF beam, the horizontal shearing stress is a maximum at the 8.____

A. midpoint of the beam
B. outermost fiber of the compression flange
C. outermost fiber of the tension flange
D. point of intersection of web and flange

9. The maximum load allowed on a 3/8" fillet weld, 6" long, when the allowable shearing stress is 13,000 #/sq.in. is MOST NEARLY, in pounds,

A. 20,700   B. 21,900   C. 24,300   D. 26,370

10. A closed level circuit was run starting at BM A. The elevation of A on closing the circuit was found to be 0.097 lower than at the start.
Of the following, the MOST logical reason for this error, barring mistakes, is the

A. length of the rod was not standard due either to a uniform expansion or contraction
B. level settled after the backsights had been read
C. turning points settled after the foresights had been read
D. line of sight was inclined upward and each foresight distance exceeded the corresponding backsight distance

11. The sensitivity of the bubble tube of an engineer's level can best be measured by

A. measuring the distance between etched lines on the vial
B. taking readings on a rod a known distance away with bubble in two different positions
C. making a two-peg test
D. measuring the curvature of the etched surface of the vial

12. Of the following, the MOST important source of accidental error in ordinary leveling work is

A. change in length of leveling rod due to change in temperature
B. axis of level tube not perpendicular to vertical axis
C. eye piece is not focused accurately
D. failure to wave rod

13. When taking a single measure of the horizontal angle between two points which differ greatly in elevation, the MOST important of the following relationships in the transit is

A. axis of long bubble parallel to line of sight
B. transverse axis perpendicular to vertical axis
C. index correction of vertical arc equal to zero
D. vertical cross-hair in plane perpendicular to transverse axis

14. Of the following factors, the one that is LEAST important in determining the total amount of superelevation required at the edge of pavement on a horizontal curve is

A. speed of vehicle   B. weight of vehicle
C. radius of curve   D. width of pavement

15. If the horizontal circle of a transit is graduated to 20' and 39 divisions on the limb equal 40 civisions on the vernier, then the LEAST count of the vernier is

A. 14"   B. 28"   C. 30"   D. 1'6"

16. The slump test for concrete is used to determine the 16.____

 A. strength B. consistency
 C. water ratio D. segregation

17. The following notes are taken from the survey of a closed traverse with five sides: 17.____

at	Deflection Angles
A	R 65° 25'
B	L 45° 14'
C	R 135° 42'
D	R 92° 17'
E	

 The value of the deflection angle at E is MOST NEARLY
 A. 111°22' B. 111°34' C. 111°46' D. 111°50'

18. A Williot-Mohr diagram is used to determine 18.____

 A. deflection in trusses
 B. wind stress in framed bents
 C. diagonal shear in beams
 D. uplift pressure on the base of a cam

19. A reinforced concrete beam is 10" wide by 16" effective depth. If fs = 20,000 lb./sq.in., fc 19.____
 = 1350 lb./sq.in. and n = 10, then the value of k is MOST NEARLY

 A. .367 B. .373 C. .403 D. .419

20. Of the following concrete structures, the one in which gunite is MOST likely to be used is 20.____

 A. footings B. piles C. walls D. beams

21. For soil sampling in hardpan, the BEST method to use is 21.____

 A. jet probing B. wash boring
 C. auger boring D. core boring

22. The bending moment at the ends of a beam fully restrained at both ends which supports 22.____
 a uniform load of w pounds per foot throughout its entire length l is

 A. $\dfrac{wl^2}{8}$ B. $\dfrac{wl}{10}$ C. $\dfrac{wl^2}{10}$ D. $\dfrac{wl^2}{12}$

23. A reinforced concrete beam 10" wide by 16" effective depth is subjected to an end shear 23.____
 of 15,000 lbs.
 If fs = 20,000 #/sq.in., fc = 2500 #/sq.in., u = 187 #/sq.in., and j = .857, the perimeter of
 steel required to reinforce against the shear, in inches, is MOST NEARLY

 A. 2.38 B. 3.72 C. 5.85 D. 6.94

24. A precast reinforced concrete beam 20'0" long, weight 50 #/ft. is to be lifted by two slings 24.____
 symmetrically placed.
 For minimum bending stress in the beam, the distance from an end to a point of support, in feet, is MOST NEARLY

A. 3.98   B. 4.15   C. 4.35   D. 5.15

25. For maximum stress in ab, the distance the load P should be from the wall is MOST NEARLY
    A. 10'7"
    B. 11'9"
    C. 13'3"
    D. 15'0"

25._____

KEY (CORRECT ANSWERS)

1. D   11. B
2. B   12. C
3. D   13. B
4. D   14. B
5. D   15. C

6. A   16. B
7. C   17. D
8. A   18. A
9. A   19. C
10. D   20. C

21. D
22. D
23. C
24. B
25. D

TEST 2

DIRECTIONS: Each question or incomplete statement is followed by several suggested answers or completions. Select the one that BEST answers the question or completes the statement. *PRINT THE LETTER OF THE CORRECT ANSWER IN THE SPACE AT THE RIGHT.*

1. The rod reading at Sta. 100+27 is 4.26. With the same H.I., the rod reading at Sta. 103+16 is 6.34.
   The grade between the two stations is MOST NEARLY

   A. +0.72%   B. +0.79%   C. -0.72%   D. -0.79%

   1.____

2. In taping a distance known to be 2000 ft. long, the distance is found to be 1900.02 ft. The error is MOST probably caused by

   A. neglecting temperature correction
   B. neglecting to record one tape length
   C. tension on tape not standard
   D. wind blowing tape out of line

   2.____

3. The sum of the deflection angles for a closed traverse, where *n* equals the number of sides of the traverse, is

   A. (n-2)180°   B. 180°n   C. (n-l)360°   D. 360°

   3.____

4. When a level rod is *waved,* the correct reading is the

   A. largest reading
   B. smallest reading
   C. average of the largest and the smallest reading
   D. difference between the largest and the smallest reading

   4.____

5. A topographic map to a scale of 1:2400 has a 5-foot vertical interval. A straight line on the map connecting two adjacent contours is 0.437 inches long.
   The slope of this line is, in percent, MOST NEARLY

   A. 5.6   B. 5.7   C. 5.8   D. 6.0

   5.____

6. A Philadelphia rod is fully extended and the distance from the 1-foot mark to the 11-foot mark is measured and found to be 10.005.
   In a level circuit, a high-rod reading on this rod is

   A. 0.005 too large
   B. 0.005 too small
   C. considered correct since the errors will balance out
   D. correct if the rod is waved

   6.____

7. A differential leveling circuit without sideshots was run between two bench marks. The level was set up x times.
   The number of turning points used was

   A. 2x   B. x-2   C. x-1   D. x

   7.____

8. A closed traverse is usually preferred to an open traverse because

   8.____

A. more ground can be covered
B. a mathematical check on the work is provided
C. the area can be determined
D. the computations are easier

9. The difference in elevation between two points on the hydraulic gradient of a pipe of uniform diameter is a measure of the loss of _____ head.

   A. potential   B. pressure   C. velocity   D. total

10. Of the following values of f in the formula $h = f \dfrac{l}{d} \dfrac{V^2}{2g}$, the one which would MOST probably apply to a smooth pipe is

    A. 0.02   B. 0.11   C. 0.31   D. 0.41

11. The required cross-sectional area of a culvert is a function of

    A. width of roadway   B. depth of fill
    C. drainage area served   D. headwall area

12. The value of k for a particular reinforced concrete beam is 0.400. The value of j for this beam is MOST NEARLY

    A. 0.873   B. 0.870   C. 0.867   D. 0.865

13. A steel bar one inch in diameter is imbedded a distance of 30 inches in a mass of concrete.
    If the bar is subjected to axial pull of 10,000#, the bond stress is, in pounds per square inch, MOST NEARLY

    A. 106   B. 108   C. 112   D. 116

14. The slump test for concrete is a measure of

    A. water-cement ratio   B. consistency
    C. strength   D. size of aggregate

15. The term *special anchorage* in concrete construction refers to

    A. an anchor bolt to tie a beam to a wall
    B. tieing the reinforcement to a steel beam
    C. a *U*-shaped bar to take care of shearing stresses
    D. a hook at the end of a reinforcing bar

16.

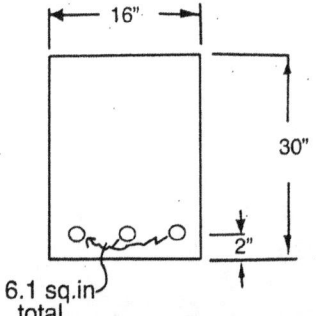

$k = \dfrac{1}{2} f_c \, k_2 \, j = 236$

Assuming exactly balanced design, the maximum bending moment that can be carried by the reinforced concrete beam in the accompanying sketch is, in inch pounds, MOST NEARLY

    A. 2,960,000   B. 3,420,370   C. 4,160,500   D. 5,180,600

17. The maximum deflection of a simple beam on a span 1 carrying a uniformly distributed load of w per unit length is $\dfrac{5}{384}\dfrac{w}{EI}$ multiplied by

    A. 1^2 B. 1^3 C. 1^4 D. 1^7

18. The section modulus of a beam is

    A. $\int y^2 dA$ B. $\dfrac{V}{Ib}A\bar{y}$ C. $\dfrac{\sqrt{I}}{A}$ D. $\dfrac{I}{c}$

19. A timber beam 3" x 12" (actual dimensions) is simply supported on a clear span of 9'0" and carries a uniform load of 1000 #/ft. throughout its entire length.
The maximum bending stress in the beam is, in lbs./sq.in., MOST NEARLY

    A. 1570   B. 1690   C. 1745   D. 1860

20. A wooden beam 8 inches wide by 12 inches deep (actual dimensions) carries a uniform load of 600 pounds per foot including its own weight on a simple span of 16'0".
The MAXIMUM shear stress intensity in the beam is, in pounds per square inch,

    A. 70   B. 71   C. 72   D. 75

21. The horizontal component of the reaction at joint B in the accompanying diagram is MOST NEARLY

    A. 32^K
    B. 36^K
    C. 40^K
    D. 44^K

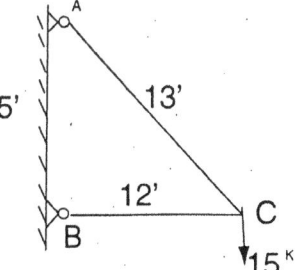

22. The yield point of a ductile metal is that unit stress at which

    A. the stress ceases to be proportional to the strain
    B. there is an increase in deformation with no increase in stress
    C. the material ruptures
    D. the metal ceases to act as an elastic material

Questions 23-27.

DIRECTIONS: Questions 23 through 27 refer to the sketch of the beam and girder connection shown below.

4 (#2)

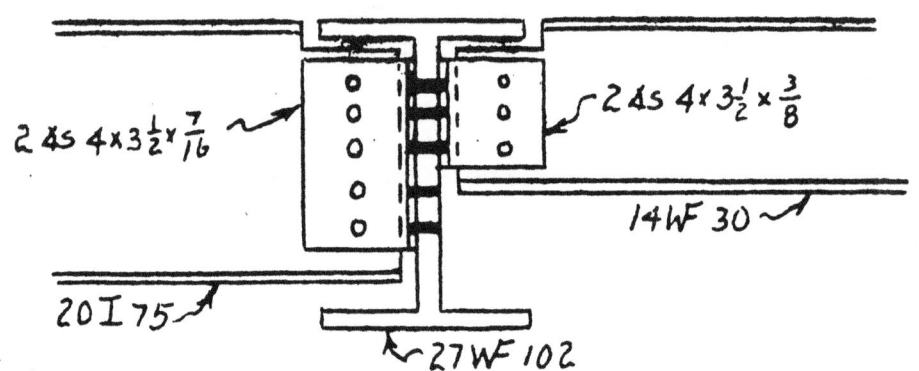

23. The diameter of the rivets used would MOST likely be

   A. 5/8"   B. 7/8"   C. 1 3/16"   D. 1 5/8"

24. Of the following allowable stresses, the only one that would be used in determining the number of rivets connecting the angles to the 20 I 75 is the allowable stress in

   A. single shear   B. end bearing
   C. web shear   D. enclosed bearing

25. The allowable load on rivet A is determined by the allowable stress in

   A. double shear   B. single shear
   C. tension   D. torsion

26. Both beams shown are

   A. chased   B. blocked   C. squared   D. clipped

27. The number of field rivets required in the connection is

   A. 4   B. 6   C. 9   D. 10

28. The term *batter* in concrete work refers to

   A. bracing of forms
   B. slope of finished surface
   C. consistency of concrete
   D. pressure of wet concrete in forms

29. Of the following items, the one that is LEAST related to the others is

   A. B.O.D.   B. Imhoff tank
   C. effluent   D. liquid limit

30. A beam on a simple span of 16'0" carries a concentrated load of 20 kips 5'0" from the left support and a uniform load of 3 kips per foot over the entire span.
    The distance from the left support to the point of maximum moment is, in feet, MOST NEARLY

   A. 5.92   B. 5.97   C. 6.02   D. 6.07

31. A beam has a trapezoidal cross-section which is symmetrical about a vertical axis. The top width is 4 inches, the bottom width 8 inches, and the depth 6 inches.
    The distance from the bottom of the beam to the neutral axis is, in inches,

| A. 2.83 | B. 2.75 | C. 2.67 | D. 2.59 |

32. The ends of a steel bar 1 inch square are set in rigid walls spaced 4'0" in the clear. Another square steel bar 2 inches on a side is set in rigid walls spaced 8'0" in the clear. The ratio of the unit stress in the longer bar to that in the shorter bar due to an increase in temperature is

   A. 3/8 B. 5/8 C. 1 D. 3/2

Questions 33-35.

DIRECTIONS: Questions 33 through 35 refer to the truss shown below.

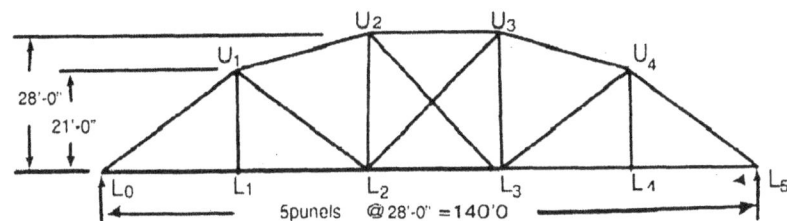

33. To obtain the stress in U_1L_2, the truss should be cut between U_1L_1 and U_2L_2 and moments taken about

   A. U_2
   B. L_1
   C. L_0
   D. a point to the left of L_0

34. The stress in member L_1L_2 for a load of one kip per foot extending over the entire span is, in kips, MOST NEARLY

   A. 74.67 B. 75.33 C. 75.67 D. 76.00

35. The stress in member U_2U_3 for a load of one kip per foot extending over the entire span is, in kips, MOST NEARLY

   A. 83.15 B. 83.30 C. 83.45 D. 84.00

36. In taping a distance on a 6% slope, the slope distance was measured. The correction per hundred feet to be applied to the measured distance is, in feet,

   A. 0.09 B. 0.12 C. 0.15 D. 0.18

37. The linear error of closure of a traverse is computed to be 0.04 feet. The sum of the lengths of the sides is 793.26 ft.
    The precision of the survey should be recorded as

   A. $\dfrac{0.04}{600}$ B. $\dfrac{4}{79326}$ C. $\dfrac{4}{793.26}$ D. $\dfrac{1}{19800}$

38. Errors due to eccentricity in the plates of a transit can be eliminated by

    A. reading the angle twice, once with the telescope normal, the second time with the telescope inverted
    B. using the averaged reading of the A and B verniers
    C. accurate leveling of the transit
    D. using two observers

39. A transit is set up at Sta. B and the deflection angle to Sta. C is measured (backsight on Sta. A) and found to be 22°15' R.
    The value of the angle ABC, measured clockwise from A to C, is

    A. 69°30'   B. 108°45'   C. 144°15'   D. 202°15'

40. The elevations of the P.V.C., P.V.I., and P.V.T. of a symnetrical vertical curve are 100.26, 103.26, and 98.76, respectively.
    The elevation of the midpoint of the vertical curve is MOST NEARLY

    A. 98.63   B. 99.72   C. 101.38   D. 103.17

KEY (CORRECT ANSWERS)

1. C	11. C	21. B	31. C
2. B	12. C	22. B	32. C
3. D	13. A	23. B	33. D
4. B	14. B	24. D	34. A
5. B	15. D	25. B	35. D
6. A	16. A	26. B	36. D
7. C	17. C	27. D	37. D
8. B	18. D	28. B	38. B
9. D	19. B	29. D	39. D
10. A	20. D	30. A	40. C

TEST 3

DIRECTIONS: Each question or incomplete statement is followed by several suggested answers or completions. Select the one that BEST answers the question or completes the statement. *PRINT THE LETTER OF THE CORRECT ANSWER IN THE SPACE AT THE RIGHT.*

1. In highway work, the degree of curve is commonly defined as the angle   1.____

    A. at the center subtended by an arc 100 ft. in length
    B. at the center subtending the entire curve
    C. at which the two tangents to the curve intersect
    D. between a tangent and a chord 100 ft. in length

2. The term *magnetic declination* refers to the   2.____

    A. attraction on a magnetic needle of nearby metallic objects
    B. dip of a magnetic needle
    C. angle between a given line and the meridian
    D. angle between true north and magnetic north

3. The bearings of the sides of a closed quadrilateral are: 3.____
    AB - N12°15'W
    BC - N15°10'E
    CD - S60°20'E
    DA - S18°30'W
    The interior angle CDA of the quadrilateral is

    A. 87°25'   B. 10°110'   C. 126°40'   D. 154°15'

4. In a given triangle, side *a* = 220 ft. and the angle opposite is 30°00'.   4.____
    If angle *B* = 45°00', then the side opposite angle *B*, in feet, is MOST NEARLY

    A. 311   B. 327   C. 346   D. 411

5. Of the following statements, the one that is CORRECT is: 5.____

    A. Blue ink is used when making tracings for blueprint work
    B. If ink lines on a tracing do not dry quickly, they should be blotted
    C. Vertical dimensions should be lettered so that they read from the right side of the sheet
    D. Dimension lines should be of the same weight as lines used in the views

6. A common method of lengthening the life of a wooden pile is by impregnating it with   6.____

    A. white lead   B. red lead
    C. sodium silicate   D. creosote

7. The MOST common unit for measuring excavation is   7.____

    A. cubic yard   B. cubic foot
    C. ton   D. pound

8. The width of each lane in a modern two-lane highway would MOST likely be

   A. 8'   B. 12'   C. 16'   D. 20'

Questions 9-11.

DIRECTIONS: Questions 9 through 11 refer to the figure shown below. (Any trigonomatic computation required is to be done by slide rule.)

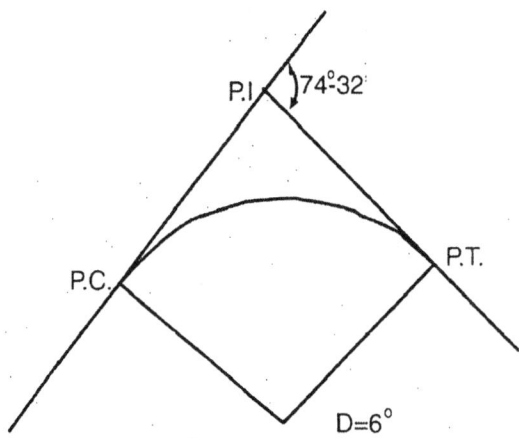

9. The station of the P.C. is 17+57.2.
   The deflection angle from the P.C. to Sta. 19 is MOST NEARLY

   A. 2°39'   B. 3°17'   C. 4°17'   D. 6°17'

10. The radius of the curve is, in feet, MOST NEARLY

    A. 955   B. 960   C. 970   D. 980

11. The station of the P.T. is MOST NEARLY

    A. 29+99.2   B. 29+99.4   C. 29+99.6   D. 30+00.4

12. Two cylindrical tanks with vertical axes lie one above the other. The lower tank is 8'0" in diameter and 8'0" high. The upper tank is 4'0" in diameter and 40'0" high with its base at the level of the top of the lower tank. The lower tank is full of water, and the upper tank is empty.
    The energy, in foot-pounds, required to pump the water from the lower to the upper tank is MOST NEARLY

    A. 502,000   B. 505,000   C. 508,000   D. 511,000

Questions 13-18.

DIRECTIONS: Questions 13 through 18 refer to the sketch of the plate girder shown below.

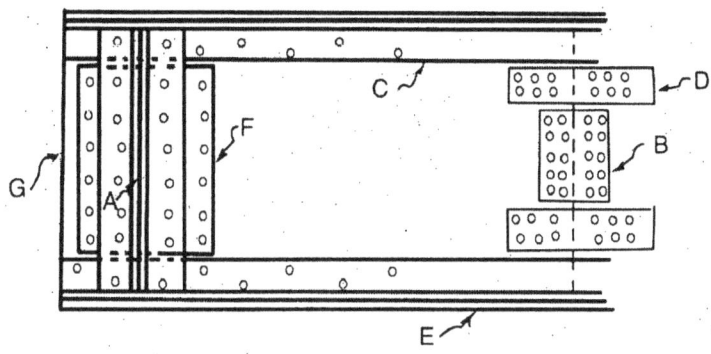

For each of the parts of the plate girder listed below in Questions 13 through 18, select the letter representing that part in the sketch above. For each of questions 13 through 18, the correct answer is

   A. A   B. B   C. C   D. D   E. E   F. F   G. G

13. Flange angle 13.____

14. Shear splice 14.____

15. Stiffener 15.____

16. Cover plate 16.____

17. Web 17.____

18. Filler plate 18.____

19. Of the following symbols, the one that represents the ratio of the modulus of elasticity of steel to the modulus of elasticity of concrete in concrete design is 19.____

   A. k   B. v   C. p   D. n

20. A rectangular gate 4'0" wide by 6'0" high is submerged in water with the 4'0" side parallel to and 2'0" below the water surface. The gate is in a vertical plane. 20.____
 The total pressure on the gate is, in pounds, MOST NEARLY

   A. 7480   B. 7590   C. 7660   D. 7720

21. The distance from the top of the gate to the center of pressure of the water on one side of the gate described in the preceding question is, in feet, MOST NEARLY 21.____

   A. 3.60   B. 3.70   C. 3.80   D. 3.90

22. Reservoir A is connected to Reservoir B by two parallel pipes, one 6 inches in diameter, the other 12 inches in diameter. The friction factor, f, is the same for each pipe. 22.____
 If the flow in the 12-inch pipe is 6 cubic feet per second, the flow in the 6-inch pipe is, in cubic feet per second, MOST NEARLY

   A. 1.01   B. 1.03   C. 1.05   D. 1.06

23. The hydraulic radius of a rectangular channel 6'0" wide with, a 4'0" depth of water is, in feet, MOST NEARLY 23.____

A. 1.71 B. 1.75 C. 1.79 D. 1.83

24. On a transit, the tangent screw is used to

    A. clamp the telescope in either erect or inverted position
    B. adjust the level bubbles
    C. focus the objective lens
    D. rotate the telescope small distances

25. The tangent of angle A is equal to

    A. $\sqrt{1-\cos^2 A}$ B. $\dfrac{\sec A}{\cos A}$ C. $\sin A \cos A$ D. $\dfrac{\sin A}{\cos A}$

26. If two stations on a mass diagram for earthwork have equal ordinates, the

    A. elevations of the two stations are the same
    B. end areas at the two stations are equal
    C. volume of cut equals the volume of fill between the two stations
    D. volume of fill between the two stations may be moved with equal economy to either station

27. The primary cause of parallax in a telescope is

    A. atmospheric disturbances
    B. maladjustment of the cross hairs
    C. improper focusing of the objective
    D. improper focusing of the eyepiece

28. The notes for a three level section for a roadway 20 ft. wide are as follows:

    $$\dfrac{c12}{16} \quad \dfrac{c13}{0} \quad \dfrac{c16}{18}$$

    The side slopes of the embankment are _____ horizontal to _____ vertical.
    A. 1; 2 B. 1; 1 C. 2; 1 D. 2; 3

29. Various combinations of the known parts of a triangle are given below. The combination which does NOT describe a unique triangle (i.e., one triangle and one only) is

    A. three sides
    B. two sides and the included angle
    C. one side and two angles
    D. two sides and an acute angle opposite one of the sides

30. To permit easier operation of vehicles, a tangent is MOST frequently connected to a horizontal circular curve by means of a

    A. reversed curve   B. spiral
    C. parabola   D. hyperbola

31. An alidade is MOST commonly used in conjunction with a

    A. transit   B. plane table
    C. barometer   D. tide gauge

32. The increase in length of a 100-foot stool tape due to a temperature rise of 15°F is, in feet, MOST NEARLY   32._____

    A. 0.0001   B. 0.0005   C. 0.01   D. 0.05

33. An instrument used to measure the area of a closed traverse, plotted to scale, is a   33._____

    A. integraph   B. clinometer
    C. planimeter   D. pantograph

Questions 34-35.

DIRECTIONS: Questions 34 and 35 refer to the following diagrams on the following page.

(Diagram for question 34.)   (Diagram for question 35.)

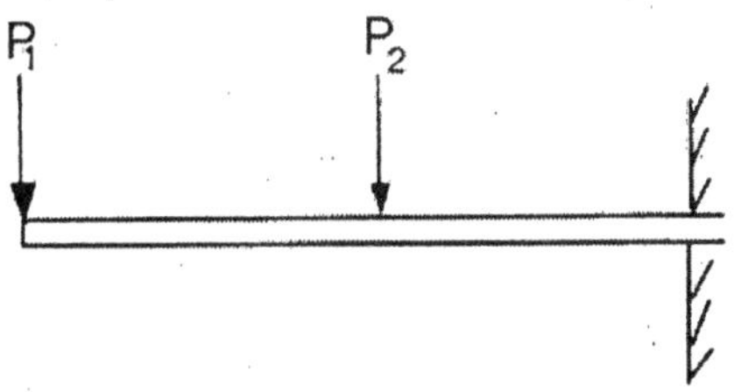

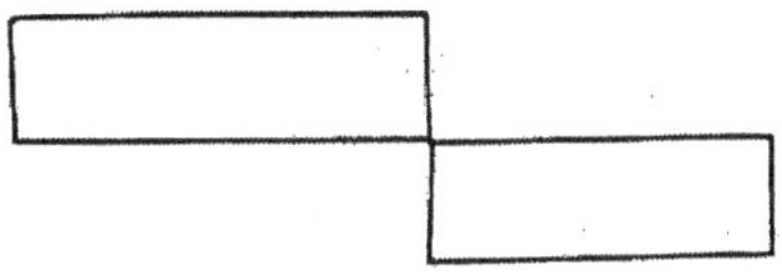

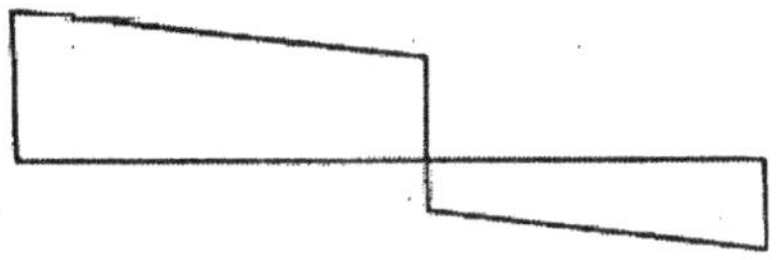

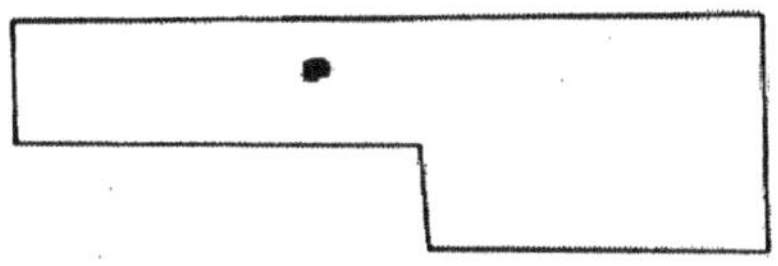

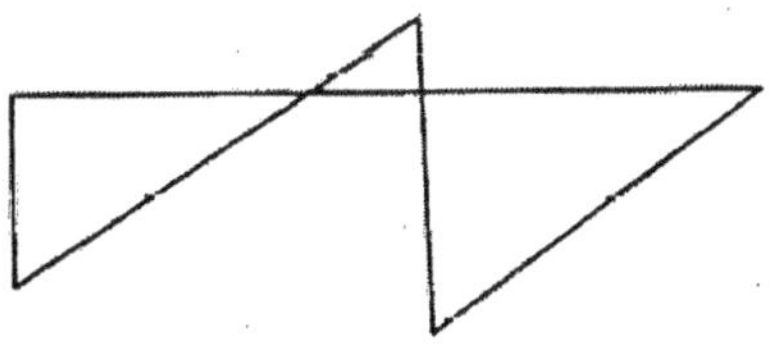

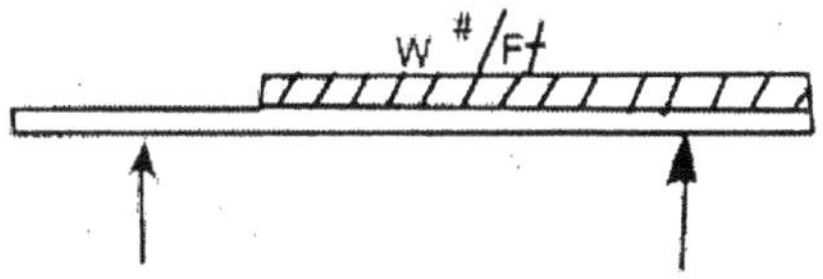

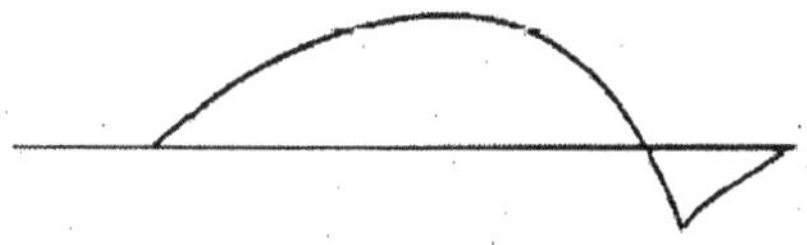

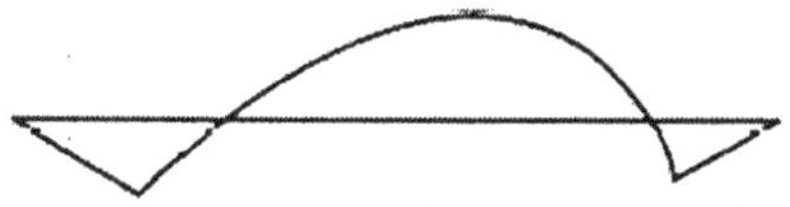

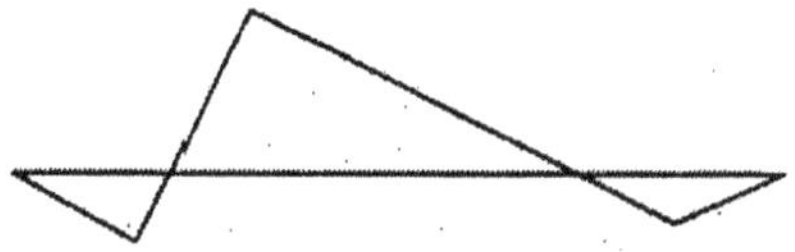

34. The shear diagram for the beam shown in the above diagram is (neglecting the weight of the beam)   34._____

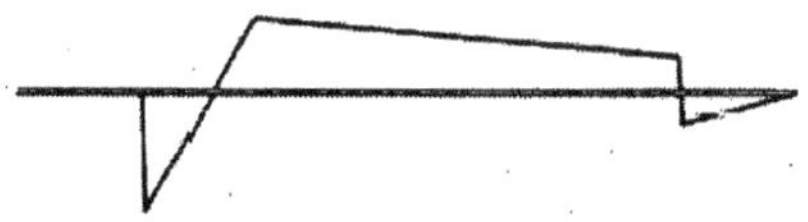

    A. A   B. B   C. C   D. D

6 (#3)

35. The moment diagram for the beam shown in the above diagram is (neglecting the weight of the beam) 35.___

    A. A   B. B   C. C   D. D

Questions 36-40.

DIRECTIONS: In Questions 36 through 40, the plan and front elevation of an object are shown on the left, and on the right are shown four figures, one of which, and only one, represents the right side elevation. Print in the space at the right the letter which represents the right side elevation. In the sample shown below, which figure correctly represents the right side elevation?

    A. A   B. B   C. C   D. D

The correct answer is A.

In Questions 36 through 40, which figure correctly represents the right side elevation?
    A. A   B. B   C. C   D. D

36.   36.___

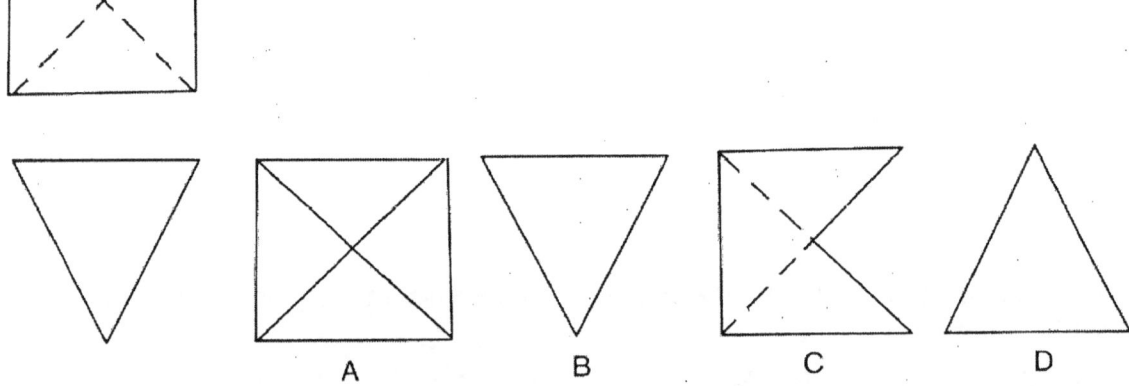

37. Questions 37-40. 37._____

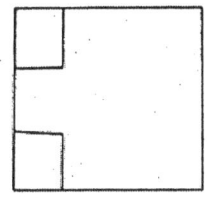

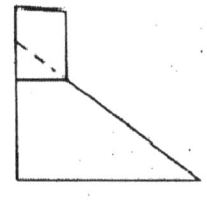 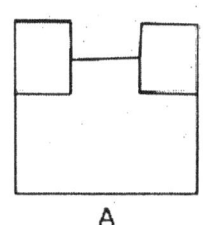 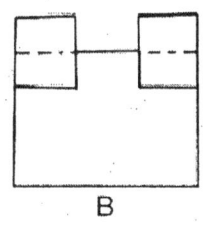 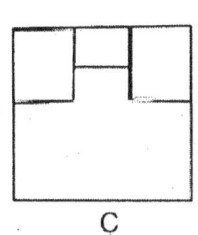 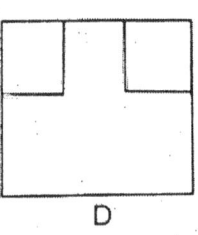
  A   B   C   D

38. 38._____

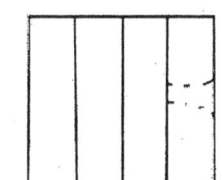

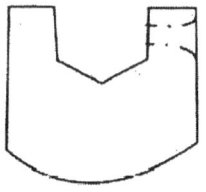 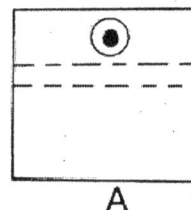 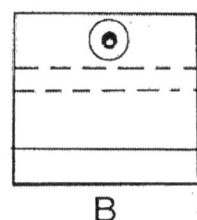 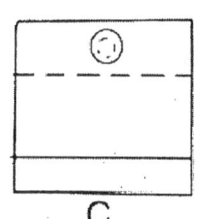 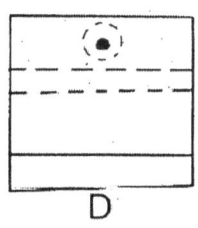
  A   B   C   D

39. 39._____

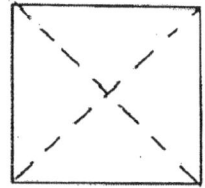

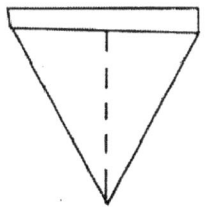 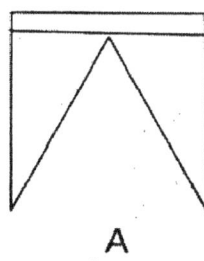 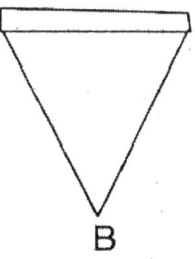 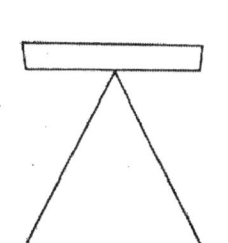 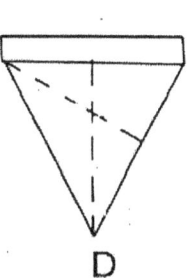
       A   B   C   D

8 (#3)

40.

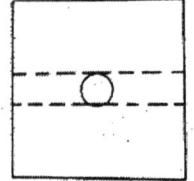

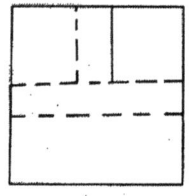
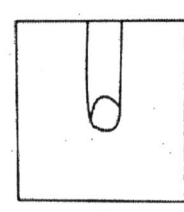
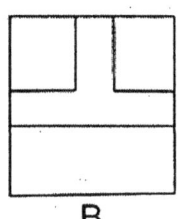
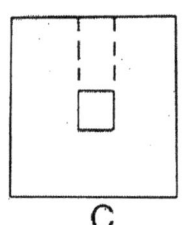
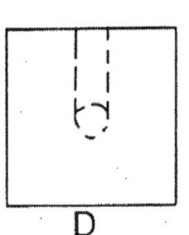

A B C D

KEY (CORRECT ANSWERS)

1. A	11. B	21. A	31. B
2. D	12. A	22. D	32. C
3. B	13. C	23. A	33. C
4. A	14. B	24. D	34. C
5. C	15. A	25. D	35. A
6. D	16. E	26. C	36. B
7. A	17. G	27. D	37. A
8. B	18. F	28. A	38. B
9. C	19. D	29. D	39. A
10. A	20. A	30. B	40. C

EXAMINATION SECTION
TEST 1

DIRECTIONS: Each question or incomplete statement is followed by several suggested answers or completions. Select the one that BEST answers the question or completes the statement. *PRINT THE LETTER OF THE CORRECT ANSWER IN THE SPACE AT THE RIGHT.*

1. A traffic sign states that parking is permitted on Sundays and Holidays. According to the traffic regulations of the city, the holiday on which parking is NOT permitted in the area covered by the sign is

    A. New Year's Day
    B. Memorial Day
    C. Thanksgiving Day
    D. Lincoln's Birthday

2. An intrastate bus is a bus that runs

    A. only in one state
    B. in 2 states only
    C. between the United States and Canada
    D. between any states in the Union

3. According to the traffic regulations of the Department of Traffic, a pedestrian facing a red signal at an intersection

    A. has the right of way over automobiles having a green signal
    B. has the right of way over trucks having a green signal
    C. may not enter the intersection facing the red signal
    D. may enter the intersection, facing the red signal, if he can do so safely without interfering with traffic

4. This sentence was taken from the traffic regulations of the City Department of Traffic with respect to yield signs:
   Proceeding past such sign with resultant collision or other impedance or interference with traffic on the intersecting street shall be deemed prima facie in violation of this regulation. The words prima facie mean MOST NEARLY

    A. probably
    B. possibly or likely
    C. literally or completely
    D. guilty

5. Where signs on city streets do not indicate otherwise, the MAXIMUM speed limit in the city is, in miles per hour,

    A. 15   B. 20   C. 25   D. 30

6. Making a U-turn in the city is NOT permissible on any

    A. street
    B. street in a residential district
    C. street in a business district
    D. 2-way street

7. A person stops his car in front of a hydrant and remains in the car. According to the traffic regulations of the City Department of Traffic,

A. this is illegal if he is within 15 feet of the hydrant
B. it is legal
C. he does not have to move if so ordered by a policeman
D. he may remain there provided he is far enough away from the hydrant so as not to interfere with hose lines

8. Taxicabs are

    A. not permitted to cruise
    B. permitted to cruise in residential areas only
    C. permitted to cruise in business areas only
    D. permitted to cruise in all boroughs except Manhattan

9. Of the following, the one that is the MAIN cause of fatal accidents is

    A. direction signals not working
    B. windshield wipers not working
    C. improper alignment of the wheels
    D. defective brakes

10. The capacity of an approach to an intersection is prinarily dependent upon

    A. slope of through band
    B. cycle length
    C. offsets
    D. through band width

11. To handle heavy traffic movements which tend to cause congestion at an intersection, it is often necessary to

    A. use a standard 3-color (RAG) traffic control signal on all four corners
    B. add arrow indications to traffic signals permitting movements in a certain direction when other traffic is halted
    C. use 2-color instead of 3-color traffic signals
    D. install a flasher caution signal facing the direction of heavy traffic flow

12. Elm Street and Oak Street are one-way streets that intersect.

    A. Cars may turn either right from both streets or left from both streets depending on the direction of travel.
    B. If cars may turn right into one street, they may not turn right into the other.
    C. Only right turns are permitted in both streets.
    D. Only left turns are permitted in both streets.

13. Of the following intersections where one street dead ends into another, the one that is SAFEST is

C. [diagram showing 45° angle]   D. [diagram showing 30° angle]

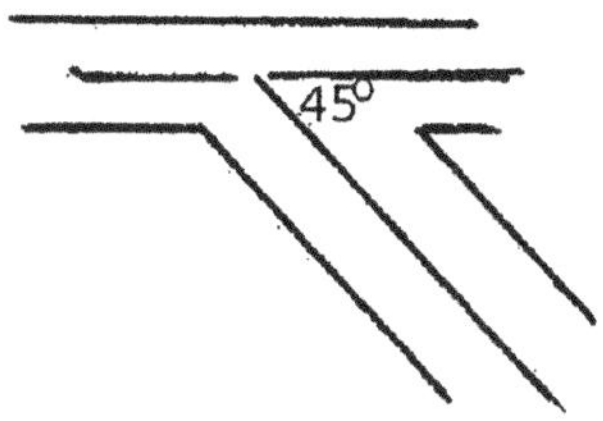

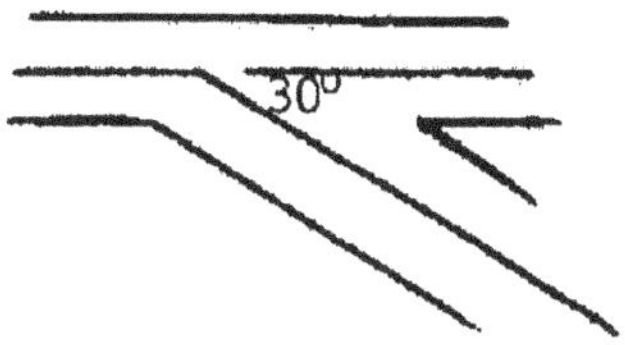

14. Driver interview, tag on vehicle, and postal cards are all methods of obtaining information relative to   14.____

    A. vehicle miles traveled
    B. accident data
    C. motor vehicle registration
    D. origin and destination

15. A study of motor vehicle volume normally includes all but one of the following: 15.____

    A. Directional movements
    B. Motor vehicle occupancy
    C. Motor vehicle classification
    D. Number of vehicles per unit of time

16. Counts made with automatic recorders must always be supplemented with manual observations to ascertain   16.____

    A. hourly distribution
    B. directional distribution
    C. vehicle classification
    D. turning movements

17. A cordon count is USUALLY made on a   17.____

    A. weekday   B. Saturday   C. Sunday   D. holiday

18. Of the following vehicles, the one that need NOT be stopped at an origin and destination station is a   18.____

    A. bus   B. foreign car
    C. station wagon D. coal truck

19. A turning movement count is USUALLY taken at   19.____

    A. a toll station   B. a highway intersection
    C. a bus terminal   D. the end of a highway

20. A manual traffic count is   20.____

    A. a mechanical counter tabulating pedestrians
    B. the number of manuals issued in a traffic survey
    C. an estimated volume of traffic
    D. the number of motor vehicles counted by the person assigned

21. Traffic counts that are made within the city limits are _____ counts.

   A. rural
   B. suburban
   C. urban
   D. sample

22. When questioning a driver in a traffic survey, the interviewer should

   A. explain briefly the reason for the interview
   B. insist on having his questions answered
   C. get the signature of the person interviewed
   D. report the person interviewed, if he did not cooperate

23. In gathering data for a traffic survey, it was decided to use only the period from 6:00 A.M. to 10:00 P.M.
    The reason for choosing this period is MOST likely that

   A. employee morale would drop if the inspectors were required to work during the night
   B. the public would not cooperate during the late night or early morning hours
   C. it is inconsiderate to disturb the public in the middle of the night
   D. the information obtained at that time would be considered adequate

24. Of the following data, the one that is MOST significant in a traffic survey is the

   A. locations between which the car travels
   B. number of cars in the driver's family
   C. number of drivers operating the car
   D. average annual mileage of the car

25. The MAIN purpose for making a motor vehicle volume survey of a particular route is to provide basic data for determining

   A. the extent of group riding
   B. whether prevailing speeds are too fast for conditions
   C. a plan of traffic control
   D. where and how much parking space may be needed

26. Of the following studies, the one which is LEAST related and would probably NOT be included in making a traffic safety survey is

   A. street and off-street parking
   B. driver observance of stop signs
   C. pedestrian observance of traffic signals
   D. accident records and facts

27. Of the following, the one which would NOT usually require a traffic survey is

   A. revision of parking time limits to assure most efficient usage of curb space
   B. creation of off-street parking facilities
   C. important trends in traffic characteristics and transportation demands
   D. complaints from residents in a particular area on the disturbance caused by heavy traffic moving through that area

28. A *spot-map* is a graphic method which is used to

    A. show types of traffic signals located at the main intersections in a community
    B. analyze the distribution of accidents within a community area
    C. arrive at reasonable accident rates
    D. show grades, width, roadway surface, and merging traffic streams in a community

29. A survey was made for the purposes of installing traffic control signals at a certain intersection of a main street and cross street in a certain area. The survey shows that although traffic is relatively heavy during the day, it becomes very light at night.
    In such a situation, it would be MOST desirable to

    A. continue the full sequence of indications as in the daytime
    B. continue operation of the signals, but lengthen the cycle of intervals
    C. completely extinguish the signals leaving the intersection uncontrolled
    D. extinguish the signals but provide a flasher mechanism on the controller

30. If the capacity of an approach to an intersection is 3600 vehicles per hour of green and the go phase on this approach is 40 seconds out of a 60-second cycle, the equivalent volume is _____ vehicles per hour.

    A. 2400   B. 3600   C. 5400   D. 2000

31. If a section of a highway 10 miles long carries an annual daily traffic of 5,000 vehicles and there are two deaths in a year, the death rate is

    A. 2.0 deaths per 5,000 vehicles
    B. 11.0 deaths per 100 million vehicle miles
    C. 11.0 deaths per million vehicle miles
    D. 2.0 deaths per 50,000 vehicle miles

32. If the difference in elevation between two intersections 300 feet apart is 6 feet, the grade along the street is

    A. 2%   B. 2   C. 0.002   D. 6%

33. If on a highway a car passes a given point every 5 seconds, the number of cars per hour passing the given point on the highway is

    A. 360   B. 480   C. 600   D. 720

34. The cost of concrete paving for a strip of driveway 50 feet long, 10 feet wide, and 6 inches deep, if concrete in place costs $30 per cubic yard, is, in dollars, MOST NEARLY
    (27 cubic feet = 1 cubic yard)

    A. 278   B. 318   C. 329   D. 380

Questions 35-38.

DIRECTIONS: Questions 35 through 38 relate to the sketch below.

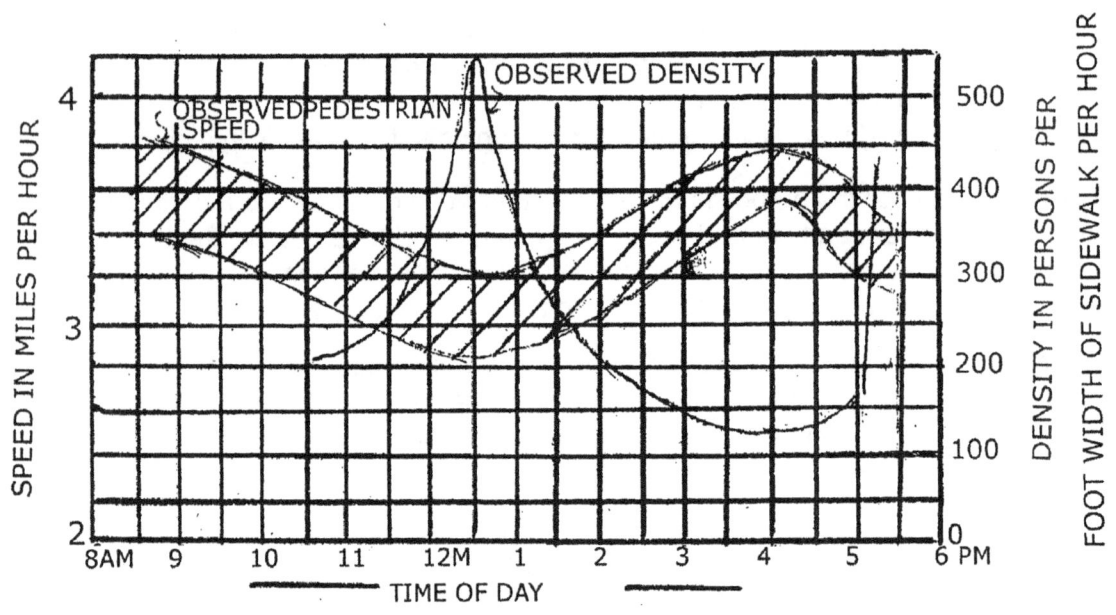

35. Assuming a 10' wide sidewalk, the number of people that would pass the given point at 12:00 M in 10 minutes is MOST NEARLY

    A. 580   B. 680   C. 780   D. 880

36. At 10:00 A.M., you could expect a person to be walking at a speed

    A. of 3 miles per hour
    B. between 300 and 420 feet per hour
    C. between 3.2 and 3.65 miles per hour
    D. of 4.5 feet per second

37. The highest average number of people using the sidewalk will USUALLY occur at

    A. 9 A.M.   B. 12:30 P.M.   C. 4 P.M.   D. 5 P.M.

38. Of the following statements relating to the diagram, the one that is MOST NEARLY CORRECT is

    A. the minimum walking speed observed is 2 miles per hour
    B. data for the survey was taken continuously for 24 hours
    C. as the number of people using the sidewalk increases, the speed at which they walk decreases
    D. the minimum observed density is 300 people per hour per foot width of sidewalk

39. A vehicle moving at 30 miles per hour is moving at a speed, in feet per second, MOST NEARLY

    A. 30   B. 44   C. 52   D. 60

40. A street map is to a scale 1 inch equals 600 feet. A distance of 1/2 inch on the drawing represents a distance on the ground, in feet, MOST NEARLY

    A. 300   B. 600   C. 900   D. 1,200

Questions 41-42.

DIRECTIONS: Questions 41 and 42 refer to the sketches below.

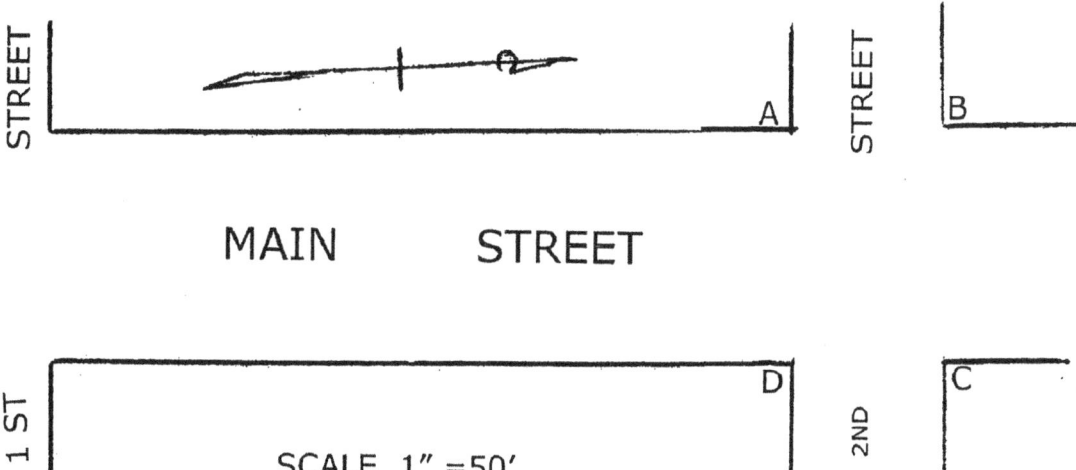

41. The length of block from 1st Street to 2nd Street is MOST NEARLY

    A. 150'   B. 250'   C. 350'   D. 450'

42. The northeast corner of Main and 2nd is

    A. A   B. B   C. C   D. D

43. The sketch shown at the right shows a right triangular island at the intersection of three streets on which is installed traffic signals A and B. Traffic conditions have increased and require than an additional traffic light be installed at point C. Electric power for signal C is to be taken from the junction box located at the base of post A and extended to C as shown by the broken line.
With the distances given as shown, the length of conduit, in feet, required to extend power from A to C is MOST NEARLY

    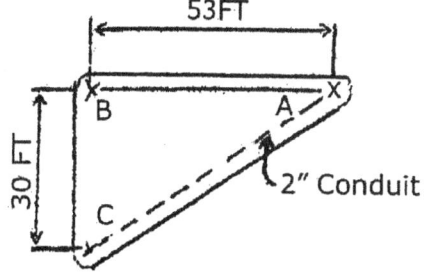

    A. 44   B. 60   C. 83   D. 75

44. The volume of traffic at a certain location increased frori 1,000 to 1,500 vehicles per hour. The percentage increase of traffic is MOST NEARLY

    A. 33%   B. 50%   C. 60%   D. 40%

45. A collision diagram would MOST likely NOT show

    A. direction of movement of each vehicle or pedestrian involved
    B. distance of the accident to the nearest building line
    C. date and hour of the accident
    D. weather and road conditions

46. A graphical representation of the detailed nature of accidents occurring at a location is known as a   46._____

    A. collision diagram
    B. condition diagram
    C. accident summary
    D. accident spot map

47. Which one of the following remedies is MOST appropriate to eliminate high accident frequency involving collisions with fixed objects?   47._____

    A. Installation of advance warning signs
    B. Reroute traffic
    C. Application of paint and reflectors to fixed object
    D. Installation of center dividing strip

48. One of the reasons for making a study of driver observance of stop signs is to study the   48._____

    A. need for retaining or removing stop signs
    B. desirability of replacing stop sign with a police officer
    C. desirability of installing pedestrian crosswalk lines
    D. need for speed zoning

49. Which one of the following remedies is MOST appropriate to eliminate high accident frequency involving pedestrian-vehicular collisions at intersections?   49._____

    A. Installation of turning guide lines
    B. Installation of painted pavement lane lines
    C. Installation of pedestrian cross-walk lines
    D. Removal of view obstruction

50. The driver of a vehicle approaching a yield sign is required to   50._____

    A. proceed without changing speed
    B. slow down if there is a vehicle in the intersection
    C. stop
    D. slow down and proceed with caution

KEY (CORRECT ANSWERS)

1. D	11. B	21. C	31. B	41. B
2. A	12. B	22. A	32. A	42. C
3. C	13. A	23. D	33. D	43. B
4. C	14. D	24. A	34. A	44. B
5. C	15. B	25. C	35. A	45. B
6. C	16. C	26. A	36. C	46. A
7. A	17. A	27. D	37. B	47. C
8. A	18. A	28. B	38. C	48. A
9. D	19. B	29. D	39. B	49. C
10. D	20. D	30. A	40. A	50. D

TEST 2

DIRECTIONS: Each question or incomplete statement is followed by several suggested answers or completions. Select the one that BEST answers the question or completes the statement. *PRINT THE LETTER OF THE CORRECT ANSWER IN THE SPACE AT THE RIGHT.*

1. No person shall stop, stand, or park a vehicle closer to a fire hydrant than 1.____

   A. 17' B. 10' C. 15' D. 12'

2. When stopping is prohibited by signs or regulations and no conflict exists with other traffic, the driver of a vehicle is 2.____

   A. permitted to stop temporarily
   B. not permitted to stop
   C. permitted to stand
   D. permitted to park

3. Where there is a *No Parking* sign, a person may 3.____

   A. not stop his vehicle
   B. stop his vehicle to discharge passengers
   C. stop his vehicle and leave it unattended for a maximum of 10 minutes
   D. stop his vehicle and leave it unattended for a maximum of 5 minutes

4. Of the following, the MOST restrictive parking sign is 4.____

   A. no standing   B. no parking
   C. taxi stand   D. bus stop

5. A highway sign that is classified as a Guide sign is 5.____

   A. Stop   B. No Passing
   C. Narrow Road   D. North Bound

6. A highway sign that is classified as a Warning sign is 6.____

   A. No U Turn   B. Hill
   C. Speed Limit 50   D. Do Not Enter

7. A highway sign that is classified as a Regulatory sign is 7.____

   A. One Way   B. Men Working
   C. RR   D. Detour

8. A traffic device that has the same effect as a stop sign is a 8.____

   A. flashing yellow   B. flashing red
   C. yield sign   D. detour sign

9. A warrant for a certain type of traffic control device is a(n) 9.____

   A. official order to install the device
   B. application from a local community for the device
   C. reason for installing the device
   D. request to remove the device

10. Shapes of signs on state highways convey definite information. The sign to the right means
    A. steep hill - slow down
    B. come to a full stop
    C. you may proceed with caution
    D. approaching narrow bridge

11. Where flasher mechanisms must be installed at intersections of a main street and a cross street as a warning signal, it would be BEST to have flashing
    A. amber on the main street and flashing red on the cross street
    B. red on the main street and flashing amber on the cross street
    C. red on the main street only
    D. amber on the cross street only

12. The primary purpose of *progressive timing* of traffic control signals is to
    A. allow the largest volume of traffic flow at the safest speed along a particular route
    B. permit slow drivers to travel at an increased speed
    C. permit the largest volume of pedestrian traffic to cross safely at the same time
    D. reduce traveling speed so that motorists have vehicles under constant control

13. A hazard marker, for example, at the end of a dead-end street, would MOST likely be
    A. yellow background with black letters
    B. yellow background with red letters
    C. a reflector type marker
    D. a warning sign

14. Of the following, the BEST reason for having markings that are uniform in design, position, and application is that
    A. less skill is required to provide the markings
    B. they cost less when they are uniform
    C. there is no harm done in providing them even where there is no need
    D. they may be recognized and understood instantly

15. If numerous pedestrian accidents occur at a signalized intersection, a pertinent study to help evaluate the problem would be
    A. signal timing
    B. motor vehicle volume
    C. pedestrian observance of traffic signals
    D. driver observance of pedestrian right of way

16. Which one of the following types of fixed-time signal systems is MOST desirable?_____ system.
    A. Flexible progressive   B. Alternate
    C. Simple progressive   D. Simultaneous

17. Of the following statements relating to traffic actuated signals, the one that is CORRECT is

    A. it is especially useful at little used intersections
    B. the length of time the green light is on is not constant
    C. it can only be used at the intersection of one-way streets
    D. it can only be used at the intersection of two-way streets

18. An advantage of the three lens signal (red, yellow, and green) over the two lens signal (red and green) is that it

    A. enables cars within the intersection to clear
    B. allows pedestrians to cross the intersection safely
    C. may be operated as a traffic actuated signal
    D. may be used as a caution signal when not used as a stop and go signal

19. A fixed time signal is one by which traffic stops and goes

    A. for equal time periods
    B. according to a predetermined time schedule
    C. by manual control
    D. according to the volume of traffic

20. The proper installation of vehicle detectors is MOST important for a

    A. pedestrian push-button installation
    B. fixed time signal system
    C. traffic actuated signal
    D. progressive system

21. Of the following, the one that is NOT considered a disadvantage in the use of pavement markings is they

    A. may be obliterated by snow
    B. may not be clearly visible when wet
    C. must be used with other devices such as traffic signs or signals
    D. are subject to traffic wear

22. *It is often desirable to mark lines on the pavement to indicate the limits and the clearance of the overhang on turning streetcars.*
    This safety measure is NOT required in this city because

    A. there are no streetcars in this city
    B. city traffic is controlled by other suitable devices
    C. city traffic is not fast enough to require it
    D. streetcars in this city turn only at the depot and not in the streets

23. A yellow curb marking may be used at all but one of the following:

    A. A fire hydrant
    B. A bus stop
    C. A depressed curb leading to a loading platform
    D. Where parking is prohibited from 8 A.M. to 6 P.M.

24. Stop lines or limit lines are used to indicate

    A. parking space limits to prevent encroachment on a fire hydrant zone
    B. the marking of stalls where parking meters are used
    C. the point behind which vehicles must stop in compliance with a traffic signal
    D. where pedestrians are permitted to cross a street

25. An island, as applied to traffic control,

    A. provides a safe area for a traffic patrolman
    B. segregates pedestrians and vehicles
    C. provides a clear area for a bus stop
    D. establishes a barrier between opposite lanes of traffic

26. Of the following, the one which is NOT a method for providing channelization of traffic is by

    A. permanent islands or strips
    B. pavement markings
    C. use of stanchions
    D. mounting traffic signal at center of intersection

27. The PRIMARY purpose for marking the pavement of heavily traveled thoroughfares into lanes is to

    A. slow up traffic
    B. prevent accidents
    C. speed up traffic
    D. keep slow drivers on the right side of the road

28. When parking is not otherwise restricted in the city, no person shall park a commercial vehicle in excess of ___ hours.

    A. 2   B. 4   C. 3   D. 6

29. A condition which need NOT be considered in making a general parking survey is

    A. reasons for parking at various locations
    B. street and roadway widths and surfaces
    C. average time vehicles remained at various locations
    D. sidewalk obstructions, such as lamp posts and fire posts

30. Concerning the purpose of parking meters, the statement which is NOT true is

    A. assist in reducing overtime parking at the curb
    B. increase parking turnover
    C. eliminate the need for off-street parking facilities
    D. facilitate enforcement of parking regulations

31. The MOST efficient layout of parking spaces in a large lot is to place the stalls _____ to the aisles.

    A. parallel   B. at right angles
    C. at a 30° angle   D. at a 60° angle

32. The time limits set by cities for parking on city streets during the daytime   32.____

    A. is considered strictly a policing problem
    B. is shorter in concentrated business areas
    C. will vary directly with the amount of traffic on the street
    D. is uniform for all sections of the city

33. Four parts of a survey report are listed below, not necessarily in their proper order: 33.____
    I. Body of report
    II. Synopsis of report
    III. Letter of transmittal
    IV. Conclusions

    Which one of the following represents the BEST sequence for inclusion of these parts in a report?

    A. III, IV, I, II   B. II, I, III, IV
    C. III, II, I, IV   D. I, III, IV, II

34. A traffic control inspector recommends that an illuminated advertising sign near a signal light be removed.   34.____
    The reason for this recommendation is MOST likely that

    A. a driver's attention may be attracted to the sign rather than the road
    B. the similarity of colors may cause confusion
    C. such signs mar the beauty of the roadside
    D. the sign encroaches upon public property

35. Of the following, the MOST important value of a good report is that it   35.____

    A. reflects credit upon the person who submitted the report
    B. provides good reference material
    C. expedites official business
    D. expresses the need for official action

36. The MOST important requirement in report writing is   36.____

    A. promptness in turning in reports
    B. length
    C. grammatical construction
    D. accuracy

37. You have discovered an error in your report submitted to the main office.   37.____
    You should

    A. wait until the error is discovered in the main office and then correct it
    B. go directly to the supervisor in the main office after working hours and ask him unofficially to correct the answer
    C. notify the main office immediately so that the error can be corrected if necessary
    D. do nothing, since it is possible that one error will have little effect on the total report

38. The use of *radar* by police as a means of apprehending motorists who exceed the speed limit has recently been challenged in court on the grounds that   38.____

    A. the motorists are not forewarned
    B. the speed limits have not been posted

C. the equipment does not give reliable results
D. there is no sworn evidence that a speed violation took place

39. Of the following, the one which is generally classified as a commercial vehicle is a

   A. station wagon
   B. chauffeur-driven passenger car
   C. taxicab
   D. truck

40. A divided arterial highway for through traffic with full or partial control of access is generally referred to as an

   A. expressway   B. parkway
   C. freeway   D. major street

41. Of the following, the MOST important advantage to be gained by converting a two-way north-south street to a one-way street is

   A. *decrease* the number of accidents
   B. *decrease* the need for bus service
   C. *increase* the average speed of traffic
   D. *increase* the turnover at curbs

42. Of the following, the BEST road for heavy traffic is

   A. two lane   B. three lane
   C. four lane undivided   D. four lane divided

43. When weekend traffic differs greatly from weekday traffic,

   A. the average daily traffic figure is used in estimating weekend traffic
   B. weekend traffic counts should be made as well as weekday counts
   C. the traffic count for another road in the area should be used
   D. traffic counts should be made at different seasons of the year

44. Work is now going on to approximately double the car-carrying capacity of which one of the following?

   A. Car parkways   B. Bridges
   C. Tunnels   D. HOV lanes

45. The MOST recent major change in the specifications of the federally aided highway program is

   A. increasing the permissible grades or roads
   B. requirements for drainage
   C. lane width
   D. vertical clearance under bridges

46. A recent newspaper article reported that small cars are considered a danger to the federally aided highway program.
    Of the following, the one that may be considered as the reason for this danger is

A. they consume less gas providing less taxes for the highway program
B. the lanes of the new highways are too wide for these cars, disorganizing the traffic flow pattern
C. the two-car family is upsetting the estimates of traffic flow
D. foreign cars are hurting American business

47. Span-wire mountings of fixed traffic control signals is generally   47._____

    A. used in the city at heavily traveled intersections
    B. used in the city at intersections in isolated areas
    C. not used in the city
    D. used at locations where more than two streets intersect

48. A map depicting straight lines drawn from points of vehicle origin to points of vehicle destination is known as _____ map.   48._____

    A. desire line   B. traffic flow
    C. bar   D. pie

49. Brake reaction time for most people is APPROXIMATELY _____ seconds.   49._____

    A. 0.6   B. 2.0   C. 0.1   D. 1.4

50. Trucks should travel along prescribed truck routes if their overall length is equal to or exceeds   50._____

    A. 27'   B. 41'   C. 30'   D. 33'

KEY (CORRECT ANSWERS)

1. C	11. A	21. C	31. B	41. C
2. B	12. A	22. A	32. B	42. D
3. B	13. C	23. D	33. C	43. B
4. A	14. D	24. C	34. B	44. D
5. D	15. C	25. B	35. C	45. D
6. B	16. A	26. D	36. D	46. A
7. A	17. B	27. C	37. C	47. C
8. B	18. D	28. C	38. C	48. A
9. C	19. B	29. D	39. D	49. A
10. B	20. C	30. C	40. A	50. D

EXAMINATION SECTION
TEST 1

DIRECTIONS: Each question or incomplete statement is followed by several suggested answers or completions. Select the one that Best answers the question or completes the statement. *PRINT THE LETTER OF THE CORRECT ANSWER IN THE SPACE AT THE RIGHT.*

Questions 1-4.

DIRECTIONS: Answer Questions 1 to 4 based on the information given in the traffic volume table below.

TRAFFIC VOLUME COUNTS

Time (A.M.)	Main Street Northbound	Main Street Southbound	Cross Street Eastbound	Cross Street Westbound
7:00- 7:15	100	100	70	60
7:15- 7:30	110	100	80	70
7:30- 7:45	150	140	110	100
7:45- 8:00	170	160	140	130
8:00- 8:15	210	190	120	110
8:15- 8:30	180	170	90	80
8:30- 8:45	160	140	70	60
8:45- 9:00	150	160	70	50
9:00- 9:15	140	150	50	50
9:15- 9:30	130	120	40	20
9:30- 9:45	120	110	30	30
9:45-10:00	120	100	30	30

1. The hour during which traffic, moving in both directions on Main Street, reached its *peak* was

    A. 7:30 - 8:30
    B. 7:45 - 8:45
    C. 8:00 - 9:00
    D. 8:15 - 9:15

2. The hour during which traffic volume, moving in both directions on Cross Street, reached its *peak* was

    A. 7:30 - 8:30
    B. 7:45 - 8:45
    C. 8:00 - 9:00
    D. 8:15 - 9:15

3. The HIGHEST average hourly volume over the three-hour period 7:00 to 10:00 was recorded for

    A. Main Street northbound
    B. Main Street southbound
    C. Cross Street eastbound
    D. Cross Street westbound

4. The *peak* 15-minute traffic volume for all directions of travel occurred between

    A. 7:30 - 7:45
    B. 7:45 - 8:00
    C. 8:00 - 8:15
    D. 8:15 - 8:30

5. Which of the following statements relating to one-way streets is CORRECT?
   One-way streets

71

A. increase turning movement conflicts between vehicles
B. decrease street capacity
C. decrease accident hazards for pedestrians
D. make it impossible to time traffic signals to control speeds

Questions 6-11.

DIRECTIONS: Answer Questions 6 to 11 based on the information given in Figure 1 below.

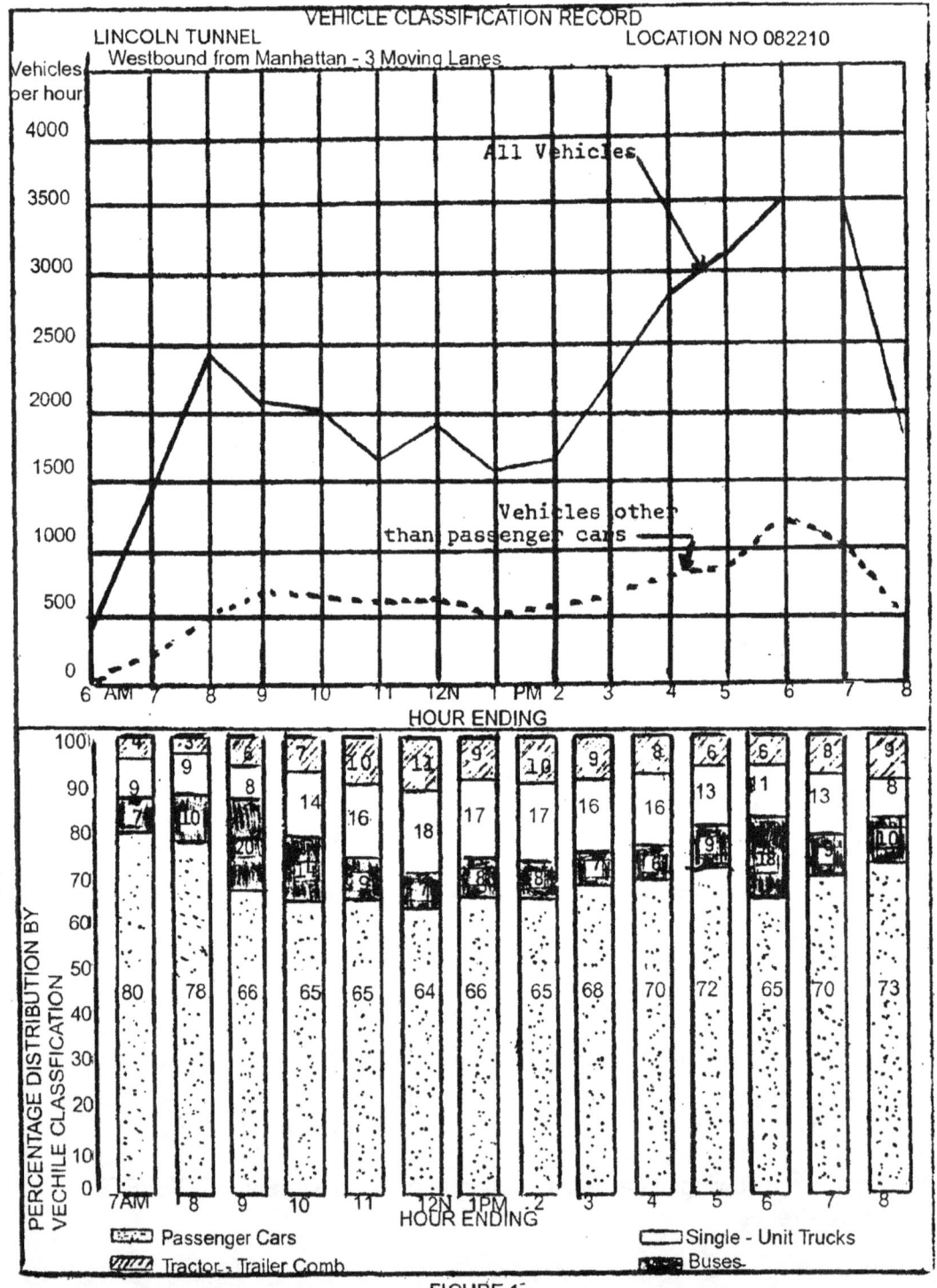

FIGURE 1

6. The total number of all vehicles traveling through the Lincoln Tunnel westbound from Manhattan between the hours of 6 A.M. and 12 Noon is *most nearly* 6.____

   A. 5,500   B. 7,500   C. 9,500   D. 11,500

7. The number of passenger cars recorded during the hour ending at 7 P.M. was *most nearly* 7.____

   A. 235   B. 1160   C. 2450   D. 3500

8. Excluding passenger cars, the AVERAGE number of vehicles per moving lane recorded during the peak hour was *most nearly* 8.____

   A. 420   B. 1180   C. 1250   D. 3550

9. The percentage of buses recorded between 6 A.M. and 8 P.M. ranged between 9.____

   A. 3% and 11%   B. 8% and 18%
   C. 6% and 20%   D. 64% and 80%

10. During the study period, the percentage of single unit trucks *exceeded* the percentage of buses for _____ hours. 10.____

    A. 4   B. 5   C. 9   D. 10

11. For all vehicles recorded, the recorded traffic volume during the morning peak hour was *most nearly* _____ of the volume during the evening peak hour. 11.____

    A. 40%   B. 50%   C. 60%   D. 70%

12. In urban areas, traffic volume is usually LOWEST during the month of 12.____

    A. January   B. March   C. August   D. October

13. In urban shopping areas, the *peak* traffic activity USUALLY occurs during 13.____

    A. Monday afternoon and Friday night
    B. Friday night and Saturday afternoon
    C. Thursday night and Saturday afternoon
    D. Monday night and Friday night

14. In the metric system, the unit that is closest to a mile is a 14.____

    A. centimeter   B. liter
    C. millimeter   D. kilometer

Questions 15-16.

DIRECTIONS: Questions 15 and 16 refer to the diagram at the top of the following Page 4.

15. Vehicle X in the diagram is heading in which direction? 15.____

    A. Southeast   B. Southwest
    C. Northeast   D. Northwest

16. If Vehicle X in the diagram makes a right turn at the intersection, it will be headed 16.____

    A. southeast   B. southwest
    C. northeast   D. northwest

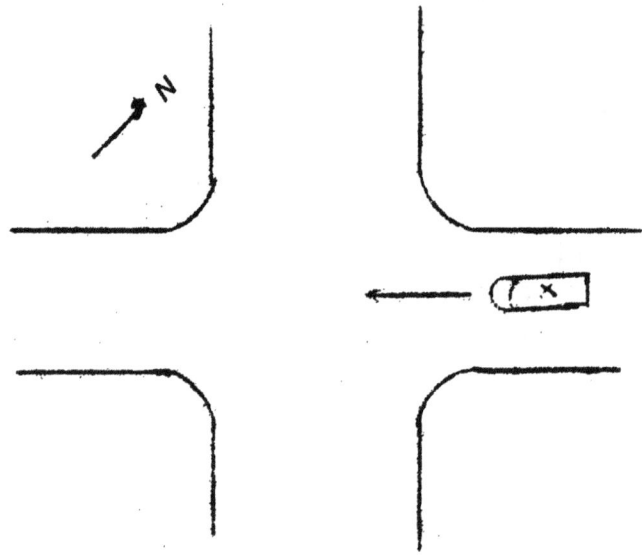

17. The one of the following that is NOT a function of channelization is   17.____

    A. control the angle of conflict
    B. favor certain turning movements
    C. protect pedestrians
    D. increase the pavement area within an intersection

18. The time of display of the yellow signal indication following the green signal indication is called the   18.____

    A. clearance interval   B. time cycle
    C. traffic phase   D. interval sequence

19. A lane constructed for the purpose of allowing vehicles entering a highway to increase speed to a rate that is safe for merging with through traffic is called a(n) _____ lane.   19.____

    A. auxiliary   B. through
    C. acceleration   D. deceleration

20. A traffic volume count which records the number and types of vehicles passing a given point is called a _____ count.   20.____

    A. rate-of-flow   B. capacity
    C. classification   D. roadway

21. On highways, the MAIN purpose served by barriers between traffic going in opposite directions is to   21.____

    A. stop cars if they get out of lane
    B. minimize the glare from oncoming cars
    C. prevent cars from overturning if they have blowouts
    D. prevent head-on accidents

22. Control count stations are USUALLY used to 22.____

    A. establish seasonal and daily traffic volume characteristics
    B. make short manual traffic counts
    C. classify traffic
    D. count traffic on weekends only

23. The MAIN purpose of off-center traffic lanes is to 23.____

    A. protect slow-moving traffic from the hazards of fast-moving traffic
    B. permit the use of special traffic control
    C. provide additional capacity in one direction of travel
    D. provide a slow-down area for disabled vehicles

24. Reserved transit lanes are used to 24.____

    A. make sure buses stop at the curb
    B. reduce bus and passenger car accidents
    C. decrease transit travel times by reducing friction between buses and other vehicles
    D. make it easier for people to get on and off buses

25. The slope or grade between points X and Y shown in the diagram below is 25.____

    A. 4%   B. 10%   C. 25%   D. 50%

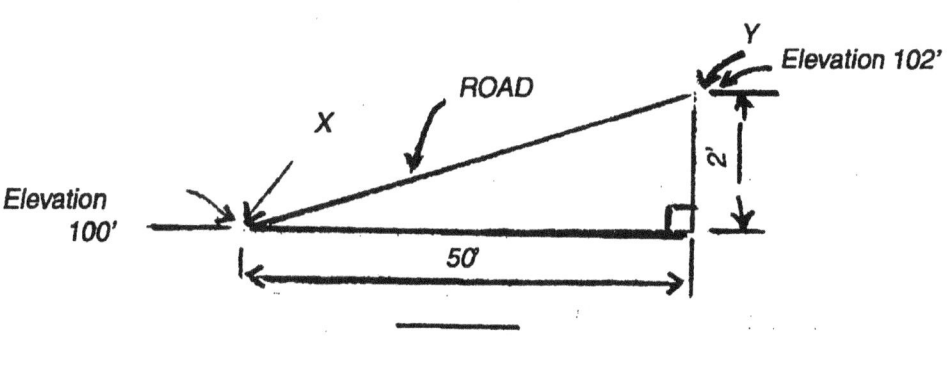

KEY (CORRECT ANSWERS)

1. B
2. A
3. A
4. C
5. C

6. D
7. C
8. A
9. C
10. C

11. D
12. A
13. B
14. D
15. B

16. D
17. D
18. A
19. C
20. C

21. D
22. A
23. C
24. C
25. A

———

TEST 2

DIRECTIONS: Each question or incomplete statement is followed by several suggested answers or completions. Select the one that BEST answers the question or completes the statement. *PRINT THE LETTER OF THE CORRECT ANSWER IN THE SPACE AT THE RIGHT.*

1. In the city, when parking is not otherwise restricted, commercial vehicles can park   1.____

   A. up to a maximum of one hour
   B. up to a maximum of three hours
   C. up to a maximum of eight hours
   D. without a time limitation

2. In the city, with respect to loading an parking, commercial vehicles are allowed to   2.____

   A. load or unload merchandise expeditiously in a no-standing zone
   B. park for one hour in a no-parking zone
   C. load or unload merchandise expeditiously in a no-parking zone
   D. park for one hour in a no-standing zone

3. On the Federal national highway system, highways ending in an even number run   3.____

   A. in the east-west direction
   B. both east-west or north-south
   C. in the north-south direction
   D. around cities and not through them

4. The *current* maximum allowed speed limit on Federal interstate highways is _____ miles per hour.   4.____

   A. 50   B. 55   C. 60   D. 65

5. In the city, when a vehicle is too long for a single parking meter space, the vehicle may   5.____

   A. not be parked in the parking meter area
   B. be parked using more than one space but a coin must be deposited in the meter designated for each space occupied
   C. be parked using more than one space and a coin must be deposited only in the forward parking meter
   D. be parked using more than one space and a coin must be deposited only in the rear parking meter

6. In the city, some signs indicate that stopping, standing, or parking regulations are in effect every day except Sundays. Where this sign is used, stopping, standing, or parking regulations would apply on   6.____

   A. Washington's Birthday   B. Brooklyn Day
   C. Columbus Day   D. Election Day

7. In the city, unless signs are posted indicating specific hours during which play street regulations are in effect, such regulations are in effect on designated streets FROM   7.____

   A. 7 A.M. until 4 P.M.
   B. 8 A.M. until 1/2 hour before sunset

77

C. 8 A.M. to 1/2 hour after sunset
D. 8 A.M. to 8 P.M.

8. When preparing to make a turn while driving a vehicle on a roadway, a driver should signal his intention to turn AT LEAST _____ feet in advance of the turn.

   A. 50   B. 100   C. 150   D. 200

9. Unless otherwise permitted or prohibited by posted signs, the MAXIMUM continuous period during which a vehicle may be parked on any roadway in the city is hours.

   A. 8   B. 12   C. 24   D. 48

10. In the city, commercial vehicles may angle stand or angle park in

    A. any area where no parking signs are installed, provided the street is wide enough to allow the vehicle to park at an angle
    B. on any one-way street where standing is not prohibited, provided the street is wide enough to allow the vehicle to park at an angle
    C. on a two-way street in areas authorized by signs, provided that the vehicle shall not occupy more than a parking lane plus one moving lane
    D. on a two-way street in areas authorized by signs, provided that the vehicles shall not extend more than 10 feet from the curb

11. Which of the following is MOST restrictive to drivers of passenger cars?

    A. Regulations relating to parking in front of fire hydrants
    B. No parking regulations
    C. No standing regulations
    D. No stopping regulations

12. The MAXIMUM permitted speed limit in the city, unless signs indicate otherwise, is _____ mph.

    A. 25   B. 30   C. 35   D. 40

13. With regard to right-of-way at an intersection that is NOT controlled by a traffic control device, the one of the following statements that is CORRECT is

    A. the car on your right has the right-of-way
    B. the car on your left has the right-of-way
    C. a car preparing to enter the intersection has the right-of-way over a car in the intersection
    D. a car turning left has the right-of-way over a vehicle going straight ahead

14. At an intersection controlled by traffic signals, a red arrow pointing to the right means that a right turn may

    A. be made after coming to a full stop
    B. be made providing the driver yields the right-of-way to all other vehicles and pedestrians
    C. not be made during the period that the red arrow is illuminated
    D. be made only if there is another indication showing a round green signal light

15. A flashing red traffic signal has the SAME meaning as a

   A. stop sign
   B. yield sign
   C. flashing yellow traffic signal
   D. hazardous intersection warning sign

16. Traffic signals are MOST frequently installed to reduce _____ collision accidents.

   A. right-angle
   B. rear-end
   C. side-swipe
   D. head-on

17. The CORRECT color combination for warning signs is

   A. yellow lettering or symbols on a black background
   B. white lettering or symbols on a red background
   C. black lettering or symbols on a yellow background
   D. black lettering or symbols on a white background

18. A PROGRESSIVELY timed traffic signal system will

   A. turn all the signals red or green at the same time
   B. usually increase the number of rear-end accidents but reduce the number of right-angle accidents
   C. make it more hazardous for pedestrians to cross at the signalized intersections
   D. decrease the number of stops traffic is required to make

19. The EFFECT of traffic signals on accidents is that traffic signals

   A. always decrease accidents
   B. sometimes increase accidents
   C. never increase accidents
   D. have no real effect on accidents

20. With respect to traffic devices, which of the following situations should receive the LOWEST priority in terms of repair or replacement?

   A. Inoperative or malfunctioning traffic signals at an intersection
   B. Missing "No Standing - Rush Hour" regulation signs
   C. Missing "Yield" signs controlling the intersection of a minor street with a major street
   D. Inoperative parking meters along one block in a retail shopping area

21. Of the following, the BEST reason why a stop sign would be used instead of a yield sign to control traffic at an intersection is

   A. there are a larger number of rear-end accidents on the street being controlled
   B. the street being controlled is less than 36 feet wide
   C. visibility is limited at the intersection
   D. the approaches to the intersection are offset to each other

22. The USUAL color combination used on interstate signs is _____ lettering and symbols on a _____ background.

   A. white; green
   B. green; white
   C. white; black
   D. black; white

23. The geometrical shape of a railroad crossing sign is that of a(n)   23.____

    A. octagon   B. circle   C. rectangle   D. triangle

24. The STANDARD pedestrian walking speed used in timing pedestrian signals is _____ per second.   24.____

    A. 1 foot   B. 4 feet   C. 8 feet   D. 12 feet

25. A driver approaching an intersection where a sign authorizes a right turn on a red traffic signal indication may make such a turn AND   25.____

    A. has the right-of-way over all vehicles in the intersection
    B. must yield right-of-way to all vehicles and pedestrians within the intersection
    C. must yield right-of-way only to vehicles and pedestrians on the cross street
    D. has the right-of-way over other turning vehicles

KEY (CORRECT ANSWERS)

1. B
2. C
3. A
4. D
5. C

6. B
7. C
8. B
9. C
10. C

11. D
12. B
13. A
14. C
15. A

16. A
17. C
18. D
19. B
20. D

21. C
22. A
23. B
24. B
25. B

EXAMINATION SECTION
TEST 1

DIRECTIONS: Each question or incomplete statement is followed by several suggested answers or completions. Select the one that BEST answers the question or completes the statement. *PRINT THE LETTER OF THE CORRECT ANSWER IN THE SPACE AT THE RIGHT.*

1. A *basic* method of operation that a *good* supervisor should follow is to

    A. check the work of subordinates constantly to make sure they are not making exceptions to the rules
    B. train subordinates so they can handle problems that come up regularly themselves and come to him only with special cases
    C. delegate to subordinates only those duties which he cannot do himself
    D. issue directions to subordinates only on special matters

2. To do a *good* job of performance evaluation, it is BEST for a supervisor to

    A. compare the employee's performance to that of another employee doing similar work
    B. give greatest weight to instances of unusually good or unusually poor performance
    C. leave out any consideration of the employee's personal traits
    D. measure the employee's performance against standard performance requirements

3. Of the following, the MOST important reason for a supervisor to have private face to face discussions with subordinates about their performance is to

    A. help employees improve their work
    B. give special praise to employees who perform well
    C. encourage the employees to compete for higher performance ratings
    D. discipline employees who perform poorly

4. Of the following, the CHIEF purpose of a probationary period for a new employee is to allow time for

    A. finding out whether the selection processes are satisfactory
    B. the employee to make adjustments in his home circumstances made necessary by the job
    C. the employee to decide whether he wants a permanent appointment
    D. determining the fitness of the employee to continue in the job

5. When a subordinate resigns his job, it is MOST important to conduct an exit interview in order to

    A. try to get the employee to remain on the job
    B. learn the true reasons for the employee's resignation
    C. see that the employee leaves with a good opinion of the agency
    D. ask the employee if he would consider a transfer

6. Chronic lateness of employees is generally LEAST likely to be due to

    A. distance of job location from home   B. poor personnel administration
    C. unexpressed employee grievances   D. low morale

7. Of the following, the LEAST effective stimulus for motivating employees toward inproved performance over a long-range period is

   A. their sense of achievement
   B. their feeling of recognition
   C. opportunity for their self-development
   D. an increase in salary

8. Suppose that NOT ONE of a group of employees has turned in an idea to the employees suggestion system during the past year.
   The *most probable* reason for this situation is that the

   A. money awards given for suggestions used are not high enough to make employees interested
   B. employees in this group are not able to develop any good ideas
   C. supervisor of these employees is not doing enough to encourage them to take part in the program
   D. methods and procedures of operation do not need improvement

9. A subordinate tells you that he is having trouble concentrating on his work due to a personal problem at home.
   Of the following, it would be BEST for you to

   A. refer him to a community service agency
   B. listen quietly to the story because he may just need a sympathetic ear
   C. tell him that you cannot help him because the problem is not job related
   D. ask him questions about the nature of the problem and tell him how you would handle it

10. For you as a supervisor to give each of your subordinates *exactly* the same type of supervision is

    A. *advisable,* because doing this insures fair and impartial treatment of each individual
    B. *not advisable,* because individuals like to think that they are receiving better treatment than others
    C. *advisable,* because once a supervisor learns how to deal with a subordinate who brings a problem to him, he can handle another subordinate with this problem in the same way
    D. *not advisable,* because each person is different and there is no one supervisory procedure for dealing with individuals that applies in every case

11. A senior employee under your supervision tells you that he is reluctant to speak to one of his subordinates about his poor work habits, because this worker is "strong-willed" and he does not want to antagonize him.
    For you to offer to speak to the subordinate about this matter yourself would be

    A. *advisable,* since you are in a position of greater authority
    B. *inadvisable,* since handling this problem is a basic supervisory responsibility of the senior employee
    C. *advisable,* since the senior employee must work more closely with the worker than you do
    D. *inadvisable,* since you should not risk antagonizing the employee yourself

12. Some of your subordinates have been coming to you with complaints you feel are unimportant. For you to hear their stories out is

    A. *poor practice,* you should spend your time on more important matters
    B. *good practice,* this will increase your popularity with your subordinates
    C. *poor practice,* subordinates should learn to come to you only with major grievances
    D. *good practice,* it may prevent minor complaints from developing into major grievances

13. Assume that an agency has an established procedure for handling employee grievances. An employee in this agency, comes to his immediate supervisor with a grievance. The supervisor investigates the matter and makes a decision.
    However, the employee is not satisfied with the decision made by the supervisor. The BEST action for the supervisor to take is to

    A. tell the employee he will review the matter further
    B. remind the employee that he is the supervisor and the employee must act in accordance with his decision
    C. explain to the employee how he can carry his complaint forward to the next step in the grievance procedure
    D. tell the employee he will consult with his own superiors on the matter

14. Subordinate employees and senior employees often must make quick decisions while in the field. The supervisor can BEST help subordinates meet such situations by

    A. training them in the appropriate action to take for every problem that may come up
    B. limiting the areas in which they are permitted to make decisions
    C. making certain they understand clearly the basic policies of the bureau and the department
    D. delegating authority to make such decisions to only a few subordinates on each level

15. Studies have shown that the CHIEF cause of failure to achieve success as a supervisor is

    A. an unwillingness to delegate authority to subordinates
    B. the establishment of high performance standards for subordinates
    C. the use of discipline that is too strict
    D. showing too much leniency to poor workers

16. When a supervisor delegates to a subordinate certain work that he normally does himself, it is MOST important that he give the subordinate

    A. responsibility for also setting the standards for the work to be done
    B. sufficient authority to be able to carry out the assignment
    C. written, step-by-step instructions for doing the work
    D. an explanation of one part of the task at a time

17. It is particularly important that disciplinary actions be equitable as between individuals. This statement *implies* that

    A. punishment applied in disciplinary actions should be lenient
    B. proposed disciplinary actions should be reviewed by higher authority
    C. subordinates should have an opportunity to present their stories before penalties are applied
    D. penalties for violations of the rules should be standardized and consistently applied

18. You discover that from time to time a number of false rumors circulate among your subordinates.
    Of the following, the BEST way for you to handle this situation is to

    A. ignore the rumors since rumors circulate in every office and can never be eliminated
    B. attempt to find those responsible for the rumors and reprimand them
    C. make sure that your employees are informed as soon as possible about all matters that affect them
    D. inform your superior about the rumors and let him deal with the matter

19. Supervisors who allow the "halo effect" to influence their evaluations of subordinates are *most likely* to

    A. give more lenient ratings to older employees who have longer service
    B. let one highly favorable or unfavorable trait unduly affect their judgment of an employee
    C. evaluate all employees on one trait before considering a second
    D. give high evaluations in order to avoid antagonizing their subordinates

20. For a supervisor to keep records of reprimands to subordinates about infractions of the rules is

    A. *good practice,* because these records are valuable to support disciplinary actions recommended or taken
    B. *poor practice,* because such records are evidence of the supervisor's inability to maintain discipline
    C. *good practice,* because such records indicate that the supervisor is doing a good job
    D. *poor practice,* because the best way to correct subordinates is to give them more training

21. When a new departmental policy has been established, it would be MOST advisable for you, as a supervisor, to

    A. distribute a memo which states the new policy and instruct your subordinates to read it
    B. explain specifically to your subordinates how the policy is going to affect them
    C. make sure your subordinates understand that you are not responsible for setting the policy
    D. tell your subordinates whether you agree or disagree with the policy

22. As a supervisor, you receive several complaints about the rude conduct of a subordinate. The FIRST action you should take is to

    A. request his transfer to another office
    B. prepare a charge sheet for disciplinary action
    C. assign a senior employee to work with him for a week
    D. interview the employee to determine possible reason, and warn that correction is necessary

23. A supervisor is *most likely* to get subordinates to work cooperatively toward accomplishing bureau goals if he

    A. creates an atmosphere that contributes to their feeling of security
    B. backs up subordinates even when they occasionally disobey regulations
    C. shows interest in subordinates by helping them solve their personal problems
    D. uses an authoritarian or "bossy" approach to supervision

24. A supervisor is holding a staff meeting with his senior employees to try to find an acceptable solution to a problem that has come up.
    Of the following, the CHIEF role of the supervisor at this meeting should be to

    A. see that every member of the group contributes at least one suggestions
    B. act as chairman of the meeting, but take no other active part to avoid influencing the senior employees
    C. keep the participants from wandering off into discussions of irrelevant matters
    D. make certain the participants hear his views on the matter at the beginning of the meeting

25. An employee shows you a certificate that he has just received for completing two years of study in conversational Spanish. As his supervisor, it would be BEST for you to

    A. put a note about this accomplishment in his personnel folder
    B. assign him to areas in which people of Spanish origin live
    C. congratulate him on this accomplishment, but tell him frankly that you doubt this is likely to have any direct bearing on his work
    D. encourage him to continue his studies and become thoroughly fluent in speaking the language

KEY (CORRECT ANSWERS)

1. B
2. D
3. A
4. D
5. B

6. A
7. D
8. C
9. B
10. D

11. B
12. D
13. C
14. C
15. A

16. B
17. D
18. C
19. B
20. A

21. B
22. D
23. A
24. C
25. A

TEST 2

DIRECTIONS: Each question or incomplete statement is followed by several suggested answers or completions. Select the one that BEST answers the question or completes the statement. *PRINT THE LETTER OF THE CORRECT ANSWER IN THE SPACE AT THE RIGHT.*

1. Of the following, the factor affecting employee morale which the immediate supervisor is LEAST able to control is 1.____

   A. handling of grievances
   B. fair and impartial treatment of subordinates
   C. general presonnel rules and regulations
   D. accident prevention

2. When one of your workers does outstanding work, you should 2.____

   A. explain to your other employees that you expect the same kind of work of them
   B. praise him for his work so that he will know it is appreciated
   C. say nothing, because other employees may think you are showing favoritism
   D. show him how his work can be improved still more so that he will not sit back

3. For you as a supervisor to consider a suggestion from a probationary worker for improving a procedure would be 3.____

   A. *poor practice,* because this employee is too new on the job to know much about it
   B. *good practice,* because you may be able to share credit for the suggestion
   C. *poor practice,* because it may hurt the morale of the older employees
   D. *good practice,* because the suggestion may be worthwhile

4. If you find you must criticize the work of one of your workers, it would be BEST for you to 4.____

   A. mention the good points in his work as well as the faults
   B. caution him that he will receive an unsatisfactory performance report unless his work improves
   C. compare his work to that of the other agents you supervise
   D. apologize for making the criticism

5. As a senior employee which one of the following matters would it be BEST for you to talk over with your supervisor before you take final action? 5.____

   A. One of the workers you supervise continues to disregard your instructions repeatedly in spite of repeated warnings
   B. One of your workers tells you he wants to discuss a personal problem
   C. A probationary employee tells you he does not understand a procedure
   D. One of your workers tells you he disagrees with the way you rate his work

6. If one of your subordinates asks you a question about a department rule and you do not know the answer, you should tell him that 6.____

   A. he should try to get the information himself
   B. you do not have the answer, but you will get it for him as soon as you can
   C. he should ask you the question again a week from now
   D. he should put the question in writing

7. If, as a supervisor, you realize that you have been unfair in criticizing one of your subordinates, the BEST action for you to take is to

    A. say nothing, but overlook some error made by this employee in the future
    B. be frank and tell the employee that you are sorry for the mistake you made
    C. let the employee know in some indirect way without admitting your mistake, that you realize he was not at fault
    D. say nothing, but be more careful about criticizing subordinates in the future

8. Of the following, the MOST important reason for a supervisor to write an accident report as soon as possible after an accident has happened is to

    A. make sure that important facts about the accident are not forgotten
    B. avoid delay in getting compensation for the injured person
    C. get adequate medical treatment for the injured person
    D. keep department accident statistics up to date

9. In any matter which may require disciplinary action, the FIRST responsibility of the supervisor is to

    A. decide what penalty should be applied for the offense
    B. refer the matter to a higher authority for complete investigation
    C. place the interests of the department above those of the employee
    D. investigate the matter fully to get all the facts

10. Suppose you find it necessary to criticize one of the subordinates you supervise. You should

    A. send an official letter to his home
    B. speak to him about the matter privately
    C. speak to him at a staff meeting
    D. ask another worker who is friendly with him to talk to him about the matter

11. Some of your subordinates have been coming to you with complaints you feel are unimportant. For you to hear their stories out is

    A. *poor practice,* you should spend your time on more important matters
    B. *good practice,* this will increase your popularity with your subordinates
    C. *poor practice,* subordinates should learn to come to you only with major grievances
    D. *good practice,* it may prevent minor complaints from developing into major grievances

12. Suppose that NOT ONE of a group of employees has turned in an idea to the employees' suggestion system during the past year. The *most probable* reason for this situation is that the

    A. supervisor of these employees is not doing enough to encourage them to take part in this program
    B. employees in this group are not able to develop any good ideas
    C. money awards given for suggestions used are not high enough to make employees interested
    D. methods and procedures of operation do not need improvement

13. For you as a supervisor to give each of your subordinates *exactly* the same type of supervision is

    A. *advisable,* because doing this insures fair and impartial treatment of each individual
    B. *not advisable,* because each person is different and there is no one supervisory procedure for dealing with individuals that applies in every case
    C. *advisable,* because once a supervisor learns how to deal with a subordinate who brings a problem to him, he can handle another subordinate with this problem in the same way
    D. *not advisable,* because individuals like to think that they are receiving better treatment than others

14. In evaluating personnel, a supervisor should keep in mind that the MOST important objective of performance evaluations is to

    A. encourage employees to compete for higher performance ratings
    B. give recognition to employees who perform well
    C. help employees improve their work
    D. discipline employees who perform poorly

15. A subordinate tells you that he is having trouble concentrating on his work due to a personal problem at home. Of the following, it would be BEST for you to

    A. refer him to a community service agency
    B. listen quietly to the story because he may just need a sympathetic ear
    C. tell him that you cannot help him because the problem is not job-related
    D. ask him some questions about the nature of the problem and tell him how you would handle it

16. To do a good job of performance evaluation, it is BEST for a supervisor to

    A. measure the employee's performance against standard performance requirements
    B. compare the employee's performance to that of another employee doing similar work
    C. leave out any consideration of the employee's personal traits
    D. give greatest weight to instances of unusually good or unusually poor performance

17. It is particularly important that disciplinary actions be equitable as between individuals. This statement *implies* that

    A. punishment applied in disciplinary actions should be lenient
    B. proposed disciplinary actions should be reviewed by higher authority
    C. subordinates should have an opportunity to present their stories before penalties are applied
    D. penalties for violations of the rules should be standardized and consistently applied

18. Assume that an agency has an established procedure for handling employee grievances. An employee in this agency comes to his immediate supervisor with a grievance. The supervisor investigates the matter and makes a decision. However, the employee is not satisfied with the decision made by the supervisor.
    The BEST action for the supervisor to take is to

A. tell the employee he will review the matter further
B. remind the employee that he is the supervisor and the employee must act in accordance with his decision
C. explain to the employee how he can carry his complaint forward to the next step in the grievance procedure
D. tell the employee he will consult with his own superiors on the matter

19. Of the following, the CHIEF purpose of a probationary period for a new employee is to allow time for

    A. finding out whether the selection processes are satisfactory
    B. determining the fitness of the employee to continue in the job
    C. the employee to decide whether he wants a permanent appointment
    D. the employee to make adjustments in his home circumstances made necessary by the job

20. Of the following, the subject that would be MOST important to include in a "break-in" program for new employees is

    A. explanation of rules, regulations and policies of the agency
    B. Instruction in the agency's history and programs
    C. explanation of the importance of the new employees' own particular job
    D. explanation of the duties and responsibilities of the employee

21. Suppose a new employee under your supervision seems slow to learn and is making mistakes in performing his duties. Your FIRST action should be to

    A. pass this information on to the bureau director
    B. reprimand the worker so he will not repeat these mistakes
    C. find out whether this worker understands your instructions
    D. note these facts for future reference when writing up the monthly performance evaluation

22. In training new employees to do a certain job it would be LEAST desirable for you to

    A. demonstrate how the job is done, step by step
    B. encourage the workers to ask questions if they aren't clear about any point
    C. tell them about the various mistakes other agents have made in doing this job
    D. have the workers do the job, explaining to you what they are doing and why

23. One of the workers under your supervision is resentful when you ask her to remove her jangling bracelets before she starts her tour of duty.
    Of the following, the BEST explanation you can give her for the rule against wearing such jewelry while on duty is that

    A. the jewelry may create a safety hazard
    B. employees must give up certain personal liberties if they want to keep their jobs
    C. workers cannot perform their duties as efficiently if they wear distracting jewelry
    D. citizens may receive an unfavorable impression of the department

24. Of the following, the LEAST important reason for having a department handbook and a bureau standard operating procedure is to

    A. help in training new employees
    B. provide a source of reference for department and bureau rules and procedures
    C. prevent errors in work by providing clear guidelines
    D. make the supervisor's job easy

25. On inspecting your squad prior to their tour of duty, you note an employee improperly and unacceptably dressed.
    The FIRST action you should take is to

    A. call the employee aside and insist on immediate correction if possible
    B. notify the district commander right away
    C. have the employee submit a memorandum explaining the reason for the improper uniform
    D. permit the employee to proceed on duty but warn him not to let this happen again

KEY (CORRECT ANSWERS)

1. C
2. B
3. D
4. A
5. A

6. B
7. B
8. A
9. D
10. B

11. D
12. A
13. B
14. C
15. B

16. A
17. D
18. C
19. B
20. D

21. C
22. C
23. D
24. D
25. A

PREPARING WRITTEN MATERIAL
EXAMINATION SECTION
TEST 1

DIRECTIONS: Each of Questions 1 through 5 consists of a sentence which may or may not be an example of good formal English usage. Examine each sentence, considering grammar, punctuation, spelling, capitalization, and awkwardness. Then choose the correct statement about it from the four options below it. If the English usage in the sentence given is better than any of the changes suggested in options B, C, or D, pick option A. (Do not pick an option that will change the meaning of the sentence.) *PRINT THE LETTER OF THE CORRECT ANSWER IN THE SPACE AT THE RIGHT.*

1. I don't know who could possibly of broken it. 1.____
   A. This is an example of good formal English usage.
   B. The word "who" should be replaced by the word "whom."
   C. The word "of" should be replaced by the word "have."
   D. The word "broken" should be replaced by the word "broke."

2. Telephoning is easier than to write. 2.____
   A. This is an example of good formal English usage.
   B. The word "telephoning" should be spelled "telephoneing."
   C. The word "than" should be replaced by the word "then."
   D. The words "to write" should be replaced by the word "writing."

3. The two operators who have been assigned to these consoles are on vacation. 3.____
   A. This is an example of good formal English usage.
   B. A comma should be placed after the word "operators."
   C. The word "who" should be replaced by the word "whom."
   D. The word "are" should be replaced by the word "is."

4. You were suppose to teach me how to operate a plugboard. 4.____
   A. This is an example of good formal English usage.
   B. The word "were" should be replaced by the word "was."
   C. The word "suppose" should be replaced by the word "supposed."
   D. The word "teach" should be replaced by the word "learn."

5. If you had taken my advice; you would have spoken with him. 5.____
   A. This is an example of good formal English usage.
   B. The word "advice" should be spelled "advise."
   C. The words "had taken" should be replaced by the word "take."
   D. The semicolon should be changed to a comma.

KEY (CORRECT ANSWERS)

1. C
2. D
3. A
4. C
5. D

TEST 2

DIRECTIONS: Select the correct answer. *PRINT THE LETTER OF THE CORRECT ANSWER IN THE SPACE AT THE RIGHT.*

1. The one of the following sentences which is MOST acceptable from the viewpoint of correct grammatical usage is:
    A. I do not know which action will have worser results.
    B. He should of known better.
    C. Both the officer on the scene, and his immediate supervisor, is charged with the responsibility.
    D. An officer must have initiative because his supervisor will not always be available to answer questions.

    1.____

2. The one of the following sentences which is MOST acceptable from the viewpoint of correct grammatical usage is:
    A. Of all the officers available, the better one for the job will be picked.
    B. Strict orders were given to all the officers, except he.
    C. Study of the law will enable you to perform your duties more efficiently.
    D. It seems to me that you was wrong in failing to search the two men.

    2.____

3. The one of the following sentences which does NOT contain a misspelled word is:
    A. The duties you will perform are similar to the duties of a patrolman.
    B. Officers must be constantly alert to sieze the initiative.
    C. Officers in this organization are not entitled to special privileges.
    D. Any changes in procedure will be announced publically.

    3.____

4. The one of the following sentences which does NOT contain a misspelled word is:
    A. It will be to your advantage to keep your firearm in good working condition.
    B. There are approximately fourty men on sick leave.
    C. Your first duty will be to pursuade the person to obey the law.
    D. Fires often begin in flameable material kept in lockers.

    4.____

5. The one of the following sentences which does NOT contain a misspelled word is:
    A. Offices are not required to perform technical maintainance.
    B. He violated the regulations on two occasions.
    C. Every employee will be held responable for errors.
    D. This was his nineth absence in a year.

    5.____

KEY (CORRECT ANSWERS)

1. D
2. C
3. C
4. A
5. B

TEST 3

DIRECTIONS: Select the correct answer. *PRINT THE LETTER OF THE CORRECT ANSWER IN THE SPACE AT THE RIGHT.*

1. You are answering a letter that was written on the letterhead of the ABC Company and signed by James H. Wood, Treasurer.
   What is usually considered to be the correct salutation to use in your reply?
   A. Dear ABC Company:
   B. Dear Sirs:
   C. Dear Mr. Wood:
   D. Dear Mr. Treasurer:

   1.____

2. Assume that one of your duties is to handle routine letters of inquiry from the public.
   The one of the following which is usually considered to be MOST desirable in replying to such a letter is a
   A. detailed answer handwritten on the original letter of inquiry
   B. phone call, since you can cover details more easily over the phone than in a letter
   C. short letter giving the specific information requested
   D. long letter discussing all possible aspects of the question raised

   2.____

3. The CHIEF reason for dividing a letter into paragraphs is to
   A. make the message clear to the reader by starting a new paragraph for each new topic
   B. make a short letter occupy as much of the page as possible
   C. keep the reader's attention by providing a pause from time to time
   D. make the letter look neat and businesslike

   3.____

4. Your superior has asked you to send an e-mail from your agency to a government agency in another city. He has written out the message and has indicated the name of the government agency.
   When you dictate the message to your secretary, which of the following items that your superior has NOT mentioned must you be sure to include?
   A. Today's date
   B. The full address of the government agency
   C. A polite opening such as "Dear Sirs"
   D. A final sentence such as "We would appreciate hearing from your agency in reply as soon as is convenient for you"

   4.____

5. The one of the following sentences which is grammatically preferable to the others is:
   A. Our engineers will go over your blueprints so that you may have no problems in construction.
   B. For a long time he had been arguing that we, not he, are to blame for the confusion.
   C. I worked on this automobile for two hours and still cannot find out what is wrong with it.
   D. Accustomed to all kinds of hardships, fatigue seldom bothers veteran policemen.

   5.____

KEY (CORRECT ANSWERS)

1. C
2. C
3. A
4. B
5. A

TEST 4

DIRECTIONS: Select the correct answer. *PRINT THE LETTER OF THE CORRECT ANSWER IN THE SPACE AT THE RIGHT.*

1. Suppose that an applicant for a job as snow laborer presents a letter from a former employer stating: "John Smith has a pleasing manner and never got into an argument with his fellow employees. He was never late or absent." This letter
    A. indicates that with some training Smith will make a good snow gang boss
    B. presents no definite evidence of Smith's ability to do snow work
    C. proves definitely that Smith has never done any snow work before
    D. proves definitely that Smith will do better than average work as a snow laborer

    1.____

2. Suppose you must write a letter to a local organization in your section refusing a request in connection with collection of their refuse.
    You should start the letter by
    A. explaining in detail the consideration you gave the request
    B. praising the organization for its service to the community
    C. quoting the regulation which forbids granting the request
    D. stating your regret that the request cannot be granted

    2.____

3. Suppose a citizen writes in for information as to whether or not he may sweep refuse into the gutter. A Sanitation officer answers as follows:
    Dear Sir:
      No person is permitted to litter, sweep, throw or cast, or direct, suffer or permit any person under his control to litter, sweep, throw or cast any ashes, garbage, paper, dust, or other rubbish or refuse into any public street or place, vacant lot, air shaft, areaway, backyard or court.
    Very truly yours,
John Doe
    This letter is *poorly* written CHIEFLY because
    A. the opening is not indented   B. the thought is not clear
    C. the tone is too formal and cold   D. there are too many commas used

    3.____

4. A section of a disciplinary report written by a Sanitation officer states: "It is requested that subject Sanitation man be advised that his future activities be directed towards reducing his recurrent tardiness else disciplinary action will be initiated which may result in summary discharge."
    This section of the report is *poorly* written MAINLY because
    A. at least one word is misspelled   B. it is not simply expressed
    C. more than one idea is expressed   D. the purpose is not stated

    4.____

5. A section of a disciplinary report written by an officer states: "He comes in late. He takes too much time for lunch. He is lazy. I recommend his services be dispensed with."
    This section of the report is *poorly* written MAINLY because
    A. it ends with a preposition   B. it is not well organized
    C. no supporting facts are stated   D. the sentences are too simple

    5.____

KEY (CORRECT ANSWERS)

1. B
2. D
3. C
4. B
5. C

PREPARING WRITTEN MATERIAL

PARAGRAPH REARRANGEMENT
COMMENTARY

The sentences that follow are in scrambled order. You are to rearrange them in proper order and indicate the letter choice containing the correct answer at the space at the right.

Each group of sentences in this section is actually a paragraph presented in scrambled order. Each sentence in the group has a place in that paragraph; no sentence is to be left out. You are to read each group of sentences and decide upon the best order in which to put the sentences so as to form a well-organized paragraph.

The questions in this section measure the ability to solve a problem when all the facts relevant to its solution are not given.

More specifically, certain positions of responsibility and authority require the employee to discover connection between events sometimes, apparently, unrelated. In order to do this, the employee will find it necessary to correctly infer that unspecified events have probably occurred or are likely to occur. This ability becomes especially important when action must be taken on incomplete information.

Accordingly, these questions require competitors to choose among several suggested alternatives, each of which presents a different sequential arrangement of the events. Competitors must choose the MOST logical of the suggested sequences.

In order to do so, they may be required to draw on general knowledge to infer missing concepts or events that are essential to sequencing the given events. Competitors should be careful to infer only what is essential to the sequence. The plausibility of the wrong alternatives will always require the inclusion of unlikely events or of additional chains of events which are NOT essential to sequencing the given events.

It's very important to remember that you are looking for the best of the four possible choices, and that the best choice of all may not even be one of the answers you're given to choose from.

There is no one right way to solve these problems. Many people have found it helpful to first write out the order of the sentences, as they would have arranged them, on their scrap paper before looking at the possible answers. If their optimum answer is there, this can save them some time. If it isn't, this method can still give insight into solving the problem. Others find it most helpful to just go through each of the possible choices, contrasting each as they go along. You should use whatever method feels comfortable and works for you.

While most of these types of questions are not that difficult, we've added a higher percentage of the difficult type, just to give you more practice. Usually there are only one or two questions on this section that contain such subtle distinctions that you're unable to answer confidently. And you then may find yourself stuck deciding between two possible choices, neither of which you're sure about.

EXAMINATION SECTION
TEST 1

DIRECTIONS: The sentences that follow are in scrambled order. You are to rearrange them in proper order and indicate the letter choice containing the correct answer. *PRINT THE LETTER OF THE CORRECT ANSWER IN THE SPACE AT THE RIGHT.*

1. Below are four statements labeled W, X, Y and Z.   1.____
   W. He was a strict and fanatic drillmaster.
   X. The word is always used in a derogatory sense and generally shows resentment and anger on the part of the user.
   Y. It is from the name of this Frenchman that we derive our English word, martinet.
   Z. Jean Martinet was the Inspector-General of Infantry during the reign of King Louis XIV.
   The PROPER order in which these sentences should be placed in a paragraph is:
   A. X, Z, W, Y   B. X, Z, Y, W   C. Z, W, Y, X   D. Z, Y, W, X

2. In the following paragraph, the sentences, which are numbered, have been jumbled.   2.____
   I. Since then it has undergone changes.
   II. It was incorporated in 1955 under the laws of the State of New York.
   III. Its primary purposes, a cleaner city, has, however, remained the same.
   IV. The Citizens Committee works in cooperation with the Mayor's Interdepartmental Committee for a Clean City.   3.____
   The order in which these sentences should be arranged to form a well-organized paragraph is:
   A. II, IV, I, III   B. III, IV, I, II   C. IV, II, I, III   D. IV, III, II, I

Questions 3-5.

DIRECTIONS: The sentences listed below are part of a meaningful paragraph but they are not given in their proper order. You are to decide what would be the BEST order in which to put the sentences so as to form a well-organized paragraph. Each sentence has a place in the paragraph; there are no extra sentences. You are then to answer Questions 3 through 5 inclusive on the basis of your rearrangements of these scrambled sentences into a properly organized paragraph.

In 1887 some insurance companies organized an Inspection Department to advise their clients on all phases of fire prevention and protection. Probably this has been due to the smaller annual fire losses in Great Britain than in the United States. It tests various fire prevention devices and appliances and determines manufacturing hazards and their safeguards. Fire research began earlier in the United States and is more advanced than in Great Britain. Later they established a laboratory specializing in electrical, mechanical, hydraulic, and chemical fields.

3. When the five sentences are arranged in proper order, the paragraph starts with the sentence which begins
   A. "In 1887…"   B. "Probably this…"   C. "It tests…"
   D. "Fire research…"   E. "Later they…"

3._____

4. In the last sentence listed above, "they" refers to
   A. the insurance companies
   B. the United States and Great Britain
   C. the Inspection Department
   D. clients
   E. technicians

4._____

5. When the above paragraph is properly arranged, it ends with the words
   A. "…and protection."
   B. "…the United States."
   C. "…their safeguards."
   D. "…in Great Britain."
   E. "…chemical fields."

5._____

KEY (CORRECT ANSWERS)

1. C
2. C
3. D
4. A
5. C

TEST 2

DIRECTIONS: In each of the questions numbered I through V, several sentences are given. For each question, choose as your answer the group of number that represents the MOST logical order of these sentences if they were arranged in paragraph form. *PRINT THE LETTER OF THE CORRECT ANSWER IN THE SPACE AT THE RIGHT.*

1.
   I. It is established when one shows that the landlord has prevented the tenant's enjoyment of his interest in the property leased.
   II. Constructive eviction is the result of a breach of the covenant of quiet enjoyment implied in all leases.
   III. In some parts of the United States, it is not complete until the tenant vacates within a reasonable time.
   IV. Generally, the acts must be of such serious and permanent character as to deny the tenant the enjoyment of his possessing rights.
   V. In this event, upon abandonment of the premises, the tenant's liability for that ceases.
   The CORRECT answer is:
   A. II, I, IV, III, V
   B. V, II, III, I, IV
   C. IV, III, I, II, V
   D. I, III, V, IV, II

   1.____

2.
   I. The powerlessness before private and public authorities that is the typical experience of the slum tenant is reminiscent of the situation of blue-collar workers all through the nineteenth century.
   II. Similarly, in recent years, this chapter of history has been reopened by anti-poverty groups which have attempted to organize slum tenants to enable them to bargain collectively with their landlords about the conditions of their tenancies.
   III. It is familiar history that many of the worker remedied their condition by joining together and presenting their demands collectively.
   IV. Like the workers, tenants are forced by the conditions of modern life into substantial dependence on these who possess great political aid and economic power.
   V. What's more, the very fact of dependence coupled with an absence of education and self-confidence makes them hesitant and unable to stand up for what they need from those in power.
   The CORRECT answer is:
   A. V, IV, I, II, III
   B. II, III, I, V, IV
   C. III, I, V, IV, II
   D. I, IV, V, III, II

   2.____

3.
   I. A railroad, for example, when not acting as a common carrier may contract away responsibility for its own negligence.
   II. As to a landlord, however, no decision has been found relating to the legal effect of a clause shifting the statutory duty of repair to the tenant.
   III. The courts have not passed on the validity of clauses relieving the landlord of this duty and liability.
   IV. They have, however, upheld the validity of exculpatory clauses in other types of contracts.

   3.____

105

V. Housing regulations impose a duty upon the landlord to maintain leased premises in safe condition.
VI. As another example, a bailee may limit his liability except for gross negligence, willful acts, or fraud.

The CORRECT answer is:
A. II, I, VI, IV, III, V
B. I, III, IV, V, VI, II
C. III, V, I, IV, II, VI
D. V, III, IV, I, VI, II

4. I. Since there are only samples in the building, retail or consumer sales are generally eschewed by mart occupants, and in some instances, rigid controls are maintained to limit entrance to the mart only to those persons engaged in retailing.
    II. Since World War I, in many larger cities, there has developed a new type of property, called the mart building.
    III. It can, therefore, be used by wholesalers and jobbers for the display of sample merchandise.
    IV. This type of building is most frequently a multi-storied, finished interior property which is a cross between a retail arcade and a loft building.
    V. This limitation enables the mart occupants to ship the orders from another location after the retailer or dealer makes his selection from the samples.

The CORRECT answer is:
A. II, IV, III, I, V
B. IV, III, V, I, II
C. I, III, II, IV, V
D. I, IV, II, III, V

5. I. In general, staff-line friction reduces the distinctive contribution of staff personnel.
    II. The conflicts, however, introduce an uncontrolled element into the managerial system.
    III. On the other hand, the natural resistance of the line to staff innovations probably usefully restrains over-eager efforts to apply untested procedures on a large scale.
    IV. Under such conditions, it is difficult to know when valuable ideas are being sacrificed.
    V. The relatively weak position of staff, requiring accommodation to the line, tends to restrict their ability to engage in free, experimental innovation.

The CORRECT answer is:
A. IV, II, III, I, V
B. I, V, III, II, IV
C. V, III, I, II, IV
D. II, I, IV, V, III

KEY (CORRECT ANSWERS)

1. A
2. D
3. D
4. A
5. B

TEST 3

DIRECTIONS: Questions 1 through 4 consist of six sentences which can be arranged in a logical sequence. For each question, select the choice which places the numbered sentences in the MOST logical sequent. *PRINT THE LETTER OF THE CORRECT ANSWER IN THE SPACE AT THE RIGHT.*

1. I. The burden of proof as to each issue is determined before trial and remains upon the same party throughout the trial.
    II. The jury is at liberty to believe one witness' testimony as against a number of contradictory witnesses.
    III. In a civil case, the party bearing the burden of proof is required to prove his contention by a fair preponderance of the evidence.
    IV. However, it must be noted that a fair preponderance of evidence does not necessarily mean a greater number of witnesses.
    V. The burden of proof is the burden which rests upon one of the parties to an action to persuade the trier of the facts, generally the jury, that a proposition he asserts is true.
    VI. If the evidence is equally balanced, or if it leaves the jury in such doubt as to be unable to decide the controversy either way, judgment must be given against the party upon whom the burden of proof rests.
    The CORRECT answer is:
    A. III, II, V, IV, I, VI B. I, II, VI, V, III, IV
    C. III, IV, V, I, II, VI D. V, I, III, VI, IV, II

    1.____

2. I. If a parent is without assets and is unemployed, he cannot be convicted of the crime of non-support of a child.
    II. The term "sufficient ability" has been held to mean sufficient financial ability.
    III. It does not matter if his unemployment is by choice or unavoidable circumstances.
    IV. If he fails to take any steps at all, he may be liable to prosecution for endangering the welfare of a child.
    V. Under the penal law, a parent is responsible for the support of his minor child only if the parent is "of sufficient ability."
    VI. An indigent parent may meet his obligation by borrowing money or by seeking aid under the provisions of the Social Welfare Law.
    The CORRECT answer is:
    A. VI, I, V, III, II, IV B. I, III, V, II, IV, VI
    C. V, II, I, III, VI, IV D. I, VI, IV, V, II, III

    2.____

3. I. Consider, for example, the case of a rabble rouser who urges a group of twenty people to go out and break the windows of a nearby factory.
    II. Therefore, the law fills the indicated gap with the crime of inciting to riot.
    III. A person is considered guilty of inciting to riot when he urges ten or more persons to engage in tumultuous and violent conduct of a kind likely to create public alarm.
    IV. However, if he has not obtained the cooperation of at least four people, he cannot be charged with unlawful assembly.

    3.____

107

V. The charge of inciting to riot was added to the law to cover types of conduct which cannot be classified as either the crime of "riot" or the crime of "unlawful assembly."
VI. If he acquires the acquiescence of at least four of them, he is guilty of unlawful assembly even if the project does not materialize.

The CORRECT answer is:
A. III, V, I, VI, IV, II
B. V, I, IV, VI, II, III
C. III, IV, I, V, II, VI
D. V, I, IV, VI, III, II

4.
I. If, however, the rebuttal evidence presents an issue of credibility, it is for the jury to determine whether the presumption has, in fact, been destroyed.
II. Once sufficient evidence to the contrary is introduced, the presumption disappears from the trial.
III. The effect of a presumption is to place the burden upon the adversary to come forward with evidence to rebut the presumption.
IV. When a presumption is overcome and ceases to exist in the case, the fact or facts which gave rise to the presumption still remain.
V. Whether a presumption has been overcome is ordinarily a question for the court.
VI. Such information may furnish a basis for a logical inference.

The CORRECT answer is:
A. IV, VI, II, V, I, III
B. III, II, V, I, IV, VI
C. V, III, VI, IV, II, I
D. V, IV, I, II, VI, III

4.____

KEY (CORRECT ANSWERS)

1. D
2. C
3. A
4. B

TRAFFIC ENGINEERING

BASIC FUNDAMENTALS OF TRAFFIC PLANNING

CONTENTS

	Page
CHAPTER 1 – CONCEPT	1-1
CHAPTER 2 – ORGANIZATION	2-1
CHAPTER 3 – PROCESS	3-1

Basic Fundamentals of Traffic Planning

CONCEPT

THOROUGHFARE PLANNING *is a method of identifying travel needs and filling them — to make road travel safe, economical, convenient, free-flowing, and environmentally acceptable.* Thoroughfare planners insure that roadways will accommodate traffic demands, maximize the use of roadways, and solve traffic problems.

THOROUGHFARE PLANNING *provides not only for modifications to existing roadways to meet current traffic demands; it provides also for the identification of land areas that should be reserved for roadway expansion to meet future traffic demands.* Planners, working toward established goals, may recommend that a particular street be retained or redesigned as necessary to perform a specific function. **Effective thoroughfare planning can reap savings in construction and maintenance costs, protect housing areas, and control travel and land-use patterns.**

PLANNING IS A STEP-BY-STEP PROCESS

The **planning process** is a method to:

Identify problems and establish goals and objectives.

Conduct traffic surveys, analyze the survey data, and estimate future traffic volumes and patterns.

Develop alternate solutions and test them against the goals and objectives, then select and implement a final plan.

Review and evaluate the plan on a continuing basis and adjust it as necessary to attain desired goals and objectives.

1-2

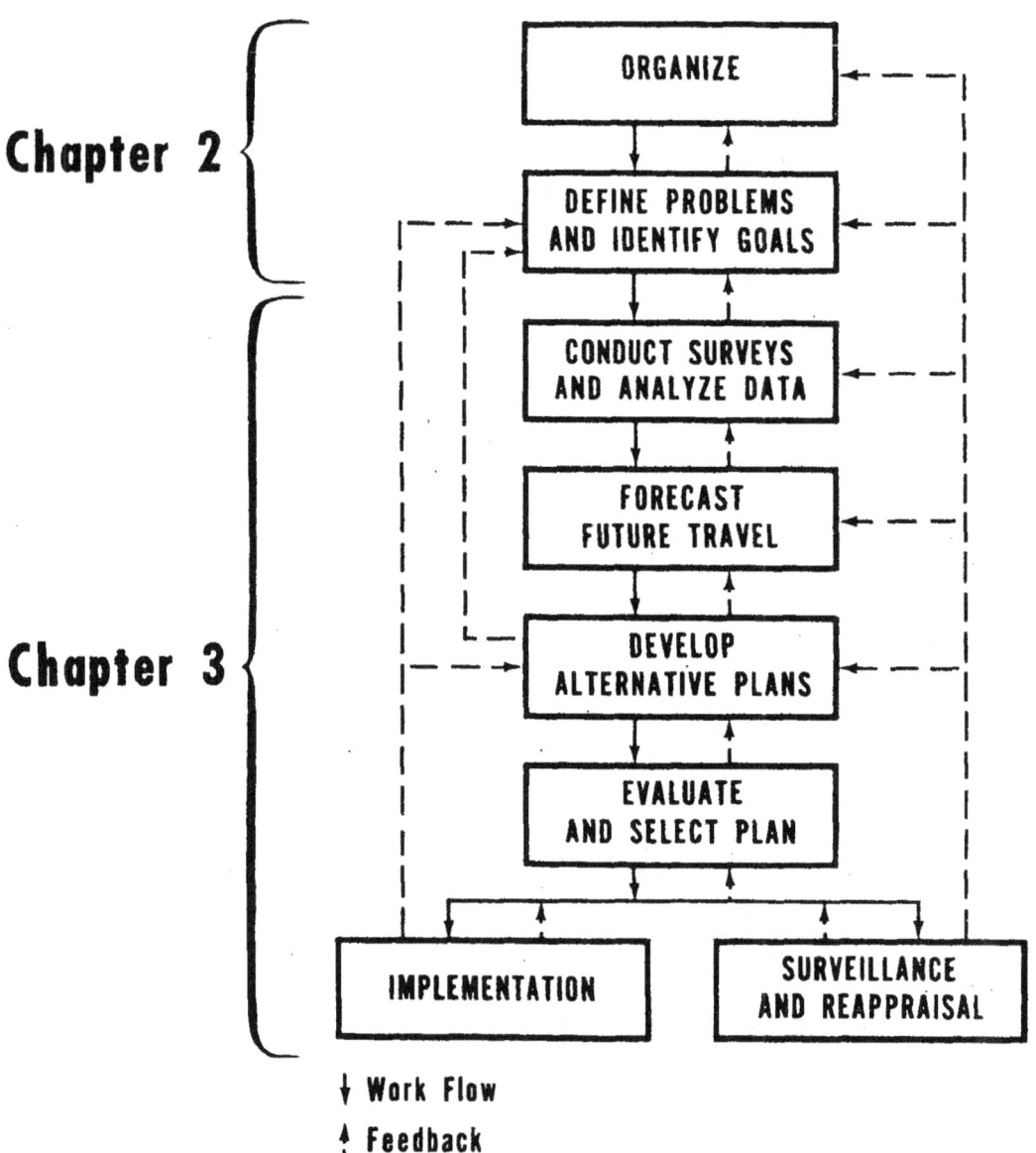

A step-by-step discussion of the planning process is presented in Chapters 2 and 3. Chapter 2 discusses the prerequisites to effective and continuing planning — that is, the formation of a planning committee, the identification of problems, and the establishment of goals. Chapter 3 summarizes the remaining steps to be taken to develop alternative plans for evaluation, selection, and implementation.

ORGANIZATION

PLANNING COMMITTEE

PROBLEM DEFINITION AND GOAL IDENTIFICATION

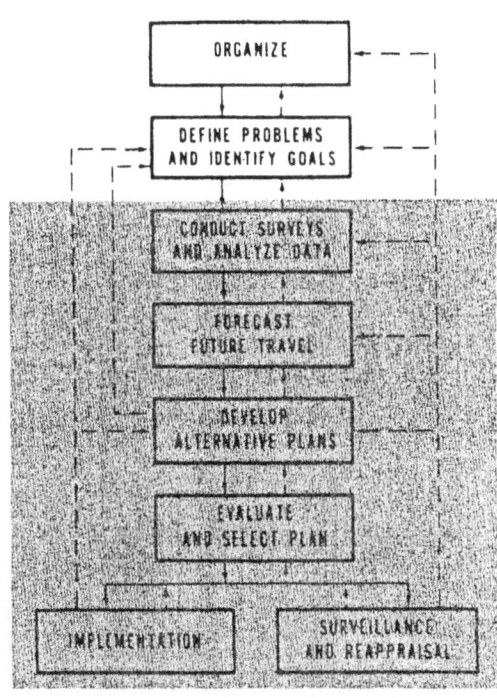

TRAFFIC PLANNING GOALS must be **determined by the installation decisionmakers,** with the **assistance of technical experts. Technical experts** should provide direction for the decisionmakers *through rational analysis of installation needs and policies.* With this information, **decisionmakers** can effectively select goals and a planning program that will insure an end product that is both workable and desirable.

2-2

PLANNING COMMITTEE

EFFECTIVE THOROUGHFARE PLANNING *requires concerted effort among policymakers and the technical and administrative staffs of the installation under study.* Each step of the planning process must be based on a simple framework in which the installation's decisionmakers can clearly understand not only the traffic problems, but also the solution to those problems. Committee members usually should be selected to represent the installation's diverse disciplines and viewpoints. For example, an individual representing each of the groups shown below would be desirable.

DECISIONMAKERS MUST

- Identify Traffic Problems
- Establish Goals to Reduce Problems
- Select Thoroughfare Plan
- Gain Support for Plan

TECHNICAL STAFF MUST

- Conduct Traffic Studies
- Estimate Future Travel
- Develop Alternate Plans
- Implement Plan

PROBLEM DEFINITION AND GOAL IDENTIFICATION

THE FIRST STEP IN THOROUGHFARE PLANNING is to **clearly identify all traffic problems of the installation** being studied.

The term *"traffic problem"* is defined as *any situation that impairs the safe and efficient flow of traffic.*

In identifying traffic problems, relativity must be considered; that is, traffic problems vary among different areas of the country. For example, a 5-minute delay in New York City is considered as negligible, while the same delay in Timbuktu would be extremely frustrating to motorists. Therefore, it must be remembered that **traffic problems are relative to the installation being studied.**

FOR EVERY TRAFFIC PROBLEM, THERE IS A POSITIVE GOAL

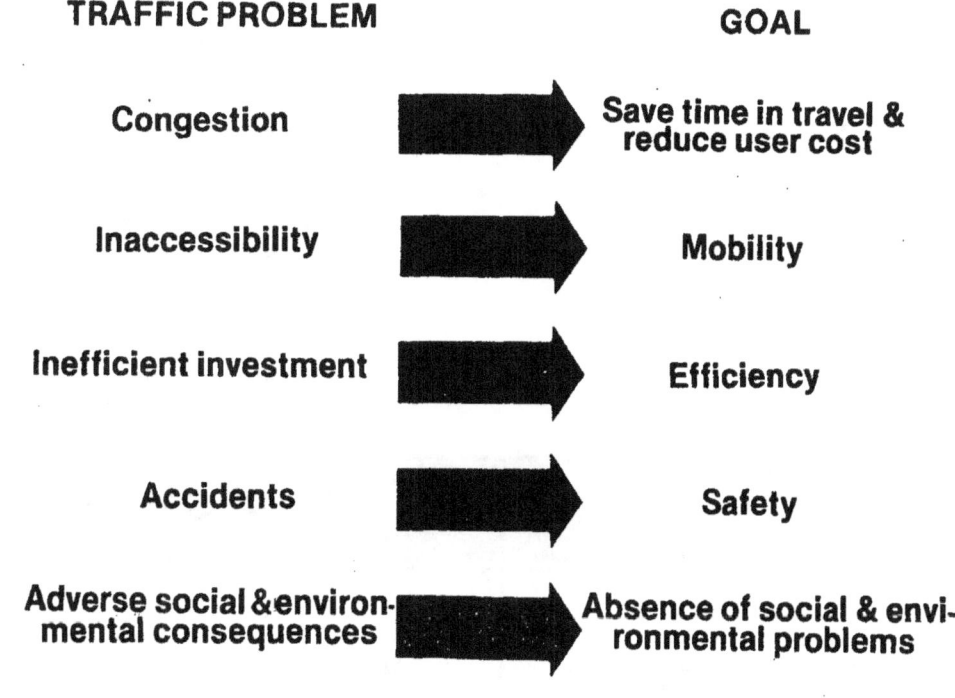

TRAFFIC PROBLEM	GOAL
Congestion	Save time in travel & reduce user cost
Inaccessibility	Mobility
Inefficient investment	Efficiency
Accidents	Safety
Adverse social & environmental consequences	Absence of social & environmental problems

2-4

PROBLEM:

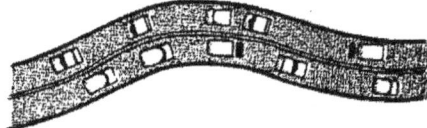

CONGESTION wastes time and increases operating costs.

CONGESTION — Motorists dislike traffic congestion primarily because of wasted time and the resulting increased operating costs. Excessive operating costs can be measured with a fair degree of precision. For example, on a 1-mile free-flowing roadway of 30 miles-per-hour speed, three stops of 30-seconds duration each will result in an increase of approximately 90 percent in total running cost of the car. Measuring the value of a motorist's time is far more difficult. However, evidence shows that, given a choice, motorists will forfeit operating economy to save time.

GOAL: TO PROVIDE EFFICIENT TRAFFIC FLOW

ADEQUATE CAPACITY saves time and reduces operating cost.

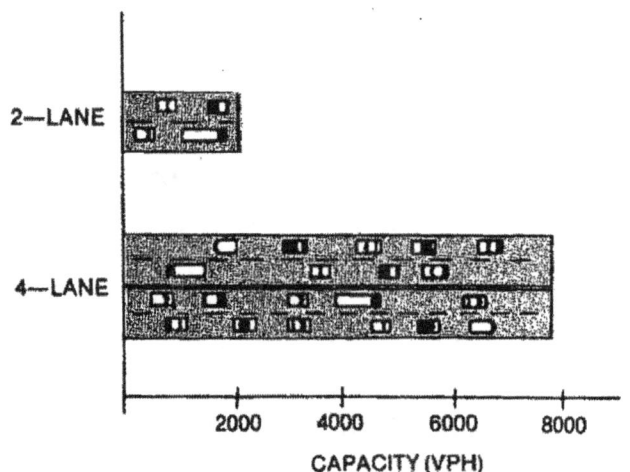

OBJECTIVE	INDICATOR
Cut travel time	Peak period travel time
Minimize congestion	Peak period volume
Reduce user cost	Vehicle user cost

2-5

PROBLEM:

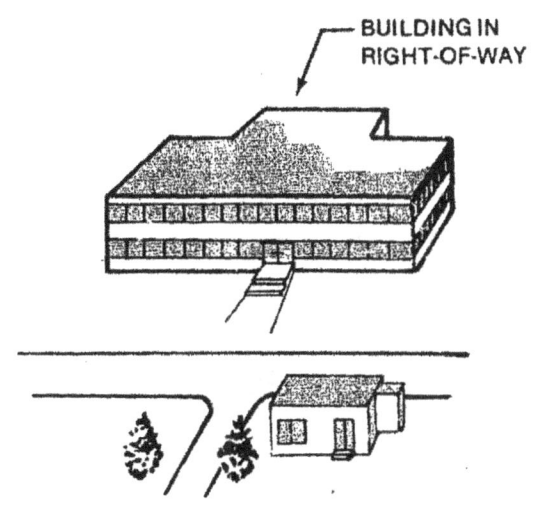

INACCESSIBILITY — Most people like to have the freedom to get where they want to go, when they want to go. High productivity is closely related to proximity in time. Without access, land cannot be developed and people cannot move to jobs, schools, hospitals, and so forth.

GOAL: **TO IMPROVE MOBILITY OF POPULATION**

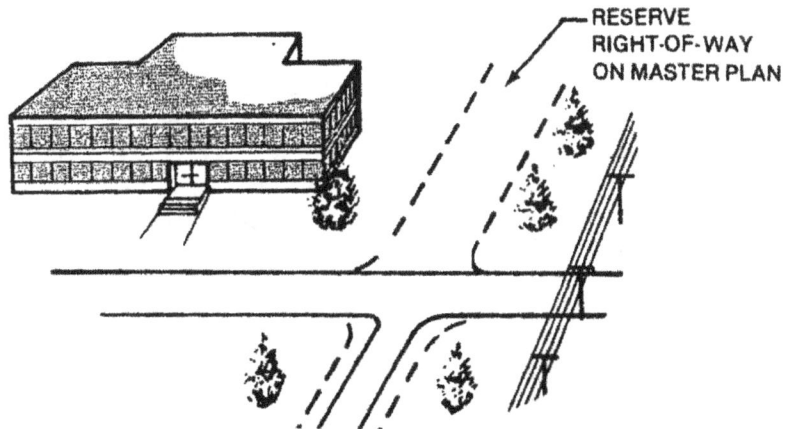

OBJECTIVE	INDICATOR
Reduce travel distance	Distance between point A and point B
Increase productivity of land and people	Changes in access caused by land development

PROBLEM:

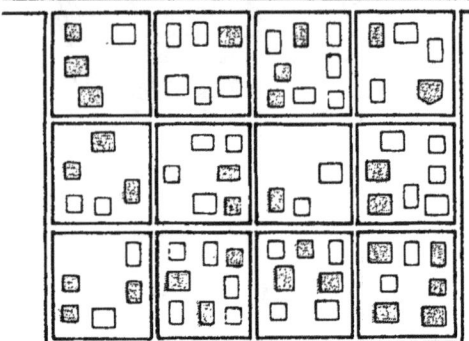

Where width of street, size of house, or size of lot is squeezed to a so-called "efficient minimum" — this is false economy.

INEFFICIENT INVESTMENT — Another universally condemned action is waste of public funds. The case of building unusable traffic facilities or misappropriating public funds is quite rare. However, the more frequent and important waste is that of false economy in traffic facilities. For example, decisions on expenditure are generally based on their budget appeal, not on their adequacy, such as patchwork improvements. The question of whether improvements may solve any particular problem is usually overlooked or avoided; example, a street-widening may prove inadequate the day it is completed and require immediate improvements. Another type of false economy results from so-called "efficient" planning, which creates waste. For example, in housing areas where the width of a street or the size of a house or the lot it occupies has been reduced to a so-called "efficient minimum" — this is false economy. EFFICIENT PLANNING IS MORE THAN AN OBSESSION TO SAVE; IT IS A METHOD TO IMPROVE.

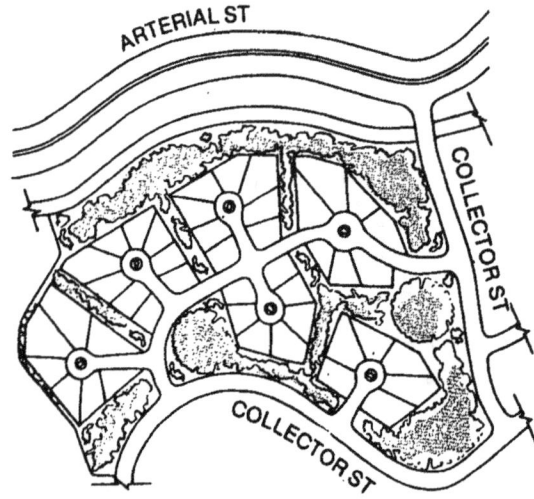

A modern residential street design preserves the neighborhood.

GOAL: TO ELIMINATE WASTE OF PUBLIC FUNDS AND PROTECT LIFE STYLE PATTERNS.

OBJECTIVE	INDICATOR
Decide expenditures based on adequacy, NOT budget appeal	Existing and desirable life-style patterns

PROBLEM:

ACCIDENTS — Accidents are the most significant of all traffic problems. In 1975 alone, approximately 58,800 motor vehicle accidents occurred on military installations, and resulted in an estimated cost of $70,000,000 to DOD and its personnel. Recent surveys of military installations revealed that the yearly accident rate ranged from 1 to over 40 per 1,000 people. This wide range indicates that the accident rate of an installation can be reduced through better traffic facilities.

ACCIDENT COST TO DOD
FATALITY — $287,175 per accident
PERSONAL INJURY — $8,085 per accident
PROPERTY DAMAGE — $520 per accident

GOAL: TO PROVIDE SAFE TRAVEL ROAD

FOUR-LANE UNDIVIDED

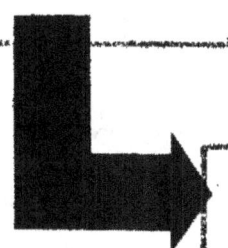

4.09 accidents per million vehicle miles

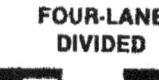
VERSUS

FOUR-LANE DIVIDED

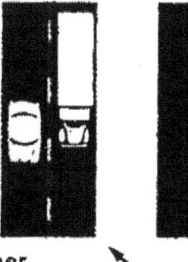

2.91 accidents per million vehicle miles

The reduction of accidents on a four-lane divided highway is 29% over the undivided highway

OBJECTIVE	INDICATOR
Reduce accidents and fatalities	Number of accidents and fatalities

PROBLEM:

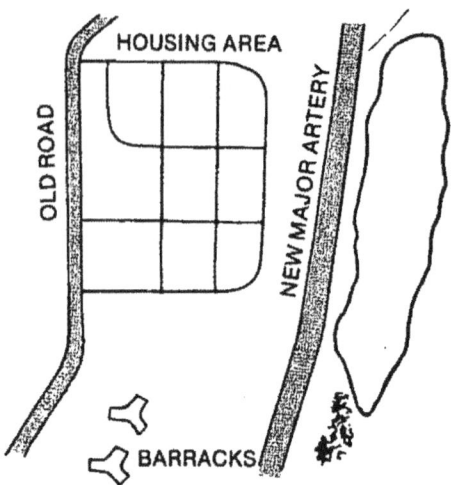

Noise Pollution.

SOCIAL AND ENVIRONMENTAL IMPACT — Ugliness, air pollution, strain, discomfort, noise, and nuisance are all components of the increasingly social nature of transportation problems. All of these problems are difficult to measure. Furthermore, problems such as ugliness are visual images that vary markedly among people, and hence it is difficult to obtain a consensus. The best way to consider these problems is in final plan selection.

GOAL: TO ENHANCE ENVIRONMENT

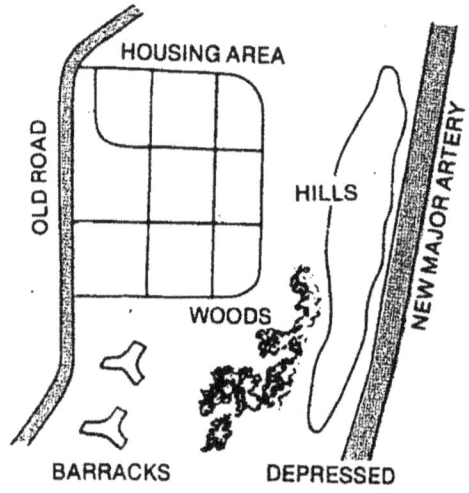

Built-In Noise Protection and Abatement

OBJECTIVE	INDICATOR
Minimize air/noise pollution	Exposure to pollution
Preserve open space	Recreational land available
Reduce travel on residential streets	Traffic volume on streets
Enhance views	Subjective judgment

BE AWARE OF CONFLICTS BETWEEN GOALS

Simply having an agreed set of goals and objectives is not enough because of the conflicts between goals. For example, the least expensive, initially, is to do nothing; whereas, the safest could very likely be the most expensive. Basically, goals should be listed and then screened to eliminate all but the most relevant. The goals selected should then be related to each other, so that losses toward one goal could be offset by gains toward another. Finally, these goals should be related to minimizing the total transportation costs.

III. PROCESS

SURVEYS

FORECAST

DEVELOPMENT

EVALUATION

IMPLEMENTATION

SURVEILLANCE AND REAPPRAISAL

THE ESTABLISHMENT OF A PLANNING PROCEDURE *is necessary in drafting a thoroughfare plan.* The process begins with **a review of existing facilities and travel characteristics. Data for present conditions** are then projected to the design year, and future deficiencies are noted. Based on these projections, **alternative improvements to present conditions** are evaluated, **a general thoroughfare plan** is selected, and **a priority schedule** is developed for implementation. The previous steps are continually reevaluated in view of the data developed at each succeeding step.

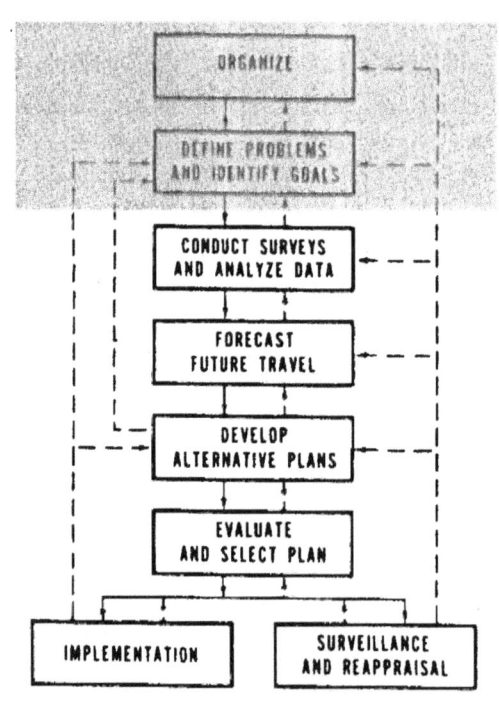

The cornerstone of the thoroughfare plan is the existing street system. Today's adequate street system, when projected to the design year, may become inadequate. **The thoroughfare plan should lead to a design that will efficiently handle traffic volumes of the average weekday peak-traffic hours for the design year.** These peak-hour flows usually are highly directional, with heavy inbound traffic in the morning and heavy outbound traffic in the evening. Occasionally, other time periods will determine a design for community service and retail-facility areas.

SURVEYS

SURVEYS are conducted to gather data on the present condition and traffic characteristics of an installation's roadways. These **data** are **analyzed** to estimate the traffic demands on the roadways and, as necessary, to redesign, evaluate, and program a road system to meet those demands.

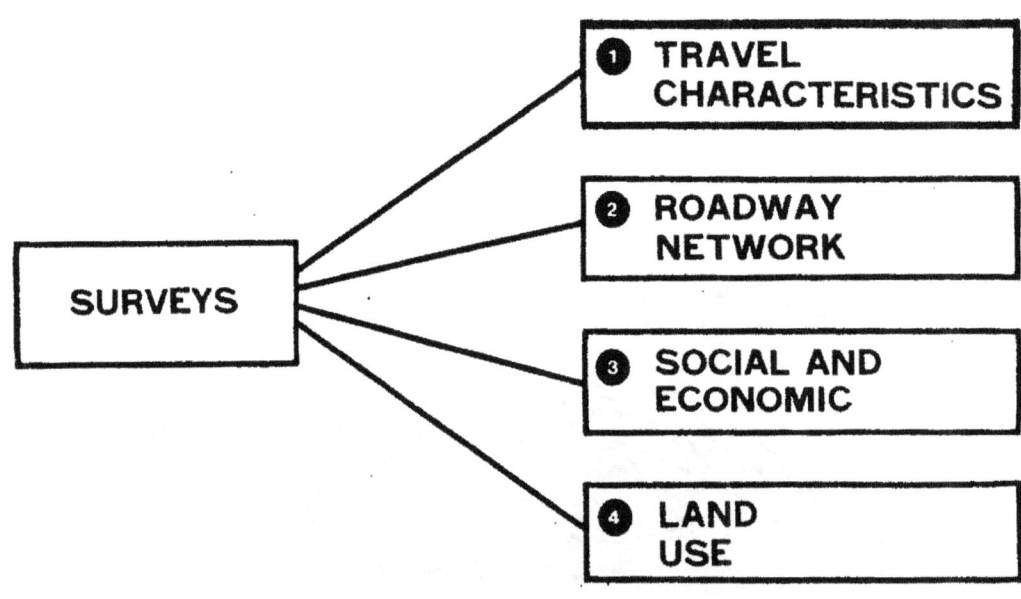

① TRAVEL CHARACTERISTICS

These surveys determine how many people use the road system, who they are, and their travel patterns. Data are gathered primarily from studies on traffic volume, vehicle occupancy, travel time and delay, and trip origin and destination. Of major interest to the installation thoroughfare planner is the employee home-to-work trip.

ESTABLISHES ROAD USAGE

② ROAD NETWORK

These surveys determine the condition and capacity of the roadway. Enough detail should be collected about the physical and operating characteristics of each segment of the route to calculate its capacity, as well as to determine its general level of service and accident history.

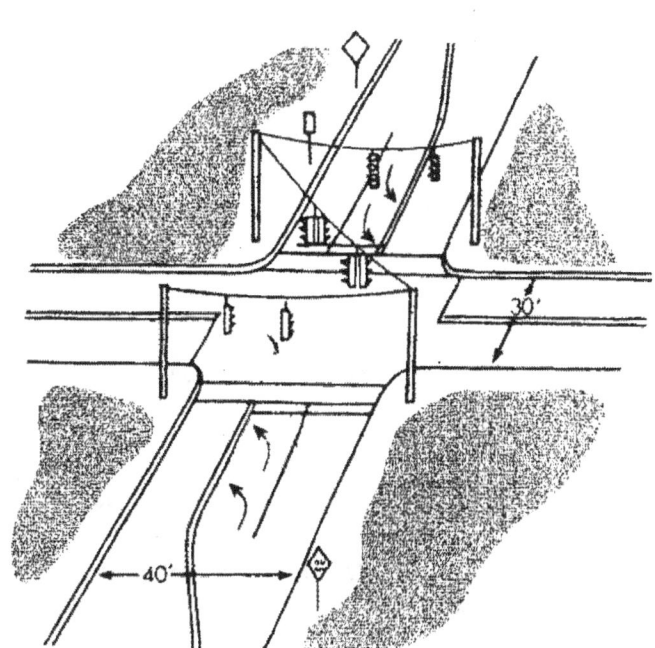

ESTABLISHES ROAD CONDITIONS

SOCIAL AND ECONOMIC

These surveys establish past and present facts about the installation road user. Typical data collected include population, employment, duty hours, housing, social services, security measures, and carpool programs. These data are used primarily as a basis for forecasting growth potential. The data are used also for origin and destination surveys and as variables to determine trip generations.

ESTABLISHES ROAD USER CHARACTERISTICS

 LAND USE

Land patterns delineate the function of the land and are basic factors in determining traffic demands of an installation.

A simplified land-use classification system should include at least five categories:

RESIDENTIAL — single-family housing, apartment housing, bachelor officer and enlisted quarters.

ADMINISTRATIVE AND COMMERCIAL — offices, training centers, and exchanges.

INDUSTRIAL AND OPERATIONAL — maintenance and production facilities, ranges, motorpools, airports, and waterfront facilities.

COMMUNITY SERVICE — dependent schools, parks, churches, and recreational facilities.

OPEN SPACE — undeveloped acreage, forest, and streams.

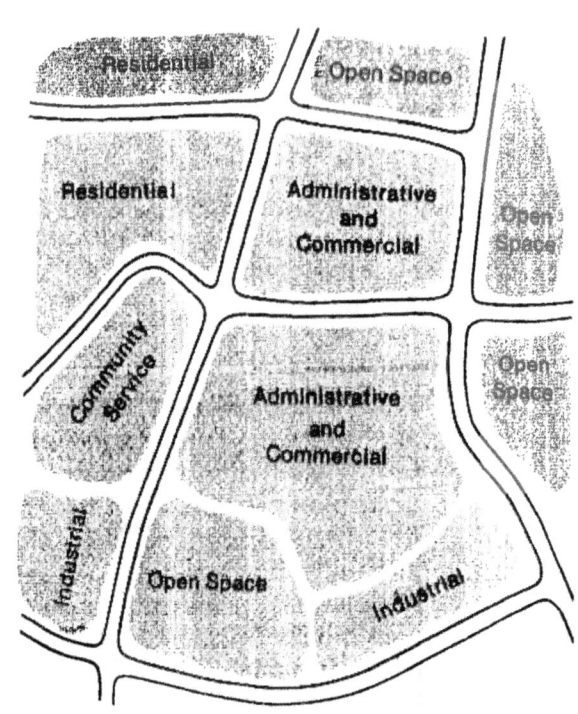

DELINEATES LAND FUNCTION

FORECAST

TRAVEL FORECASTS *are used to determine the transportation service NEED that will result from a change in land use.* For example, what roads will be needed to service a new housing area. Travel forecasts can include home-based, nonhome-based, work, nonwork, person, vehicle, and other type trips. Therefore, **the key to reducing the complexity of a travel forecast** *is to limit the forecast to only what is NEEDED to establish the maximum travel demand.* At a military installation, maximum travel demand is generally created by the highly directional employee home-to-work vehicle-trip that occurs during the morning or evening peak rush hour. Travel forecasts often need to establish only this type demand. A notable exception to this criterion is facilities that generate large traffic volumes not associated with the work trip, such as commercial and community facilities.

> TRAVEL FORECASTS QUANTIFY FUTURE TRAFFIC DEMAND

THE FORECAST PROCESS starts with the **proposed road network and land use**, along with a **thorough understanding of existing traffic flow patterns**. Based on this information, **a prediction** is made of the number of future trips to and from an activity **(trip generation)**, where these trips begin and end **(trip distribution)**, and over which routes the trips are to be made **(trip assignment)**. This process is then used to **evaluate** various alternative road systems. After each numerical evaluation, all forecasts are examined to determine if they are reasonable. If the forecast is unreasonable, the assumptions and procedures used to predict the trips should be reexamined and appropriate changes made.

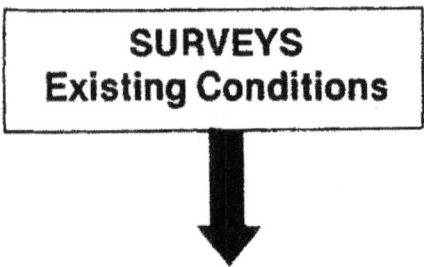

① LAND USE
Where will activities and roads be located?

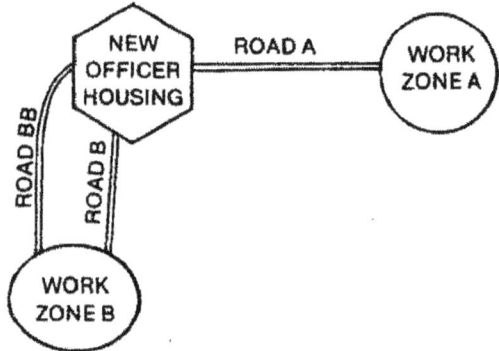

② TRIP GENERATION*
How many trips begin and end at the activity?

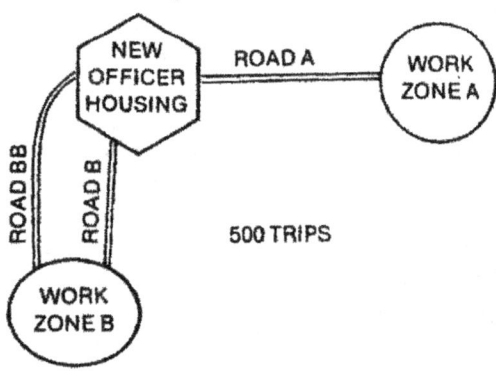

③ TRIP DISTRIBUTION*
How many trips will be made between activities?

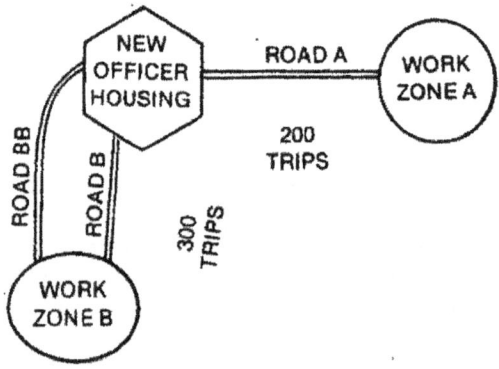

④ TRIP ASSIGNMENT*
Over which routes will trips between activities be made?

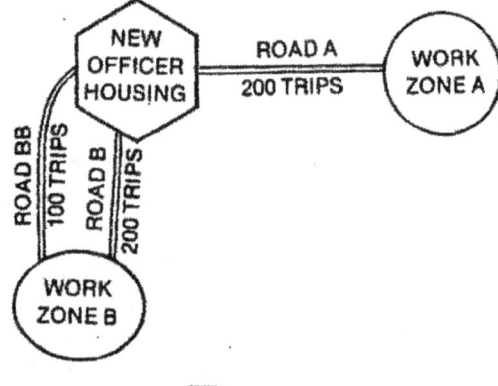

*Only peak-hour trips in direction of maximum flow are shown.

① LAND USE — Where will activities be located?

LAND-USE FORECASTS *provide estimates of future land development — location and type. These estimates* include not only *land usage,* but also *socio-economic variables, such as population, dwelling units, retail sales.* On military installations, this information is obtained from the installation master development plan. However, a major consideration in selecting locations shown on the development plan is the accessibility of that location. Therefore, as the road system is developed, proposed land uses shown on the development plan should be reexamined and changed, if necessary, to achieve a desirable future travel pattern. In every case, the road plan should provide a circulation system that maximizes access for movements between activities, giving due consideration to safety, comfort, and convenience, as well as cost.

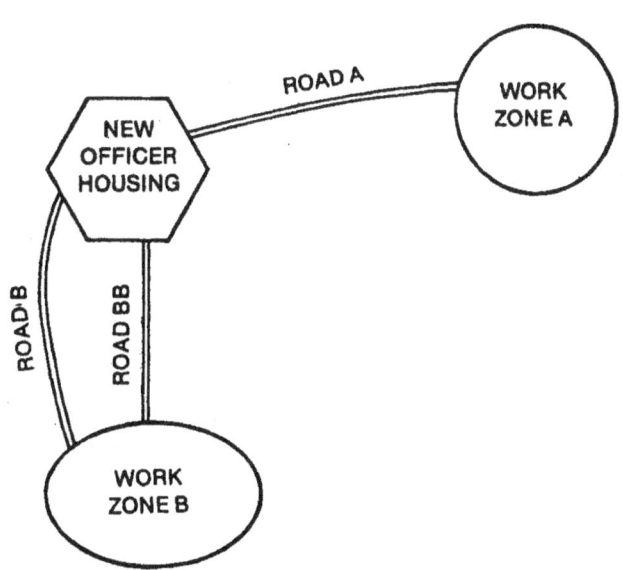

PREDICTIONS OF FUTURE TRAVEL ARE BASED ON FUTURE LAND USE

AND USE PLANNING OBJECTIVES

- Plan for people — not for automobiles and buildings.

- Arrange facilities to achieve the most attractive working and living environment.

- Improve internal traffic flow and external access.

- Consolidate various functional activities.

- Lay out commercial facilities in a way that will bring the patrons close to as many stores as possible once they have parked.

- Locate industrial sites adjacent to transportation facilities so that access is as convenient as possible.

- Provide space for future expansion of facilities and for offstreet parking.

- Locate pollution- and noise-emitting facilities away from residential and commercial areas.

- Route as much traffic as possible around dwelling areas.

- Separate pedestrian and vehicle flows.

- Provide locations that are convenient to residential areas for supplemental services — parks, schools, shops, and chapels.

2 TRIP GENERATION — How many trips begin or end at an activity?

TRIP GENERATION ANALYSIS is a way to *estimate the number of future trips that will begin or end at an activity.* Trip generation analysis provides information on the peak volume of cars to be parked and the peak volume of traffic to be moved onto the road system at any one time.

Trip generation predictions are usually based on trip-making rates that are observed at existing facilities. Because of the many variables affecting traffic generation, specific generation rates have not been developed in this guide. However, for most military installations, trip-making rates can be determined from simple counts of vehicles entering and leaving driveways at existing similar facilities. When establishing generation rates, three characteristics of land use should be evaluated: intensity, character, and location of activity. "Intensity of land use" helps relate how many people will use the land and is expressed in such terms as "employees," "1,000 square feet of floor space," and "dwelling units." "Character of land use" refers to the type of land use, such as residential or industrial; whereas, "location of activity" generally refers to either a central built-up area or a remote area. When using existing facilities to estimate trip generation rates, both facilities should be similar in intensity, character, and location.

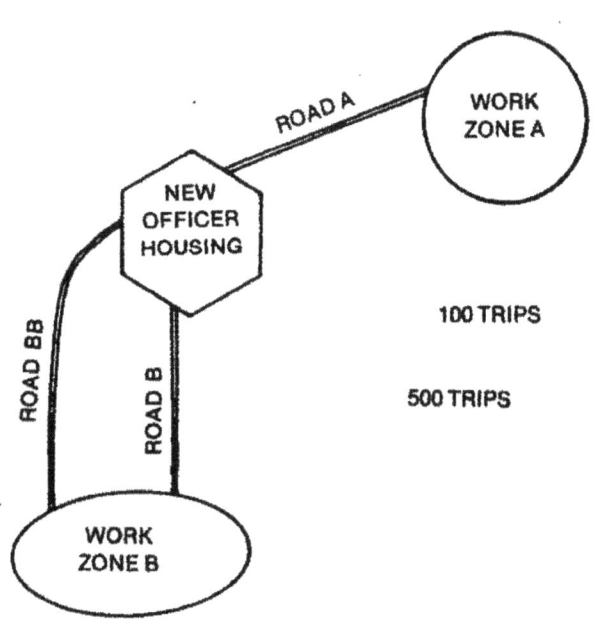

TRIP GENERATION DETERMINES PARKING AND ACCESS NEEDS

TYPICAL GENERATION UNITS

LAND USE	UNIT	LAND USE	UNIT
Bank	1,000 sq ft GFA*	Industrial	employee
Bank, drive-in	drive-in window	Institutional (schools)	student & employee
Barracks	person	Library	1,000 sq ft GFA*
Bowling alley	1,000 sq ft GFA*	Military installation	employee
Cafeteria	seat	Office building	employee
Chapel	seat	Recreation facilities	military strength
Clubs	member	Research facility	employee
Commercial	1,000 sq ft GFA*	Restaurant	seat
Dental clinic	dental chair	Service station	pump
Family housing	dwelling unit	Theater	seat
Golf club	member	Visitor center	employee
Guest house	bedroom	Warehouse	employee
Hospital	outpatient & employee	*Gross floor area	

EXAMPLE GENERATION*

A. STATE PROBLEM AND NEED

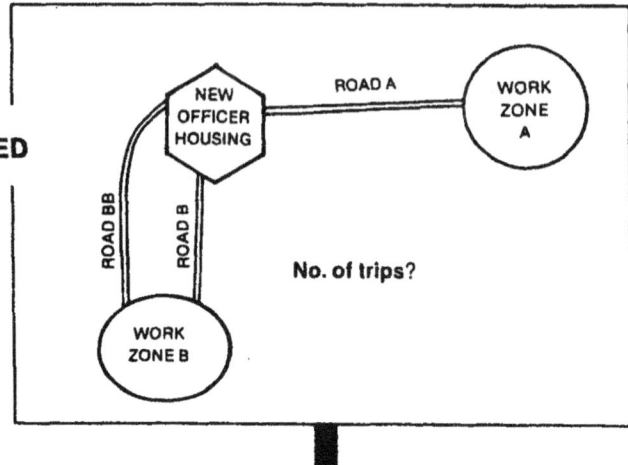

B. IDENTIFY LAND-USE FACTORS
- LOCATION
- CHARACTER
- INTENSITY

- BUILT-UP AREA
- RESIDENTIAL
- 500 HOUSES

C. DEVELOP GENERATION RATE
(Relation between trip making and land use at similar facility)

SURVEY AT SIMILAR FACILITY
- BUILT-UP AREA
- 400 HOUSES
- RESIDENTIAL
- 400 CARS EXITING IN PEAK HOUR
- TRIP RATE = 1.0 TRIPS/HOUSE

D. APPLY RELATIONSHIP TO FORECAST

- PEAK-HOUR ACCESS DEMAND = (500 HOUSES) (1.0 TRIPS/HOUSE)
  = 500 TRIPS

* Only peak-hour trips in direction of maximum flow are shown.

③ TRIP DISTRIBUTION — How many trips will be made between activities?

TRIP DISTRIBUTIONS *are analyzed to establish the number of trips that will be made between specific activity areas.* Two basic types of *mathematical models* are used to predict future trip distribution: *growth models and distribution models. Growth models* expand existing trips between zones based on an anticipated growth rate; whereas, *distribution models* estimate travel patterns based on the number of trips generated by the various zones, and then distribute these trips among the zones. The better known traffic models include the Fratar, Gravity, Intervening Opportunities, and Competing Opportunities. However, since these models require sophisticated data collection and analyses, they are not generally used at relatively small military installations.

TRIP DISTRIBUTION AT A MILITARY INSTALLATION generally can be *accomplished through* two methods. *An average-growth factor method* is used where significant changes in the zonal characteristics are not expected. When areas are almost completely undeveloped, a *proportional distribution method* is used. Both methods present reasonably accurate predictions of the future home-to-work trip. The average-growth method projects future trips between two zones by applying an average of the two zonal growth rates to the existing trips between the zones. On the other hand, the distribution method simply proportions the trips to be generated at a new facility in relation to existing concentrations at trip origins. Relationships for use in these models can be developed from origin and destination studies and/or peak-hour traffic counts.

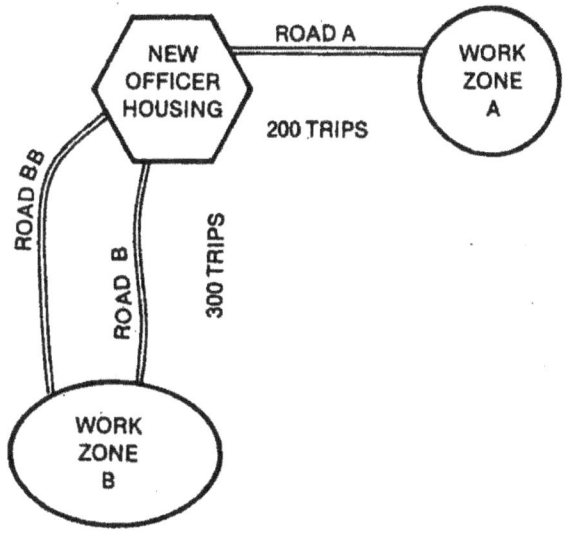

TRIP DISTRIBUTION DETERMINES TRAFFIC CORRIDOR

EXAMPLE DISTRIBUTION *

I. GROWTH MODEL

Where:

$$T_{ij} = t_{ij}\left(\frac{F_i + F_j}{2}\right)$$

T_{ij} = future trips between i & j
t_{ij} = existing trips between i & j
F_i = growth factor at i
F_j = growth factor at j

(A) DETERMINE NUMBER OF EXISTING TRIPS BETWEEN ZONES

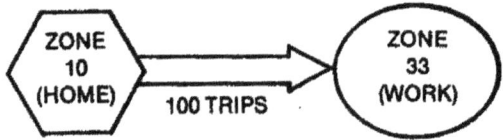

(FROM ORIGIN AND DESTINATION SURVEYS)

(B) ESTIMATE GROWTH RATES FOR BOTH ZONES

$$F_{10} = 1.6$$
$$F_{33} = 1.4$$

(INSTALLATION GROWTH ESTIMATES FROM MASTER DEVELOPMENT PLAN)

(C) COMPUTE FUTURE TRIPS

$$T_{10,33} = t_{10,33}\left(\frac{F_{10} + F_{33}}{2}\right)$$

$$= 100\left(\frac{1.6 + 1.4}{2}\right)$$

$$= 150 \text{ TRIPS}$$

II. DISTRIBUTION MODEL

Where:

$$T_{ij} = T_j\left(\frac{P_i}{\sum_{i=1}^{n} P_i}\right)$$

T_{ij} = future trips between i and j
T_j = future trips generated at j
P_i = existing trips produced at i
$\sum_{i=1}^{n} P_i$ = total trips produced

(A) DETERMINE TRIPS TO BE GENERATED AT NEW FACILITY

500 HOUSING UNITS WILL GENERATE 500 TRIPS

(B) FROM TRAVEL SURVEYS DETERMINE WHERE EXISTING TRIPS ARE DISTRIBUTED

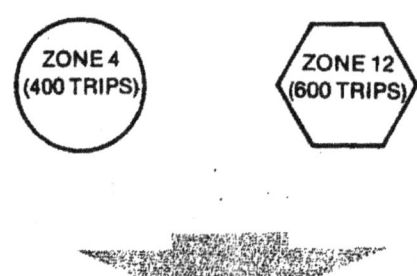

(C) DISTRIBUTE FUTURE TRIPS PROPORTIONATELY

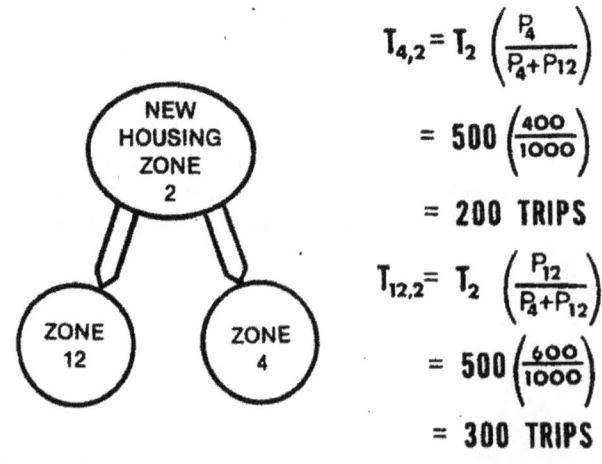

$$T_{4,2} = T_2\left(\frac{P_4}{P_4 + P_{12}}\right)$$
$$= 500\left(\frac{400}{1000}\right)$$
$$= 200 \text{ TRIPS}$$

$$T_{12,2} = T_2\left(\frac{P_{12}}{P_4 + P_{12}}\right)$$
$$= 500\left(\frac{600}{1000}\right)$$
$$= 300 \text{ TRIPS}$$

*Only peak-hour trips in direction of maximum flow are shown.

4. TRIP ASSIGNMENT — Over which routes will trips between activities be made?

The final phase of forecasting the travel demand is THE ASSIGNMENT OF VEHICLE TRIPS BETWEEN ZONES TO VARIOUS TRAFFIC ROUTES. One method of trip assignment is to simulate, from input on the travel pattern or desires of motorists, the extent to which a proposed system would be used. This technique is very complex; therefore, its use should be limited to those familiar with it.

On a military installation, the *primary technique for assigning traffic* is the *"all or nothing with capacity restraint."* In this technique, trips are allocated between zones to the one single path or route that represents the best path for a certain number of vehicles. Assignment thereafter is made to the second or next best alternate route. Frequently, the maximum traffic on a roadway is established as that capacity at which traffic can flow with only limited congestion, allowing the motorist to travel at his desired pace within legal limits. To achieve a balance in all zone-to-zone traffic, a trial-and-error assignment method generally is used; that is, minimum paths are calculated, assignments are made, roads are analyzed for travel comfort and convenience, then new assignments are made. This process continues until traffic is balanced on all routes between zones.

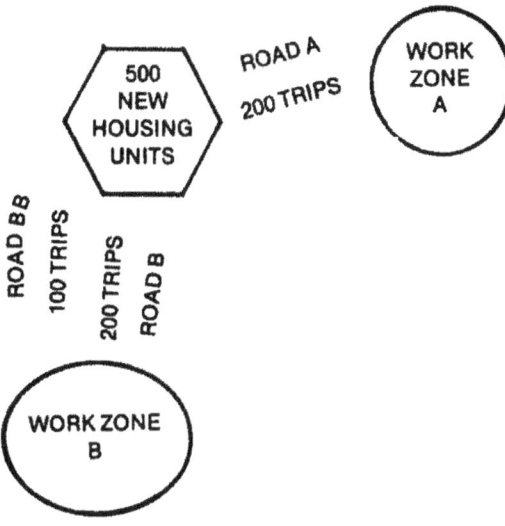

TRIP ASSIGNMENT DETERMINES ROAD WIDTH

FACTORS INFLUENCING ROUTE SELECTION

TANGIBLE	INTANGIBLE
Travel time	Human nature
Travel distance	Relative comfort and ease
Operating cost	Esthetics
Frequency of stops	Geometrics
Safety	

COMPONENTS OF ASSIGNED TRAFFIC

INDUCED TRAFFIC — new trips enticed

DIVERTED TRAFFIC — existing trips diverted from other paths

FACILITY-CREATED TRAFFIC — sightseers or traffic developed because of changes in land use

CONVERTED TRAFFIC — change in mode, such as bus to auto or auto-pool to driver

SHIFTED TRAFFIC — existing trips that show new origin and/or destination

NATURAL GROWTH TRAFFIC — result of natural growth rate

3-15

EXAMPLE ASSIGNMENT

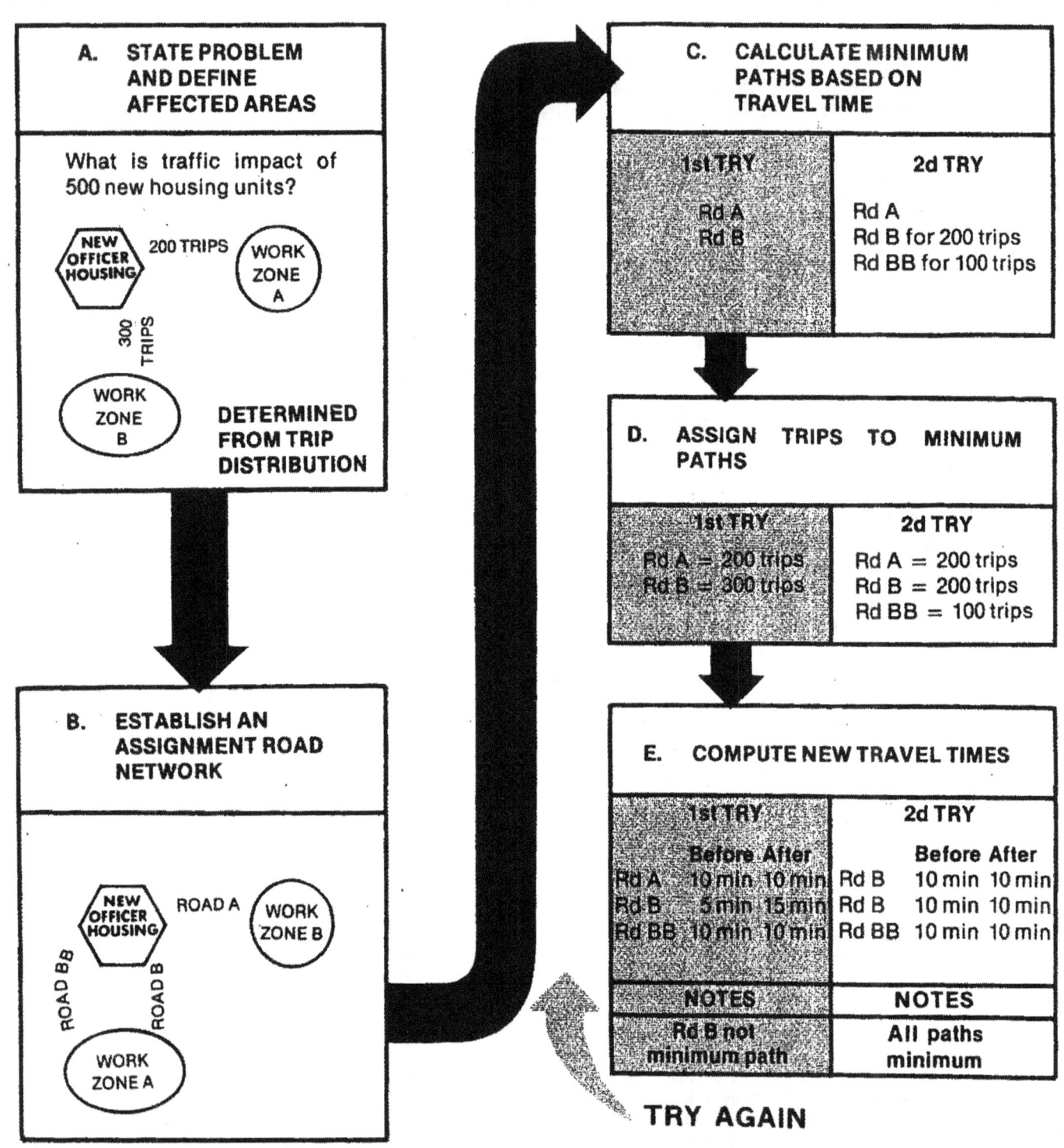

*Only peak-hour trips in direction of maximum flow are shown.

THIS PHASE OF ROAD DESIGN concerns **reducing traffic surveys and travel forecasts into various acceptable road systems.** The goal statements discussed in chapter 2 provide a basis for determining an acceptable system.

The development of alternatives, which by nature is a creative function, usually begins by estimating future travel on the existing road system. From these travel projections, problem areas and road needs can be identified. Assuming that this measure shows problems, a new trial road system is designed.

Once **one or more alternatives** are developed, the road plans are then tested to examine their performance. Congestion should be tested first. As alternatives pass the congestion test, they should be measured in more detail, such as travel time, travel distance, safety, parking, user costs, and environmental impact. The development and testing should end with a manageable number of alternatives that are acceptable in all phases of the roadway plan test. These alternatives then pass into the selection stage.

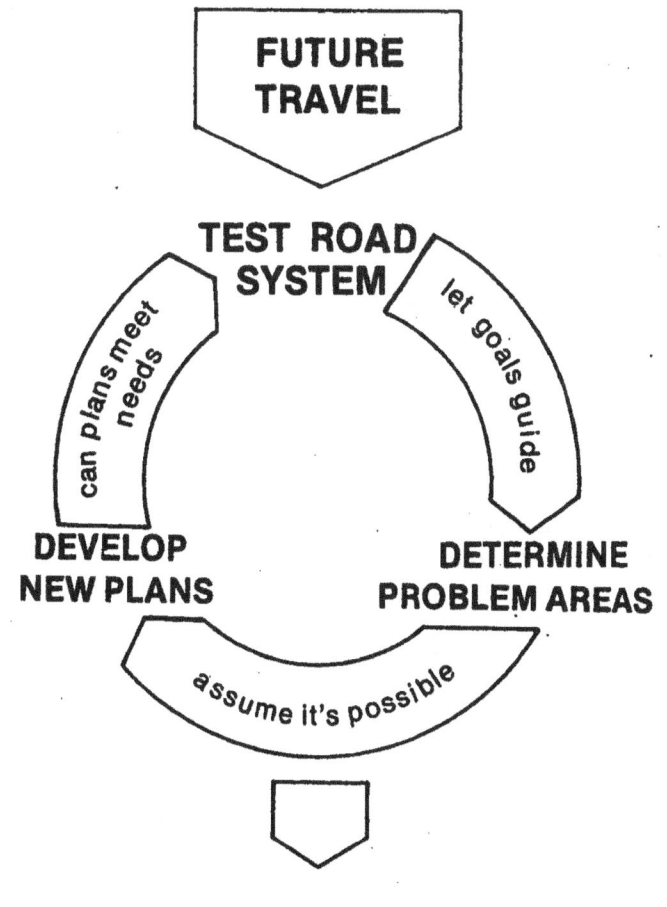

DEVELOPMENT OBJECTIVES

Although development is a creative function, the following objectives should be used to enhance the creative capacity of the road designer.

1 REDUCE CONGESTION

The test of any road system starts by measuring its capacity to handle projected traffic volumes. To eliminate capacity problems, the planner should not only insure that the congested roadways are improved, but should also consider improving remote routes in the vicinity, or even adding entire segments. For example, a bypass road can help relieve congestion on routes that are remote from it.

2 SERVE TRIP DESIRES

Analysis of vehicle trips — their origin, destination, length, and other characteristics — helps to determine installation roadway network, access-road needs, and entrance gate locations.

3 PROVIDE LAND-USE ACCESS

Alternate road systems should be developed to serve access needs identified by the installation master development plan.

4 PROVIDE SYSTEM CONTINUITY

Geometric configurations of the alternate road system should be limited to provide travel continuity, as well as practical construction and operation. When new routes are constructed, they should connect to the existing system where sufficient capacity exists to absorb the additional demand.

DEVELOPMENT OBJECTIVES

1. Reduce congestion
2. Serve trip desires
3. Provide land-use access
4. Provide system continuity

EVALUATION

IN THE EVALUATION, *all acceptable alternatives are considered and compared with one another to determine the best roadway plan.* The plan selected should provide the installation with a traffic corridor system that shows a road type or improvement for each traffic corridor. At this stage, the road plan does not show exact road location. However, each plan presented for evaluation has been found acceptable in the development phase, based on a preliminary look at the possibilities for location and design. In the evaluation phase, one plan is selected; then, in the implementation phase, the final plan is refined to show roadway location and design.

The most common method of evaluating a roadway is simply **to examine the measures of each alternative and make a judgment-based decision.** This decision usually requires trade-offs. For example, "X" minutes saved in travel are worth "Y" dwelling unit removals. As an aid in evaluating trade-offs, a weighting system applied to each evaluation criterion is suggested.

ALTERNATIVE A ALTERNATIVE B

EVALUATION

BEST PLAN
ALTERNATIVE A

EVALUATION DETERMINES BEST PLAN

EVALUATION METHOD

① ESTABLISH CRITERIA

- Accident rates
- Travel time
- Travel distance
- Exposure to pollution

② DETERMINE WEIGHT OF EACH CRITERION

CRITERIA	WEIGHT
Accident rate	4
Travel time	3
Exposure to pollution	2
Travel distance	1

③ SPECIFY RELATIVE PERFORMANCE OF EACH ALTERNATIVE IN EACH CATEGORY

CRITERIA	PERFORMANCE RATING	
	ALT A	ALT B
Accident rate	2	1
Travel time	2	1
Exposure to pollution	1	2
Travel distance	1	2

④ MULTIPLY THE WEIGHT OF EACH CRITERION BY THE PERFORMANCE RATING, THEN SUM PRODUCTS

CRITERIA	ALT A WEIGHT × PERFORMANCE = PRODUCT RATING	ALT B WEIGHT × PERFORMANCE = PRODUCT RATING
Accident rate	4 × 2 = 8	4 × 1 = 4
Travel time	3 × 2 = 6	3 × 1 = 3
Exposure to pollution	2 × 1 = 2	2 × 2 = 4
Travel distance	1 × 1 = 1	1 × 2 = 2
Total	17	13

⑤ SELECT BEST PLAN

ALT A

IMPLEMENTATION

ROADWAY IMPLEMENTATION includes location, design, right-of-way acquisition, and construction. It is not a part of the roadway planning process. Planning is only a tool for making decisions today that will meet the roadway needs of tomorrow. However, continual planning provides data and assistance for the implementation. For example, a major service is the supply of base data for locating and designing the roadway within the traffic corridor.

SURVEILLANCE AND REAPPRAISAL

ONE CHARACTERISTIC OF TRANSPORTATION PLANS is that the analysis of a few years ago may be almost obsolete today. Obsolescence of the transportation plan may be caused by changes in goals, shifts of emphasis among goals, changes in funding, changes in administration, and improvements in transportation planning. Obsolescence of the plan is also frequently caused by radical departure from some part of the plan. Each installation should monitor changes that affect the transportation plan and should estimate their effect on the validity of the plan, changing the plan as necessary.

TRAFFIC ENGINEERING

ROAD DESIGN: INTERSECTIONS

CONTENTS

	Page
I. ELEMENTS	2
TURNING ROADWAYS	3
CORNER RADII	3
AUXILIARY LANES	4
CHANNELIZATION	6
SIGHT DISTANCE	8
MEDIA OPENINGS	9
II. DESIGN	10
CLASSIFICATION	10
CONTROL	12
INTERSECTION TYPES	14
INTERSECTION DESIGN IMPROVEMENTS	16

ROAD DESIGN: INTERSECTIONS

ELEMENTS

DESIGN

THE NUMBER, TYPE, AND SPACING OF INTERSECTIONS determine to a large degree the capacity, speed, and safety of most installation roadways. This chapter discusses the elements of design as well as various geometric designs that can be used to insure efficient traffic flow. *The selection of the primary geometric and traffic control designs of the intersection are dependent on the traffic pattern during one or more peak traffic periods.*

INTERSECTIONS
CONTROL CAPACITY
AND SAFETY

I. ELEMENTS

THE MAJOR ELEMENTS OF INTERSECTIONAL DESIGN are those *elements that have the greatest impact on vehicle operations, such as medians, channelization islands, deceleration and acceleration lanes, and corner radii.* The dimensions given in this section for those elements are based on widely accepted standards, or are as recommended by the American Association of State Highway and Transportation Officials.

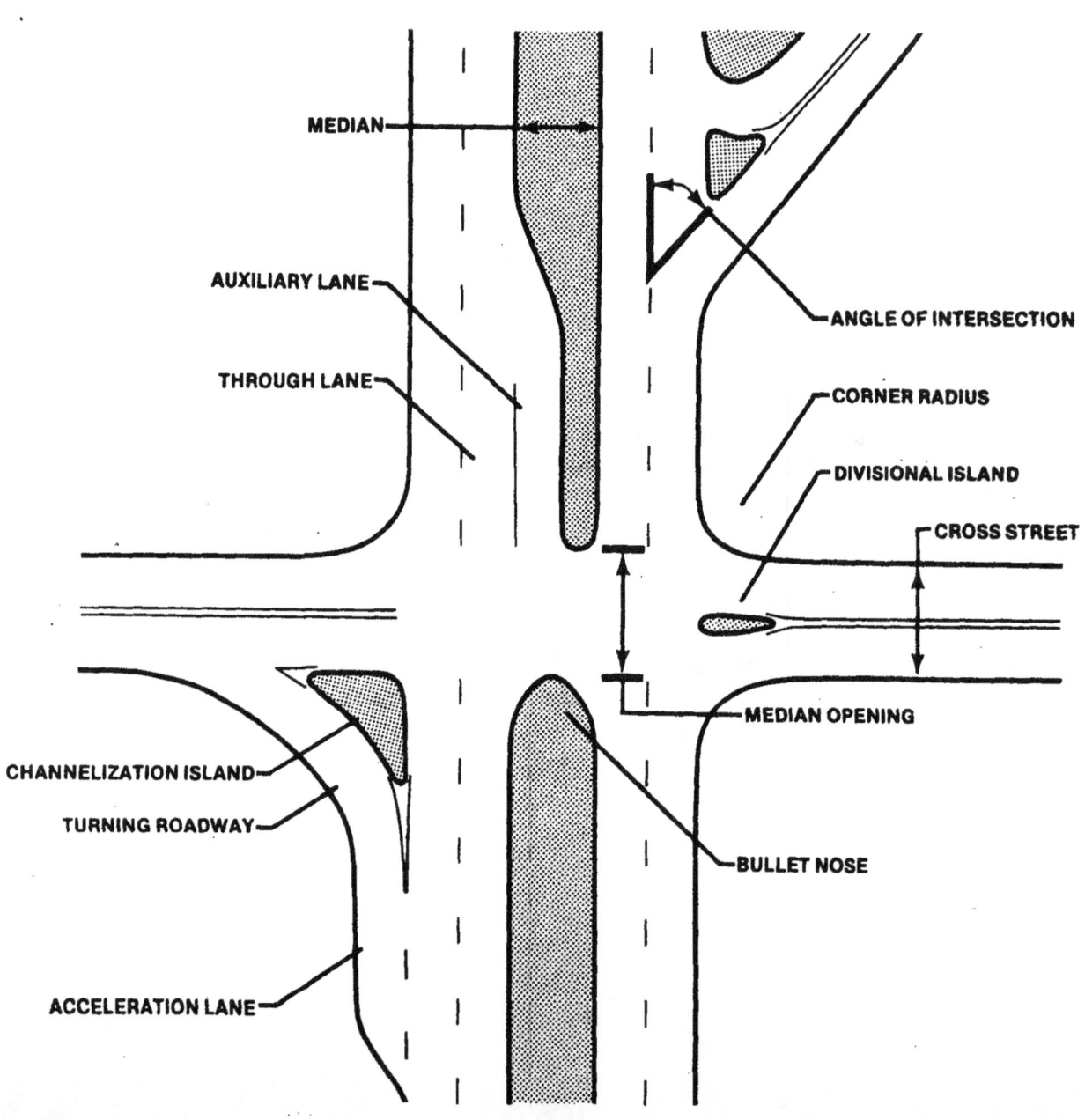

TURNING ROADWAYS

THE "TURNING ROADWAY" TECHNIQUE *connects two intersection legs. Thus, it shortens the travel path for turning vehicles, facilitates traffic control by separating turning movements, and reduces the amount of intersectional pavement by substituting islands for surfaced area. This technique can also reduce the frequency and severity of collision between right-turn vehicles and through traffic.* It is warranted, however, only where the main road traffic volume exceeds 10,000 vehicles per day, the road speed exceeds 25 miles per hour, and right-turn maneuvers exceed 30 per hour.

The critical elements of the turning-roadway design are the island area and location, the turning radius, and the roadway width. The island must be large enough to command attention and should be located at least 2 to 4 feet from the through lanes. A desirable 90-degree turning lane for buses and single-unit trucks would have a 70-foot radius and an 18-foot width. Angle-of-turn designs for other vehicles may be found in the American Association of State Highway and Transportation Officials publication, A Policy on Geometric Design of Rural Highways.

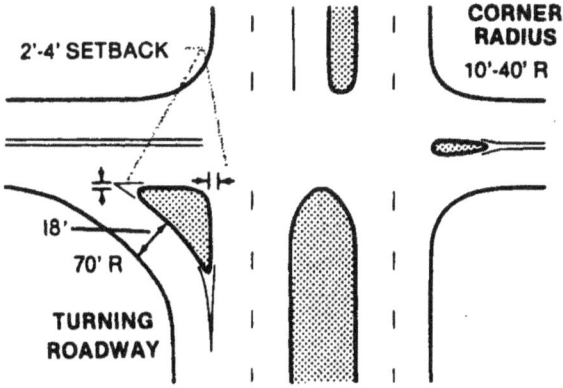

CORNER RADII

Generally, to the extent practicable, THE CORNER RADII OF INTERSECTIONS ON INSTALLATION ROADWAYS *should satisfy the requirements of the vehicles using the roadways.* However, many **factors** must be considered in **determining the corner radii** of individual intersections, such as: *availability of right-of-way, angle of the intersection, pedestrian use of the intersection, width and number of lanes on intersecting streets, and speed on the roadways.*

Radii of 10 to 20 feet may be used in built-up areas and other areas where vehicle needs must be balanced against pedestrian needs and against the need for corner setbacks.

Radii of 15 to 25 feet, adequate for passenger vehicles, may be used at minor cross streets with little truck-turning requirement. These small radii may be used also at major intersections with 10-foot-wide parking lanes at the curb and 12-foot-wide travel lanes. At these locations, even semitrailers are able to turn about a 15-foot curb radius with little or no encroachment on adjacent lanes. When using this design, parking must be restricted for at least 30 feet on the approach and 45 feet on the exit. Caution in use of these small radii is advised because traffic volumes may increase to the point where parking will be prohibited and the space used as a travel lane. Where feasible, radii of 30 feet or more should be provided at major cross streets to permit occasional truck turns without too much encroachment.

Where buses and large truck combinations turn frequently, radii of 40 feet or more should be provided. These larger radii are desirable also where speed reductions might cause problems.

AUXILIARY LANES

AUXILIARY LANES *are those lanes that adjoin the through travel lanes, but are used to supplement through traffic movement.* These lanes are used primarily as *storage for vehicles turning onto cross streets.* However, they may be used for acceleration of vehicles turning onto the major street, deceleration of vehicles leaving the major street, parking, or as climbing lanes for trucks.

The preferred design width of these lanes is 12 feet, but they may be 10 feet. The length of an auxiliary lane for turning vehicles consists of three components: deceleration length, storage length, and taper length. *The deceleration length is the distance required for a comfortable stop, and generally includes the taper. The storage length is based on the maximum number of vehicles likely to accumulate at any one time.* At unsignalized intersections, design should be based on the number of turning vehicles that arrive in an average 2-minute period within the peak hour. At signalized intersections, storage length should be based on 1.5 to 2 times the average number of vehicles that would store per cycle. In either case, the design length should be on the liberal side to avoid the possibility of through traffic being delayed by a turning vehicle.

In addition to the deceleration and storage lengths, *the taper length is an important component of the auxiliary lane.* The taper is used in transition from the normal road width to that of the auxiliary lane. For speeds of less than 30 miles per hour, a taper rate of 8:1 is standard and tapers less than 70 feet long generally are unsatisfactory.

Design for acceleration lanes is similar to that for deceleration lanes, in that widths and tapers are similar, and the total length of the lane depends on the speed difference between the through traffic and the merging traffic. A minimum length of 150 feet is recommended for these lanes.

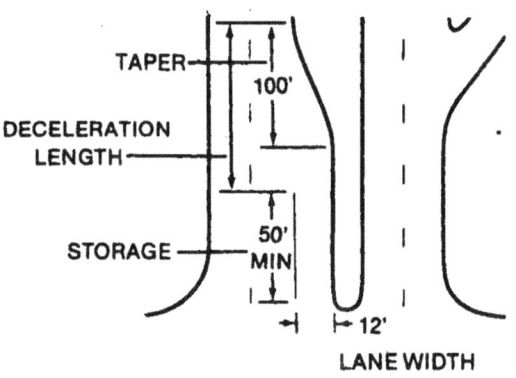

LEFT-TURN DECELERATION LANE

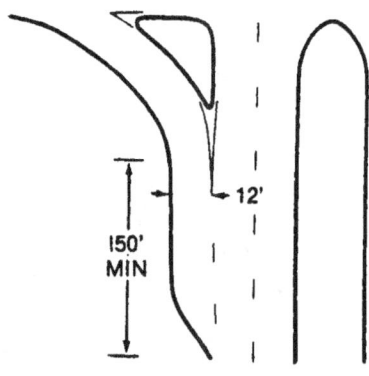

ACCELERATION LANE

DECELERATION LENGTHS (INCLUDING TAPER)

MAJOR STREET TRAVEL SPEED (mph)	LENGTH (ft)
20	160
30	250
40	370
50	500

STORAGE LENGTHS (UNSIGNALIZED)*

LEFT-TURNING VEHICLES (vph)	STORAGE (ft)
30	50
60	50
100	75
200	175
300	250

*SIGNALIZED — Storage length equals 1.5 to 2 times the average number of vehicles that would store per cycle.

ACCELERATION LENGTHS (INCLUDING TAPER)

MAJOR STREET TRAVEL SPEED (mph)	LENGTH (ft)
30	150
40	310
50	680

CHANNELIZATION

CHANNELIZATION *is the design of traffic lanes and islands in a way that will provide definite paths for vehicles to follow within the intersection. Effective channelization reduces the points of conflict in an intersection, or at least reduces the severity of any possible conflict.* In some cases, channelization can prevent wrong decisions and/or reduce the number of decisions the motorist must make. However, if improperly designed, traffic channels and islands can be not only confusing, but also exceedingly dangerous. It must be remembered that, although every intersectional detail may appear vividly in the design plan, the driver sees the intersection at a flat angle. Therefore, if it is too complicated, he may become confused in trying to interpret the intent of the channelization.

CHANNELIZATION

CHANNELIZATION SEPARATES COMPLEX INTERSECTION MOVEMENTS, AND CLEARLY DEFINES POINTS OF CONFLICT.

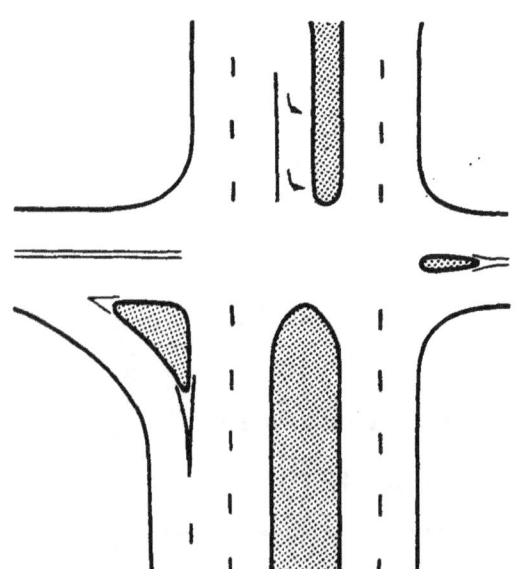

CHANNELIZATION

CHANNELIZATION REDUCES THE AMOUNT OF PAVED AREA, WHICH DECREASES VEHICLE WANDERING

CHANNELIZATION PREVENTS INCORRECT DECISIONS AND CONTROLS THE ANGLE OF CONFLICT

CHANNELIZATION FORCES RIGHT ANGLE CONFLICT GIVING MAXIMUM SIGHT DISTANCE

CHANNELIZATION

DESIGN

Traffic streams that cross should intersect at or near right angles, unless a merging or weaving maneuver is involved. In those cases, a flat angle of intersection is preferred.

Points of crossing or conflict should be well separated.

Refuge areas for turning vehicles should be provided clear of through traffic.

Prohibited turns should be blocked wherever possible.

Location of essential control devices should be established as a part of the design of a channelized intersection. Channelization may be desirable to separate the various traffic movements where multiple-phase signals are used.

Channelization islands should be designed so that the vehicle naturally moves through the islands.

Although the area of vehicle conflict should be reduced as much as possible by channelization, the number of islands should be kept to a minimum. Excessive islands can make it impossible for the driver to determine his or her course of action.

Traffic islands should be at least 4 to 6 feet wide and at least 12 to 20 feet long. Smaller islands confuse the driver.

Channelization islands should be set back 2 to 4 feet from the traffic lane so that they do not form an obstruction that tends to cause the vehicle to swerve away from the island.

CONTROL ANGLE OF CONFLICT

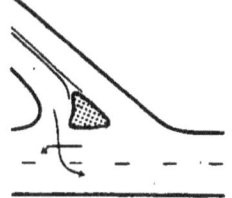

ISLAND SIZE AND LOCATION

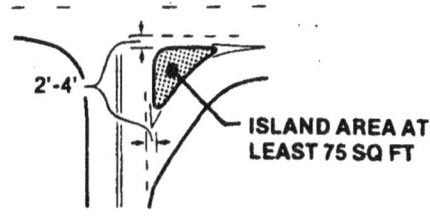

PROTECTION AND STORAGE

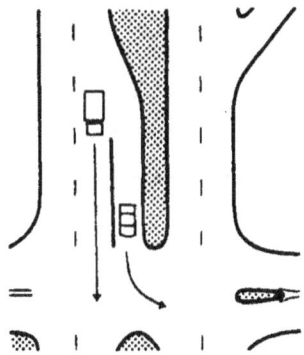

FLARED OPENINGS FOR EASY ENTRANCE

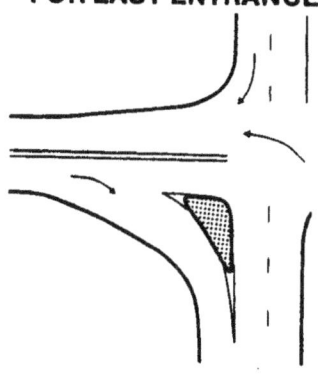

SIGHT DISTANCE

Along the roads of an intersection, as well as across all road corners, SIGHT SHOULD BE UNOBSTRUCTED FOR A DISTANCE THAT WILL ENABLE DRIVERS APPROACHING THE INTERSECTION TO SEE EACH OTHER IN TIME TO PREVENT COLLISION. The sight distance needed at a given intersection *depends on the type of traffic control at that intersection, width of the road, speed of approach, and type of vehicle.* Where no control exists, sight distance along each intersectional leg must be great enough that a driver can see any obstacle at the intersection in time to avoid it. Where cross-street traffic is controlled by STOP signs, the driver of the stopped vehicle should see enough of the major road to be able to clear the intersection before a vehicle that comes into view after he has started reaches the intersection. This distance is the basic criterion for most roadways. Where sight distance is inadequate, speed zones or signal control may be required for safety.

STOP CONTROL ON CROSS STREET		
DESIGN SPEED (MPH)	REQUIRED SIGHT DISTANCE	
	2 LANES (FT)	4 LANES (FT)
30	405	465
40	540	620
50	675	775
60	810	930

For divided roadways, medians equal to or wider than the vehicle length enable the crossing to be made in two steps. Narrower medians should be included in the width to be crossed in one step.

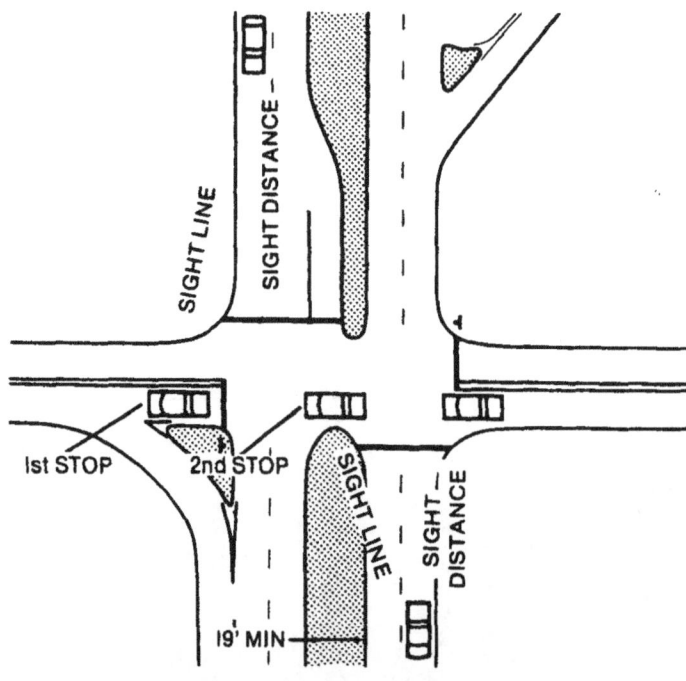

MEDIAN OPENINGS

The design of medians for intersections **depends on the character and volume of through and turning traffic.** Where nearly all vehicles travel through the intersection, and the volume is well below capacity, the simplest and least costly median opening may be adequate. Conversely, where crossing and turning movements are numerous and speeds and traffic volumes are high, the median should be of a shape and width that will permit efficient turning movements.

1 MINIMUM DESIGN

For medians requiring only a simple design, the length of the median opening and shape of the median end are determined by the vehicle turning radius. The arc of the radius is tangent to the median edge and the centerline of the crossroad. For single-unit trucks and an occasional semitrailer, a 50-foot radius with a semicircular median end is acceptable. The minimum length of the median opening should be at least 40 feet; and the maximum length no more than 100 feet.

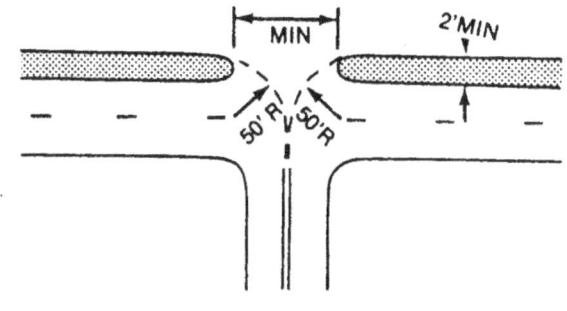

2 ABOVE-MINIMUM DESIGN

Where above-minimum designs are required, the general pattern for the simple design is used, but with larger dimensions. For example, in lieu of using a 50-foot control radius for single-unit vehicles, a 75-foot radius could be used. Also, for medians wider than 8 feet, a bullet-nose median end can be used in lieu of the semicircular end. This end treatment improves vehicle travel paths, lessens intersectional pavement, and shortens the length of the median opening.

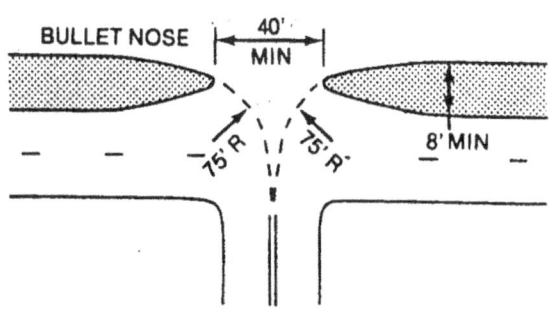

3 DESIGN FOR CROSS TRAFFIC

Where signalization is unjustified and crossing movements are unsafe, the median should be wide enough to store at least one vehicle. The controlling median width is the length of the design vehicle to be accommodated.

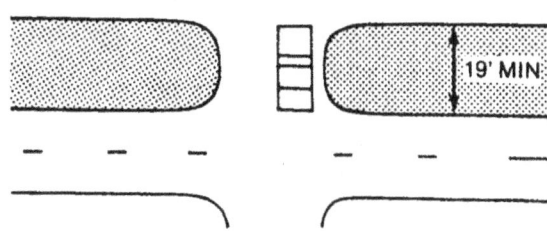

II. DESIGN

The regulated sharing of common space where two or more roadways intersect requires intersection designs and traffic controls that are drastically different from those of the open road. "INTERSECTION DESIGN" *is the process of determining the best way one traffic stream can cross another or make certain movements without conflict.* For example, where two major roadways cross, some type of bridge structure may be required to eliminate conflict. Where two minor roadways cross, however, traffic conflict may be controlled simply with a stop sign. In general, then, **traffic volume, speed, and accident rate** — *as well as the ever-present economics* — **determine the method to be applied at a given crossing.** This section illustrates various designs that can preclude conflict at roadway crossings.

CLASSIFICATION

Design requirements for intersections vary with the importance of the intersecting roadways. Therefore, the functional classification used here places *crossing roadways into three groups* in accordance with their importance: *minor/minor, major/minor, and major/major.* Each group carries a set of suggested minimum design standards, which correspond with the importance of the roadway system and the specific service each is expected to provide.

① MINOR/MINOR INTERSECTION

THE INTERSECTION OF TWO LOW-VOLUME ROADS should be kept *simple in geometry and traffic control.* Drivers need only to be able to see other approaching vehicles so as to judge their speed and distance. Design of this intersection should insure that: *paths on approach to and through the intersection are natural; horizontal and vertical alignment is compatible with the operation; and sight distance is sufficient.*

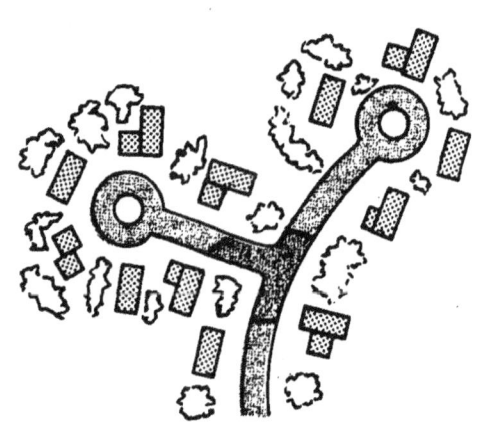

② MAJOR/MINOR INTERSECTION

Where a low *volume road* and *a high volume road* intersect, it is basic that drivers on both roads know immediately which road is major. Also, good sight distance for both roads is essential but particularly for vehicles crossing the major road. Traffic control of these intersections generally is provided with stop signs on the minor road.

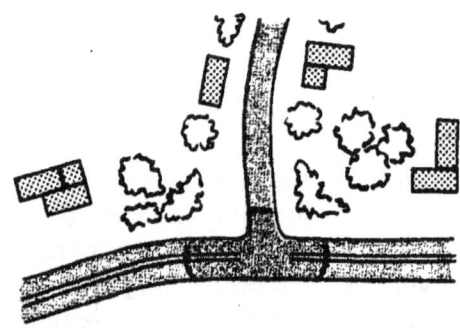

③ MAJOR/MAJOR INTERSECTION

Heavy traffic volumes where two or more roadways cross each other may require drastic changes from open road operating conditions, and capacity considerations because of the regulated sharing of common space. The configuration of the intersection is the principal determinant of operational safety and efficiency. The type of control and geometry can vary extensively. For example, *control may vary from yield signs to traffic signals, and geometry may vary from a two-lane, two-way roadway to a six-lane divided roadway with auxiliary lanes and turning roadways.* Because of extensive variations that may be required to handle heavy traffic volumes, requirements for both present and future demand should be established prior to design.

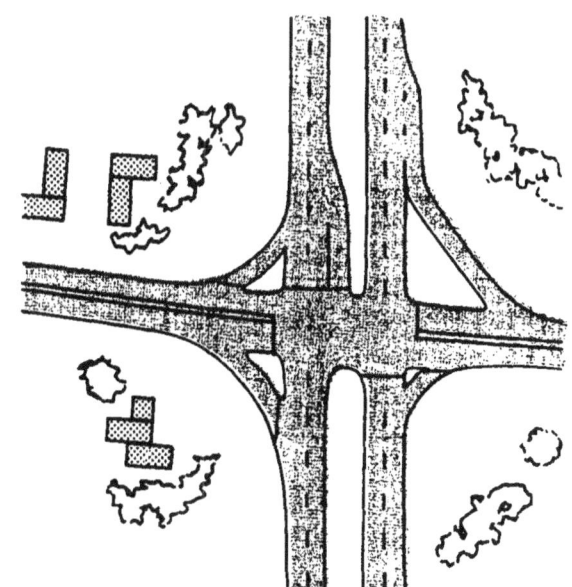

Horizontal and vertical alignment should be compatible with operational requirements.

Paths on approach and through intersection should be natural.

Traffic should be separated according to maneuvers.

Turning maneuvers should be physically accommodated.

Turning roadways should be designed for reasonable speeds.

Good transitions to turning roadways and auxiliary lanes should be provided.

Sight distances should be sufficient for conditions.

Design must be compatible with environmental conditions.

12

> **DRIVERS SHOULD BE ABLE TO:**
>
> - DETECT THE IMPORTANCE OF THE INTERSECTING ROADWAY.
>
> - DETERMINE THE REQUIRED LANE OR POSITION IN ORDER TO ACCOMPLISH THE INTENDED MANEUVER.
>
> - IDENTIFY AND RESPOND TO THE CONTROL DEVICE.
>
> - IDENTIFY THE REQUIREMENTS OF THE INTERSECTING TRAFFIC STREAM AND JUDGE THE CHARACTERISTICS OF THAT STREAM AS THEY RELATE TO THE MANEUVER.

CONTROL

Many methods may be used to enable one traffic stream to cross another or to make certain turning movements efficiently and safely. However, **basic crossing conflicts can be eliminated by** use of these devices: **yield signs, stop signs, and traffic signals.**

❶ YIELD SIGNS

YIELD SIGNS generally are *used where minor roads intersect, where traffic speeds are low, and/or where adequate sight distance is available.* The yield sign indicates to the driver that he must decide whether to continue through the intersection at 15 or 20 miles per hour or come to a complete stop. Thus, *sight distance must be sufficient for the driver to look in both directions, determine his course of action, and then either traverse the intersection or come to a complete stop.* This sign should never be used to protect entrances on major streets.

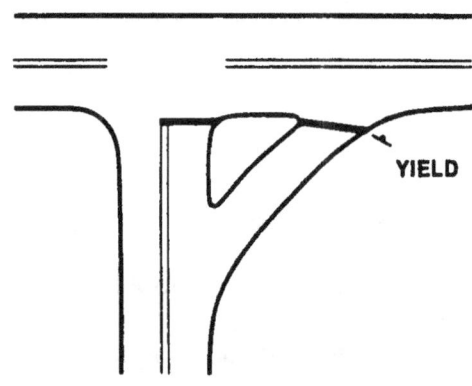

② STOP

At an *intersection of a minor roadway with an intermediate or major one*, the *crossing conflict* generally can be *controlled* by the use of a stop sign. The driver on the minor street must have sufficient sight distance to judge when it is safe to cross and must have an adequate gap in the traffic flow. It is possible to make use of a stop-and-enter crossing only when the traffic volumes on the major facility are not over approximately two-thirds of the capacity of the facility. When the major facility is flowing continuously, it will be difficult, if not impossible, to make a safe crossing. When this condition exists, more restrictive control is required.

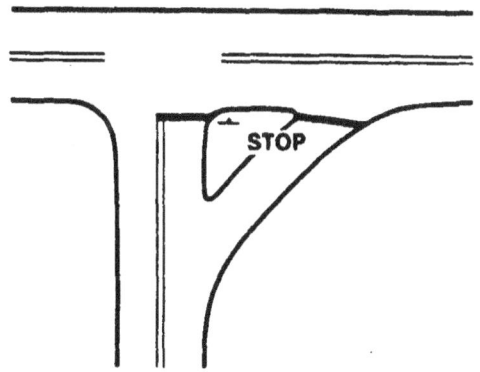

③ TRAFFIC SIGNAL

The most restrictive intersectional control — *signalization* — *should be used only at major intersections and, desirably, only where the road speed does not exceed 45 miles per hour.* The signalized intersection should be designed so as not to reduce the capacity of the street system. For example, if two major roadways are to cross at an intersection and each will operate near capacity, the traffic signal may reduce the capacity of both roads to one-half. In this case, additional traffic lanes within 1,000 feet of the intersection may be desirable.

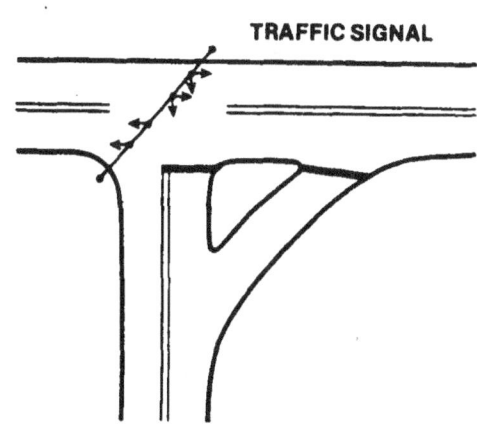

INTERSECTION TYPES

THE BASIC TYPES OF INTERSECTIONS *are determined by the number of intersecting legs;* that is, **three-leg, four-leg, multileg.** However, any one of the basic types **can vary greatly in scope, shape, and channelization.** Once the type is established, a final geometric design can be selected simply by applying the design controls and elements previously discussed. In this section, each type of intersection, with likely variations, is discussed. Traffic control for every type of intersection is not discussed; however, all types of intersections shown lend themselves to control, ranging from yield signs to traffic signals.

① THREE-LEGGED

Generally, this design is *used to terminate one roadway.* Where turning movements are hazardous, the intersection may be flared or designed with turning roadways. A Y-type design, an undesirable version of the T-intersection, generally results in operational problems.

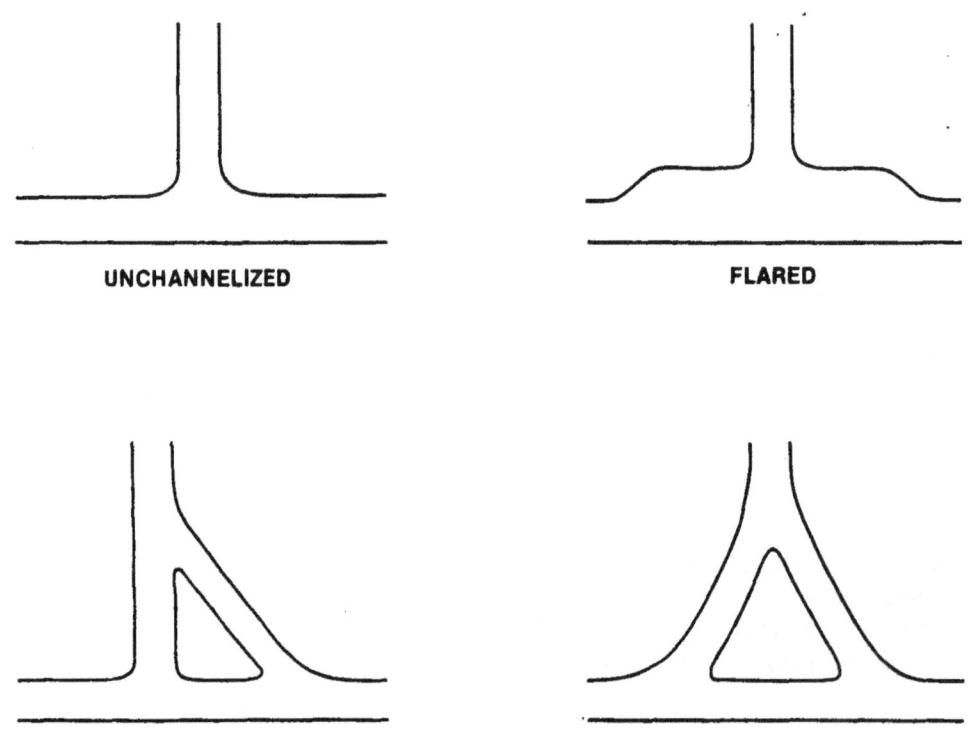

UNCHANNELIZED   FLARED

TURNING ROADWAYS

2 FOUR-LEGGED

Except that it provides for the direct crossing movement, a cross-intersection is *similar to the T-intersection.* The cross-intersection has many variations, depending on operating conditions. The *right-angle* is the common crossroad type; however, the crossroad may be skewed, even though this is undesirable.

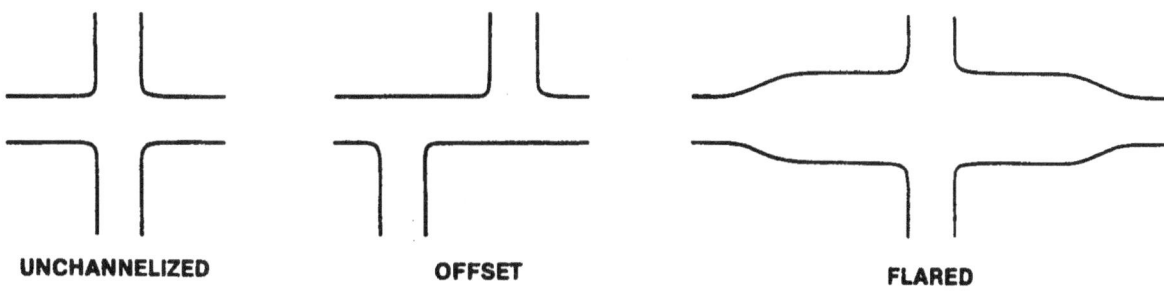

UNCHANNELIZED OFFSET FLARED

3 MULTILEGGED

This type of intersection generally *represents a total compromise of operational requirements.* Generally, either some form of channelization and signalization should be used, or one leg of the intersection should be eliminated. However, the rotary type intersection has been used for multisided intersections with heavy turning movements and low speeds. The rotary design operation depends upon weaving, and the success of such an operation depends upon the length of the weaving section in relation to traffic volume and operating speeds. In some cases, a rotary design can be improved by routing the through traffic directly through the middle of the rotary and forcing all turns onto the rotary. Minor street and turning movements may be either stop-and-enter or signalized, depending upon the volumes of traffic to be handled.

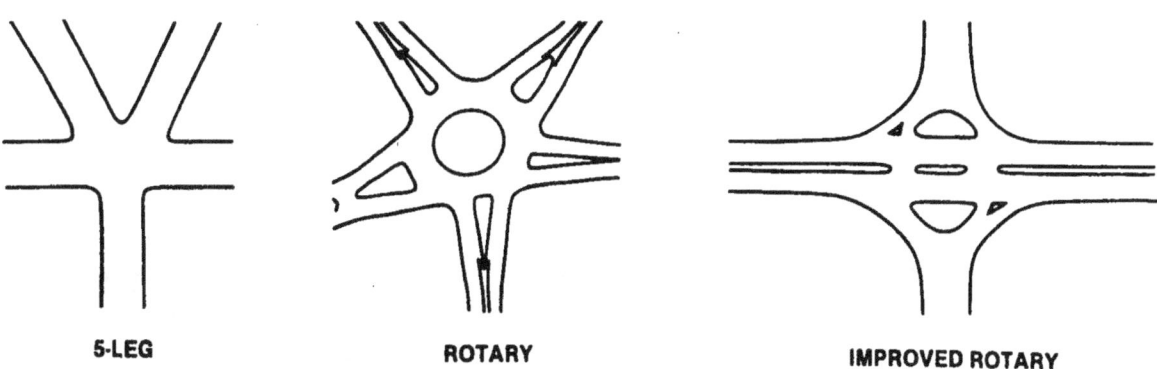

5-LEG ROTARY IMPROVED ROTARY

INTERSECTION DESIGN IMPROVEMENTS

THE TYPES OF INTERSECTION IMPROVEMENTS include a wide range of minor and major changes to intersections. For purposes of this guide, these IMPROVEMENTS have been grouped into four categories: **realignment, widening, and left- and right-turn provisions.** Not all types of improvements are included here — only the most common ones.

DESIGN PRINCIPLES

The layout should be visible to the driver, and the moves he must or can make should be apparent. A "bird's eye" or "drawing board" view is not available for a driver to study.

Intersection layouts should be simple. All drivers must be able to sense what to expect so that they are not required to hesitate or to decrease relative speeds while passing through an intersection.

Intersectional design should incorporate the informational signing necessary to guide vehicles through. Problems resulting from inadequate sign position and sign message can often be avoided by good initial design of all essential components.

The intersection should have adequate capacity for present and future traffic demands.

The intersection should be easy to cross. Excessively skewed intersections should be avoided because of the difficulties involved in crossing them.

Intersections should be planned to permit installation of additional control devices as traffic flow increases.

DESIGN IMPROVEMENTS

1. REALIGNMENT
2. WIDENING
3. LEFT TURN
4. RIGHT TURN

1. REALIGNMENT

Offset intersections — that is, intersections whose opposite halves are not in direct alignment — constitute a major traffic engineering problem. For the two halves to operate as two intersections, the offset needs to be at least 150 feet in built-up areas and at least 500 feet in outlying areas. Redesign of the intersection to match the two halves usually will reap large benefits in safety and efficiency of operation.

Intersections with high skew angles also are troublesome. The classical solutions to this problem are either: to realign or reduce the skew angle; or to separate the two halves of the intersection into two individual intersections by realigning the halves into T-intersections. Either of these realignments will reduce the potential for near head-on collisions that are inherent in the "before" condition. With either design, however, the tradeoff is a probable increase in the frequency of minor accidents.

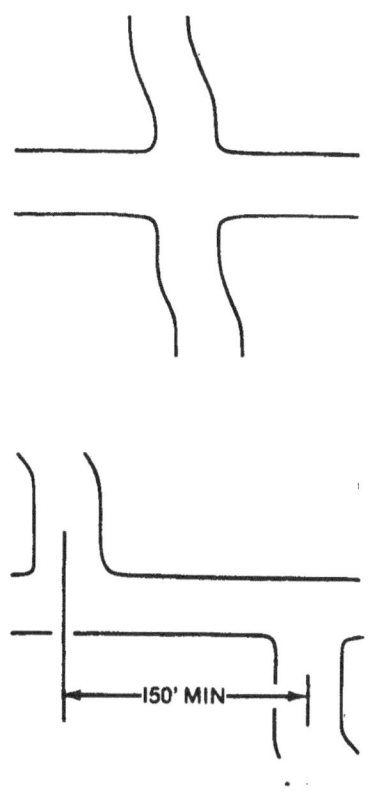

2. WIDENING

The intersection is commonly the lowest capacity element of an arterial street system. Thus, intersectional modifications that increase the number lanes in the intersectional area can more effectively balance the capacity of the facility. Flaring is an effective intersection treatment that increases the capacity, while improving operations, of the intersection. Flaring involves increasing the width of the pavement approaching the intersection. This is accomplished usually by adding a left-turn lane or, a right-turn lane, or both, as discussed under left- and right-turn provisions. Flaring can be used also to increase the number of through lanes. However, great care must be exercised to guard against operational problems downstream. To truly be effective, the merging operation downstream requires 300 to 500 feet of taper, which usually indicates midblock lane additions as well as the intersectional improvements. For this reason, flaring usually provides space for turn lanes.

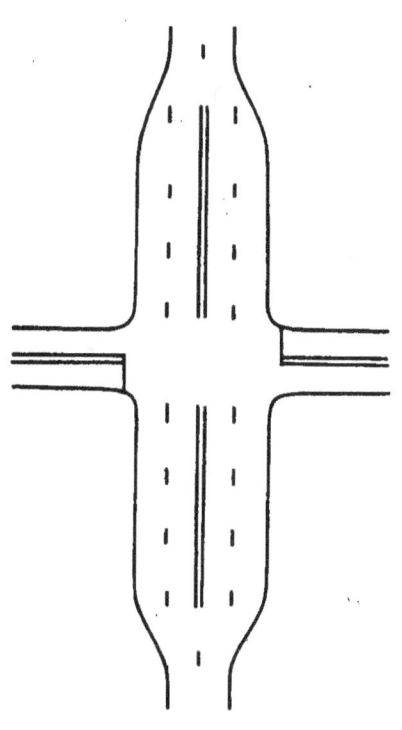

③ LEFT-TURN PROVISIONS

In general, A VEHICLE THAT LEAVES A MAJOR ROAD VIA A LEFT TURN *must come to a complete stop.* The **addition of left-turn lanes,** whether **by flaring or by taking space from an existing median,** can substantially increase the capacity and safety of the intersection by reducing the conflict between left-turning vehicles and through lanes.

SINGLE TURN

For normal **two-lane facilities, the roadway at the intersection must be widened to provide the "deceleration" lane. For a four-lane divided road, portions of the division strip may be removed to provide a median lane.** Median widths of 20 to 25 feet are desirable for median lanes; however, widths of 16 to 18 feet are adequate. A 10-foot lane with a 2-foot separator, either curbed or painted, may be used where speeds are low and the intersection is signal-controlled.

Typical traffic volumes warranting use of this technique should exceed 8,000 vehicles per day on the major road, with 100 left-turn vehicles during the peak hour.

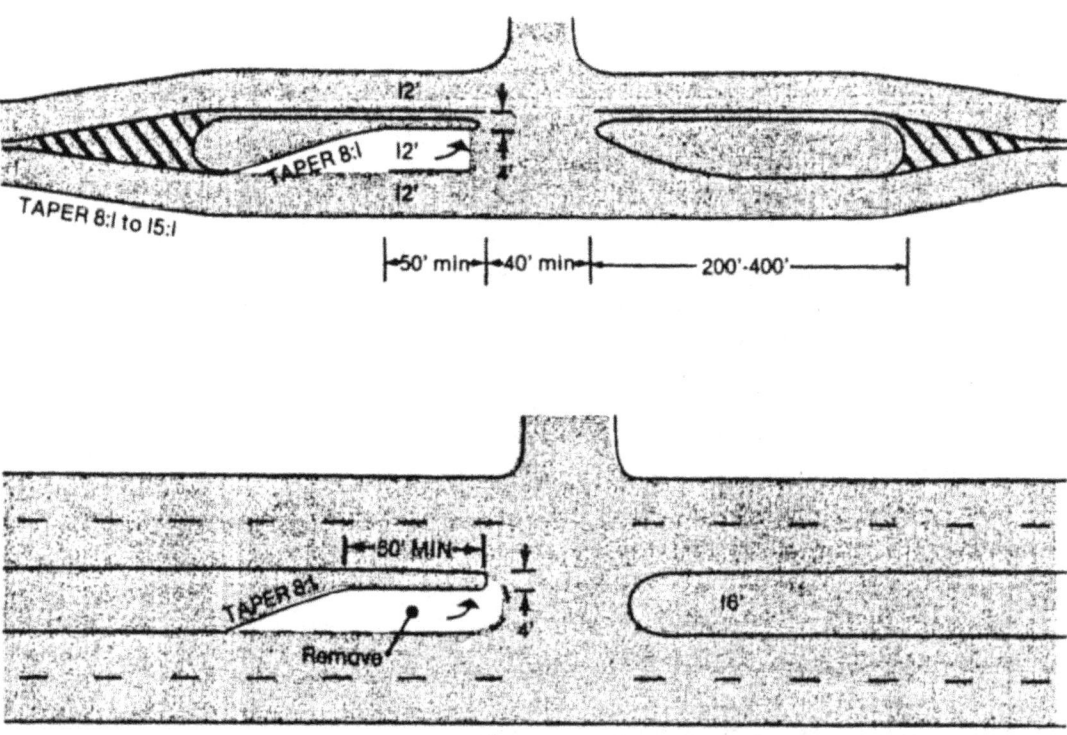

19

DUAL TURN

Where the capacity of a single left-turn lane is insufficient to accommodate the demand volume, a dual left-turning lane should be considered. Generally, the capacity of the approach controls the capacity of the intersection; thus, to maximize the flow through an intersection and to determine the quality of service afforded, a capacity analysis is necessary. However, a 75- to 80-percent left-turn capacity increase may be predicted by adding a second left-turn lane.

To provide a *left-turn bay* for a dual left-turn situation, it is necessary to *provide a wide continuous median or to "neck down" the lanes farther downstream*. Two through lanes in both directions and two left-turn lanes (all 12-foot lanes) would require a minimum pavement width of 76 feet, including a 4-foot median at the nose of the left-turn bay. This would then result in a 28-foot median downstream if the right-of-way were not narrowed. This width is desirable but often unavailable, especially in the more centralized areas where frequent dual left-turn lanes are needed. It is important, though, to provide a wide enough *"throat"* at intersection-entrance lanes to allow motorists to reach their lane safely and comfortably after a turning maneuver, without encroaching on another lane, the median, or curb. The operation of dual left-turn movements must be signalized, and is generally more favorable if the left turns have their own signalized phase, or if they are controlled on a leading or lagging green indication of the through phase.

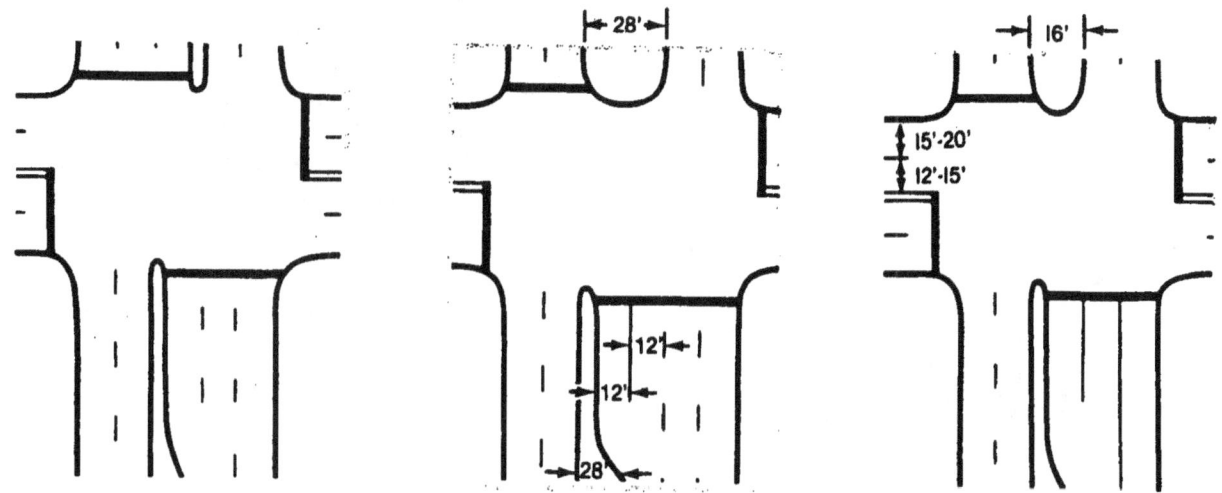

④ RIGHT-TURN PROVISIONS

RIGHT-TURNING MOVEMENTS may be enhanced by the **use of large corner radii, turning roadways, merging lanes, and deceleration lanes.** Generally, the technique that should be used is *related directly to the amount of traffic making the movement, the volume on the major street, and the vehicle speeds.*

LARGE CORNER RADII

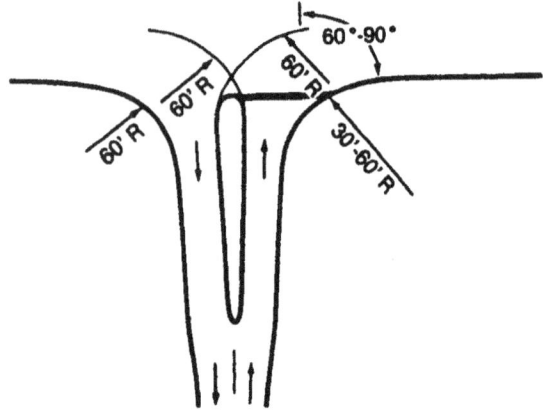

TURNING ROADWAY

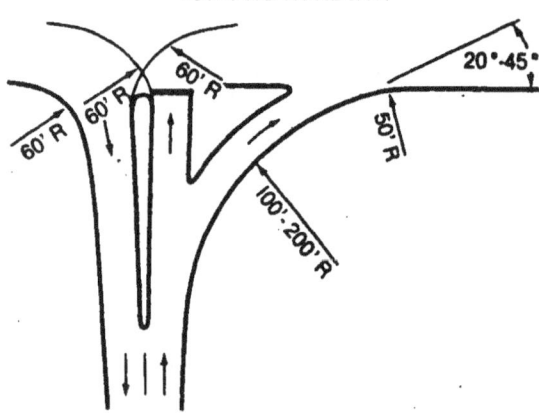

TURNING ROADWAY WITH ACCELERATION LANE

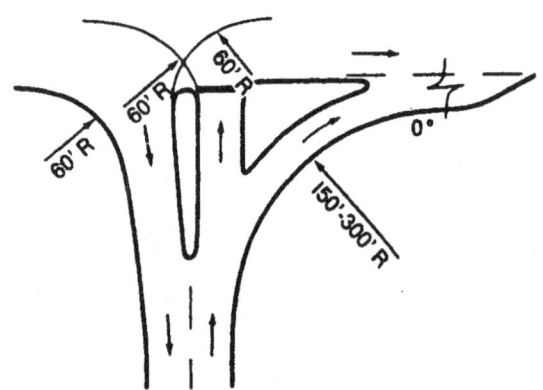

FROM MINOR TO MAJOR ROAD

Large corner radii should be used where minor volumes are making a right turn and it is desirable to minimize conflict between turning vehicles and through traffic. Where there are at least 60 turning vehicles during the peak hour and 8,000 vehicles per day on the major road, **a turning roadway** may be appropriate. With this design, the angle of entry into the road should be from 20 to 45 degrees in order for the turning vehicles to enter the through lane at a moderate speed. Finally, when major street volumes exceed 8,000 vehicles per day with at least 90 right turns from the minor road during the peak hour, it may be desirable to provide for their continuous movement into the intersection. In these cases, the angle of entry onto the through lane should be zero degrees, and vehicles must be provided with an **additional lane** that extends a sufficient distance for the vehicles to weave into the main stream of traffic. In some cases, this additional lane may be added for over a thousand feet. Where turning roadways are inappropriate, intersections may be improved by adding a **special right-turn lane.** As a general guideline, consideration should be given to installing this lane when the average number of right-turning vehicles exceeds 2 per signal cycle or 120 per hour during the peak period.

FROM MAJOR ROAD TO MINOR ROAD

Vehicles leaving a major facility via a right turn **should be permitted to make their exit at a reasonable speed so that they will not be forced to slow down to a point that will hold up traffic or create unsafe conditions.** On moderate speed routes, where traffic volumes are not in excess of 8,000 vehicles per day, the right turn can be made from a "taper" and a circular curve. *The length of the taper and the radius of the curve will depend upon whether the right-turning vehicle must come to a complete stop before merging into the minor street traffic.* Where traffic volumes are at least 8,000 vehicles per day and speeds exceed 30 miles per hour, a separate deceleration lane should be formed for the turning traffic. In general, this deceleration lane and the turning radius must be related so that the vehicle can come to a complete stop, if necessary, at the entrance to the minor road.

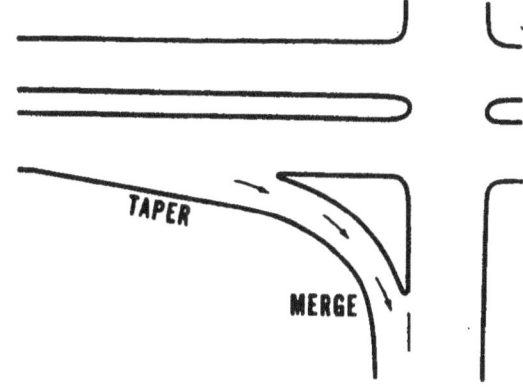

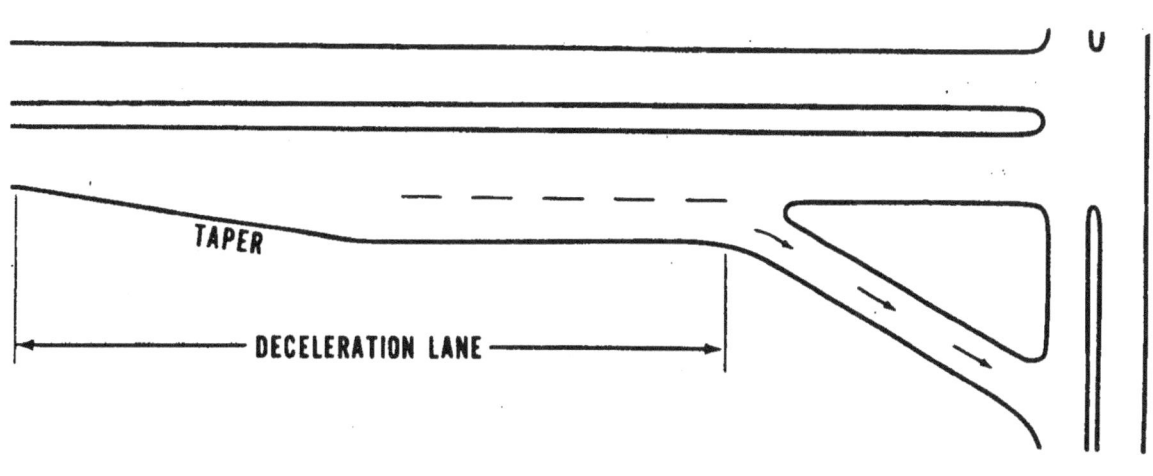

TRAFFIC CONTROL STUDIES

CONTENTS

	Page
Traffic Control Device Studies	1
Vehicle Registration Study	1
Origin-Destination Study	1
Speed Study	1
Speed-Delay Study	1
Motor Vehicle Volume Study	2
Roadway Capacity Studies	2
Vehicle Occupancy Study	2
Pedestrian Study	2
Observance of Stop Sign Study	3
Observance of Traffic Signals Study	3
Parking Studies	3
Accident Records Study	3

TRAFFIC CONTROL STUDIES

Type	Purpose	Requirement For Study	Personnel and Equipment
Traffic Control Device Studies	To inventory, locate, classify, and evaluate traffic control devices; and increase adequacy of these devices.	One initial study of all devices which is updated by periodic studies of specific areas on a routine basis.	Special two-man teams. Normal patrol equipment, and stopwatch, tape measure (100 ft), manual on uniform traffic control devices, field forms or notebook.
Vehicle Registration Study	To determine peak loads of traffic and adequacy of parking. May be used to adjust or update origin and destination study, or be used in lieu of this study.	As required to measure peak traffic in relation to existing roadways, and duty hour schedules.	Study is conducted by extraction and processing of information with ADPS. Traffic section personnel obtain input data, and ADP section processes data as required.
Origin-Destination Study	To develop data on origins and destinations of personnel entering, leaving, or traveling within an installation on a typical working day.	As required to support long-range planning, to anticipate major changes in strengths and functions, to support traffic construction requirements, and to assign traffic properly.	Varies with type and scope of study.
Speed Study	To determine if prevailing speeds are proper, to determine proper speed for new or improve roadways; to serve as a warrant for, and guide in, the placement and operation of traffic control devices, and to assist in accident research and enforcement.	Conducted for specific roadways as a result of observation, enforcement activity, and accident experience. Also required for new or renovated roadways.	Personnel may consist of one-man or two-man teams depending on the method and type of study. Equipment may consist of patrol vehicle, mirror box, stopwatch, field sheets, radar (with or without graphic recorder), and electric timer. Normally, police gear and marked vehicles are not used.
Speed-Delay Study	To determine variation in speed along a route; indicate amount, location, course, frequency and duration of delays, and provide overall speed and travel time along a route.	Conducted on specific routes as problems develop of congestion, delay and insufficient capacity. Also conducted when necessary to assign route priority, to consider use of alternate routes, to evaluate speed limits, and to check effectiveness of control devices.	Personnel will consist of a two-man team without distinctive police gear. Unmarked sedan or ¼-ton truck, standard watch and stopwatch, and field sheets as required.

Type	Purpose	Requirement For Study	Personnel and Equipment
Motor Vehicle Volume Study	To obtain an accurate record of the number, directional movements, and variation in volume of motor vehicles passing through intersections or using major routes, and to provide data for use in construction of a traffic flow map.	Conducted as required to determine street adequacy, to appraise effectiveness of traffic control measures, and to establish priorities and designs for traffic and/or road improvements and for new streets.	Two policemen are required to observe and record at a normal two-way intersection. If traffic exceeds 1500 vehicles per hour entering the intersection, one policeman may be required for each of the four approaches. Ordinary watches, field sheets, summary sheets, and (if used) manual counters are needed.
Roadway Capacity Studies	To determine the practical capacities of roadways as an adjunct to other studies; and to provide basic information required to update traffic regulations, to establish priorities for street improvements, and to aid in traffic planning.	Conducted as required to relieve congestion through appropriate corrective action in those areas where traffic volumes exceed traffic capacities.	Varies with scope of study. Normally, as a minimum, requires a two-man team equipped with tape measure, stopwatch post or engineer maps, sketch pads, and odometer (optional).
Vehicle Occupancy Study	To determine the number of occupants per motor vehicle.	As required to examine parking difficulties and congestion; to assist in planning for future traffic and parking facilities, and to evaluate the adequacy of transit services.	Either one-man or two-man teams with normal police gear depending on traffic volume. Equipment required includes ordinary watch, field sheets, and summary sheets.
Pedestrian Study	To determine the amount of pedestrian traffic at intersections and/or midblock crossing points.	As required to evaluate pedestrian-vehicle conflicts, and assist in planning control, physical protection, and enforcement measures.	Locally designed field sheets or notebooks. Either one-man or two-man teams depending on the pedestrian volume. Police gear is not worn.
Observance of Stop Sign Study	To determine the degree of drive obedience.	As required to study the relation of driver obedience to accidents at high accident frequency locations, and to assist in taking measures to increase driver obedience.	One person can normally make this study. He should not wear distinctive police equipment and should have a watch and field sheets.

2

170

Type	Purpose	Requirement For Study	Personnel and Equipment
Observance of Traffic Signals Study	To determine voluntary observance of intersection traffic control signals.	As required at intersections where congestion and high accident rates prevail.	Two policemen without distinctive police gear are normally required. On multiple approaches with heavy traffic, four or six policemen may be required. Equipment consists of an ordinary watch, field sheets, and summary sheets.
Parking Studies	To determine the adequacy, use, and location of existing parking facilities; and to provide guidance in the placement and design of parking areas for future use.	A comprehensive, installation survey is normally required only in conjunction with long-range planning for major changes in the installation. Surveys are conducted at specific areas as parking problems become evident, or in anticipation of the development of parking problems.	Field sheets, summary sheets, post map, aerial photos, and questionnaires are used as required for the specific study or survey being conducted. Personnel requirements and use of police gear depend on the type and scope of the study.
Accident Records Study	To improve enforcement, engineering, and education programs.	As needed to identify and treat high accident locations, to assist in evaluating highway design factors, to establish priorities of action, and to measure effectiveness of remedial action.	ADP equipment and trained personnel for automatic data processing. Normally, two police perform observations for condition and collision diagrams.

GLOSSARY OF TRAFFIC CONTROL TERMS

TABLE OF CONTENTS

	Page
Access Road ... Desire Line	1
Divided Street ... Left Turn Lane	2
Manual Traffic Control ... Passenger Vehicle	3
Passenger (Transit) Volume ... Separate Turning Lane	4
Shoulder ... Traffic Accident	5
Traffic Actuated Controller ... Uninterrupted Flow	6
Vehicle ... Zone (Origin-Destination Studies)	7

GLOSSARY OF TRAFFIC CONTROL TERMS

A

ACCESS ROAD - Public roads, existing or proposed, needed to provide essential access to military installation and facilities, or to industrial installations and facilities in the activities of which there is specific defense interest. Roads within the boundaries of military reservation are excluded from this definition unless such roads have been dedicated to public use and are not subject to closure.

ACCIDENT SPOT MAP - An area or installation map showing the location of vehicle accidents by means of symbols. Symbols may represent accidents classified as to daylight hours, night hours, injury or death.

ANGLE PARKING - Parking where the longitudinal axes of vehicles form an angle with the alignment of the roadway.

C

CENTER LINE - A line marking the center of a roadway between traffic moving in opposite direction.

COLLISION DIAGRAM - A plan of an intersection or section of roadway on which reported accidents are diagramed by means of arrows showing manner of collision.

COMBINED CONDITION AND COLLISION DIAGRAM - A condition diagram upon which the reported accidents are diagramed by means of arrows showing manner of collision.

CONDITION DIAGRAM - A plan of an intersection or section of roadway showing all objects and physical conditions having a bearing on traffic movement and safety at that location. Usually these are scaled drawings.

CORDON COUNTS - A count of all vehicles and persons entering and leaving a district (cordon area) during a designated period of time.

CORDON AREA - The district bounded by the cordon line and included in a cordon count.

CROSSWALK - Any portion of a roadway at an intersection or elsewhere distinctly indicated for pedestrian crossing by lines or other markings on the surface. Also, that part of a roadway at an intersection included within the connections of the lateral lines of the sidewalks on opposite sides of the traffic way measured from the curbs, or in the absence of curbs, from the edges of the traversable roadway.

D

DELAY - The time consumed while traffic or a specified component of traffic is impeded in its movement by some element over which it has no control usually expressed in seconds per vehicle.

DESIRE LINE - A straight line between the point of origin and point of destination of a trip without regard to routes of travel (used in connection with an origin-destination study).

DIVIDED STREET - A two-way road on which traffic in one direction of travel is separated from that in the opposite direction by a directional separator. Such a road has two or more roadways.

E

85 PERCENTILE SPEED - That speed below which 85 percent of the traffic unit's travel, and above which 15 percent travel.

F

FIXED-TIME CONTROLLER - An automatic controller for supervising the operation of traffic control signals in accordance with a predetermined fixed time cycle and divisions thereof.

FIXED-TIME TRAFFIC SIGNAL - A traffic signal operated by a fixed-time controller.

FLASHING BEACON - A section of a standard traffic signal head, or a similar type device, having a yellow or red lens in each face, which is illuminated by rapid intermittent flashes.

FLASHING TRAFFIC SIGNAL - A traffic control signal used as a flashing beacon.

FLOATING CAR - An automobile driven in the traffic flow at the average speed of the surrounding vehicles.

FLOW DIAGRAM - The graphical representation of the traffic volumes on a road or street network or section thereof, showing by means of bands the relative volumes using each section of roadway during a given period of time, usually 1 hour.

H

HIGH FREQUENCY ACCIDENT LOCATION - A specific location where a large number of traffic accidents have occurred.

I

INTERSECTION APPROACH - That portion of an intersection leg which is used by traffic approaching the intersection.

L

LATERAL CLEARANCE - The distance between the edge of pavement and any lateral obstruction.

LATERAL OBSTRUCTION - Any fixed object located adjacent to the traveled way which reduces the transverse dimensions of the roadway.

LEFT TURN LANE - A lane within the normal surfaced width reserved for left turning vehicles.

M

MANUAL TRAFFIC CONTROL - The use of-hand signals or manually operated devices by traffic control personnel to control traffic.

MANUAL COUNTER - A tallying device which is operated by hand.

MASS TRANSPORTATION - Movement of large groups of persons.

MULTIAXLE TRUCK - A truck which has more than two axles.

O

OCCUPANCY RATIO -The average number-of occupants per vehicle (including the driver).

ODOMETER -A device on a vehicle for measuring the distance traveled, usually as a cumulative total, but sometimes also for individual trips, with an indicator on the instrument panel where it is usually combined with a speedometer indicator, or in the hub of a wheel in some trucks.

OFF-PEAK PERIOD - That portion of the day in which traffic volumes are relatively light.

OFFSET LANES - Additional lanes used for traffic which is heavier in one direction. Also known as unbalanced lanes.

OFF-STREET PARKING - Lots and garages intended for parking entirely off streets and alleys. street and alleys (may be angle or parallel parking) for parking of vehicles.

ORIGIN DESTINATION STUDIES - A study of the origins and destinations of trips of vehicles and passengers. Usually included in the study are all trips within, or passing through, into or out of a selected area.

OVERALL SPEED - The total distance traversed divided by the travel time. Usually expressed in miles per hour and includes all delays.

OVERALL TIME - The time of travel, including stops and delays except those off the traveled way.

P

PARALLEL PARKING - Parking where the longitudinal axis of vehicles are parallel to alignment of the roadway so that the vehicles are facing in the same direction as the movement of adjacent vehicular traffic.

PARKING DURATION - Length of time a vehicle is parked.

PASSENGER VEHICLE - A free-wheeled, self-propelled vehicle designed for the transportation of persons but limited in seating capacity to not more than seven passengers, not including the driver. It includes taxicabs, limousines, and station wagons, but does not include motorcycles.
(In capacity studies, also includes light reconnaissance vehicles, and pickup trucks.)

PASSENGER (TRANSIT) VOLUME - The total number of public transit occupants being transported in a period of time.

PEAK PERIOD - That portion of the day in which maximum traffic volumes are experienced.

PEDESTRIAN - Any person afoot. For purpose of accident classification, this will be interpreted to include any person riding in or upon a device moved or designed for movement by human power or the force of gravity, except bicycles, including stilts, skates, skis, sleds, toy wagons, and scooters.

PERCENT OF GRADE - The slope in the longitudinal direction of the pavement expressed in percent which is the number of units of change in elevation per 100 units of horizontal distance.

PERCENT OF GREEN TIME - The percentage of green time allotted to the direction of travel being studies.

PROPERTY DAMAGE - Damage to property as a result of a motor vehicle accident that may be a basis of a claim for compensation. Does not include compensation for loss of life or for personal injuries.

PUBLIC HIGHWAYS- The entire width between property lines, or boundary lines, of every way or place of which any part is open to use of the public for purposes of vehicular traffic as a matter of right or custom.

PUBLIC TRANSIT - The public passenger carryi ng service afforded by vehicles following regular routes and making specified stops.

R

REFLECTORIZE - The application of some material to traffic control devices or hazards which will return to the eyes of the road user some portion of the light from his vehicle headlights, thereby producing a brightness which attracts attention.

REGULATORY DEVICE - A device used to indicate the required method of traffic movement or use of the public traffic way.

REGULATORY SIGN - A sign used to indicate the required method of traffic movement or use of the traffic way.

RIGHT TURN LANE - A lane within the normal surfaced width reserved for right turning vehicles.

ROADWAY - That portion of a traffic way including shoulders, improved, designed, or ordinarily used for vehicle traffic.

S

SEPARATE TURNING LANE - Added traffic lane which is separated from the intersection area by an island or unpaved area. It may be wide enough for one or two line operation

SHOULDER - The portion of the roadway contiguous with the traveled way for accommodation of stopped vehicles, for emergency use, and for lateral support of base and surface courses.

SIGHT DISTANCES - The length of roadway visible to the driver of a passenger vehicle at any given point on the roadway when the view is unobstructed by traffic.

SIGNAL CYCLE - The total time required for one complete sequence of the intervals of a traffic signal.

SIGNAL CONTROLLER - A complete electrical mechanism for controlling the operation of traffic control signals, including the timer and all necessary auxiliary apparatus mounted in a cabinet.

SIGNAL FACE - That part of a signal head provided for controlling traffic from a single direction.

SIGNAL HEAD - An assembly containing one or more signal faces that may be designated accordingly as one-way, two-way, multi-way.

SIGNAL PHASE - A part of the total time cycle allocated to movements receiving the right-of-way or to any combination ments receiving the right-of-way simultaneously during one

SIMPLE INTERSECTION - An intersection of two traffic ways, approaches.

SPEED - The rate of movement of a vehicle, generally expressed in miles per hour.

STOPPING SIGHT DISTANCE –The distance required by a drive of a vehicle, given speed, to bring vehicle to a stop after and object becomes visible.

STREET WIDTH - The width of the paved or traveled portion of the roadway.

T

THROUGH MOVEMENT - (See THROUGH TRAFFIC)

THROUGH STREET - A street on which traffic is given the right-of-way so that vehicles entering or crossing the street must yield the right-of-way.

THROUGH TRAFFIC - Traffic proceeding through a military installation or portion not originating in or destined to that military installation or portion thereof.

TIME CYCLE - (See SIGNAL CYCLE)

TRAFFIC - Pedestrians, ridden or herded animals, vehicles, street cars, and other conveyances, either singly or together, while using any street for purposes of travel.

TRAFFIC ACCIDENT - Any accident involving a motor vehicle in motion that results in death, injury, or property damage.

TRAFFIC ACTUATED CONTROLLER- An automatic controller for supervising the operation of traffic control signals in accordance with the immediate and varying demands of traffic as registered with the-controller by means of detectors.

TRAFFIC CONTROL - All measures except those of a structural kind that serve to control and guide traffic and to promote road safety.

TRAFFIC CONTROL DEVICE - A Traffic control device is any sign, signal, marking, or device placed or erected for the purpose of regulating, warning, or guiding traffic.

TRAFFIC DEMAND - The volume of traffic desiring to use a particular route or facility.

TRAFFIC ENGINEERING - That phase of engineering that deals with the planning and geometric design of streets, highways, and abutting lands, and with traffic operations thereon, as their use is related to the safe, convenient, and economic transportation of persons and goods.

TRAFFIC FLOW - The movement of vehicles on a roadway.

TRAFFIC FLOW PATTERN - The distribution of traffic volumes on a street or highway network~

TRAFFIC GENERATOR - A traffic producing area such as a post exchange, parking lot, or administrative center.

TRAFFIC SIGNAL INTERVAL - Anyone of the several divisions of the total time cycle during which signal indications do not change.

TRAFFICWAY - The entire width between property lines (or other boundary lines) of every way or place of which any part is open to use of public for purposes of vehicular traffic as a matter of right or custom.

TRANSIT VEHICLE - A passenger carrying vehicle, such as a bus or streetcar which follows regular routes and makes specific stops.

TRAVEL TIME- The total elapsed time from the origin to destination of a trip.

TURNING MOVEMENT - The traffic making a designated turn at an intersection.

TWO-WAY STREETS - A street on which traffic may move in opposite directions simultaneously. It may be either divided or undivided.

TYPE OF ACCIDENT - The kind of motor vehicle accident, such as head-on, right-angle, etc.

TYPE OF SURFACE - The class of surface such as concrete, asphalt, gravel, etc.

U

UNINTERRRUPTED FLOW - The flow of-vehicles under ideal conditions resulting in unrestricted movement.

V

VEHICLE - Every device in, upon, or by which any person or property is or may be transported or drawn upon a highway, except those devices moved by human power or used exclusively upon stationary rails or tracks.

VEHICULE OCCUPANCY - The average number of occupants per automobile, including the driver.

VOLUME - The number of vehicles passing a given point during a specified period of time.

W

WARNING SIGN - A sign used to indicate conditions that are actually or potentially hazardous to highway users.

WARRANT - Formally stated conditions that have been accepted as minimum requirements for justifying installation of a traffic control device or regulation.

Z

ZONE (ORIGIN-DESTINATION STUDIES) -- A division of an area established for the purpose of analyzing origin-destination studies. It may be bounded by physical barriers such as rivers and highways, or may be the location of individual work organizations that have duty stations in relatively close proximity.